DELIUS
PORTRAIT OF A COSMOPOLITAN

Frederick Delius

Delius
Portrait of a Cosmopolitan

Christopher Palmer

With a Foreword by
ERIC FENBY

 HOLMES & MEIER PUBLISHERS

New York

First published in the United States of America 1976 by
Holmes & Meier Publishers, Inc.
101 Fifth Avenue
New York, New York 10003

Library of Congress Cataloging in Publication Data

Palmer, Christopher.
  Delius : portrait of a cosmopolitan.

  Bibliography : p.
  Includes index.
  1. Delius, Frederick, 1862-1934.
ML410.D35P3   780'.92'4 [B]   76-8893
ISBN 0-8419-0274-7

PRINTED IN GREAT BRITAIN

12th November 1974 19.00

Dear Christopher,

I much enjoyed reading your
portrait of Delius. It recalled conversations I
heard at his table, well over forty years ago, on
much that you have compiled in it's pages. Your
description of him is true to life. He could not be
regarded as exclusively English; French, German,
Norwegian, English and American (when his neighbour
called) were spoken daily in his household. I am
therefore delighted to find that your book develops these
five-fold dispositions to full cosmopolitan status in Delius
both as man and as musician.

May I settle a point you raise?
Delius's voice was of light, tenor timbre;
pleasant, not harsh, but with a drawl. There was no trace
of accent that I could detect.

With best wishes for the book.

Yours sincerely,

Eric Fenby

To my Parents

Contents

Illustrations

Preface

A spirit of jealous possessiveness on the part of English writers on music has tended over the years to foster an excessively insular approach to Delius's art and a refusal to recognise the richly cosmopolitan elements of which it is compounded. It has become something of a commonplace to refer to Delius as a 'solitary and unique' figure in the history of twentieth-century music. In a sense he was, but we must beware of the temptation to view his achievement in a kind of critical vacuum, divorced from its rightful cultural, historical and cosmopolitan context. The more we probe the question, in fact, the more uncomfortably do we become aware that in classifying Delius as an exclusively English composer the English claim an unwarranted privilege, for they are but one of a number of possible contenders for the distinction of ownership. Delius was a curiously stateless man, a wanderer over the face of the earth who never really settled and struck roots anywhere. But whatever else he was or was not, he would no doubt have been less than flattered to see himself referred to constantly in dictionaries and reference books as an 'English composer'. Vaughan Williams, undisputed leader of music in England between the wars, once wrote: 'The more level-headed of us do not imagine that because Delius used an English folksong in one of his compositions it makes him into an Englishman. Those who claim England as the birthplace of Delius's art must base their arguments on more valid premises than this.' Too often has Delius been arbitrarily categorised as an English Romantic and left at that.

This book is a modest attempt to redress the balance, to view Delius in a much wider perspective, in an international, cosmopolitan framework rather than as an exclusively national phenomenon. America, Scandinavia, Germany and France – Delius lived in, knew, loved and learned from them all, and it is the nature of these contrasting milieux and the strength of their impact on Delius's personality that I have tried to determine here. Painters and writers frequently leave their mark, since Delius was never a musicians' musician: and other composers' music is discussed only insofar as it relates to Delius and illuminates his work as well as theirs. Boundary lines between countries have not been rigidly observed: for instance I found it more rational to discuss Constant Lambert, an English composer, in the context of the American chapter, and to bring the American composer Bernard Herrmann into the English chapter. Likewise the context has determined which of Delius's own compositions are to be scrutinised in any great detail. I have addressed this book more to the general music-lover with an interest in Delius (I have assumed a certain elementary knowledge of the man and his music) rather than to the specialist, so that should the latter be looking for deep technical analysis he will not find it here. Where I have lapsed into technical talk I have done so in a manner of which the composer, I hope, would have approved: not as an end in itself but as one means to the end of presenting an accurate portrayal of Delius as both man and artist.

In one way in particular is Delius's cosmopolitanism symptomatic of his entire disposition. He was a rebel as a young man and his rebellious nature *kept* him young. He detested and hit out against those pretentious fooleries which the majority of us are bamboozled and brainwashed into accepting as the realities of existence; he flouted convention not for the sake of flouting convention but because he weighed conformity in the balance of his own experience and found it wanting. So too in music. He was never lulled by the fashionable complacency endemic in certain species of artists, nor by the security and acceptability of long-tried, oft-used conventions of syntax. He asked questions all the time and judged the answers by what experience had taught him, not by what had been instilled into him from birth. He held the musical Establishment and academic respectability in music in the highest contempt; he adapted the techniques of musical composition to his own ends, knowing precisely what he was doing – and as to the validity and durability of what he did posterity has already been the judge. He made no parade of technical knowledge, but he *knew*, and it no doubt amused him to hear people with no inside experience of his scores describe him as a dilettante and an 'amateur'. But in fact he was one of the most 'professional' musicians who ever lived, and certainly one of the most musical.

So he was a rebel, then, devoid of inhibition, and an individualist; but, like all rebels and individualists, he was fundamentally a lonely person. A rebel's principles are usually so strict that few of his friends are capable of measuring up to them, and he will always act in accordance with those principles, regardless of the effect of his action on his intimates. Delius was not lacking in friends on any level, and he loved passionately at least once in his life; yet how many really *shared* his life? Jelka Rosen Delius, his wife, was prepared to subordinate her entire existence to her husband's, and one's only hope is that Delius was conscious of the magnitude of his debt to her. Probably he wasn't; probably he accepted it merely as his right. But Jelka never *shared* his life in the fullest, widest, deepest sense. And this essential loneliness is surely reflected in his cosmopolitan isolation. Delius had no home. His whole life was affected by an uprootedness, a yearning insecurity. Yet it was this very uprootedness, this isolation, this forced cosmopolitanism, which bred in him so rich and vital a creative personality – and hence the whole man, Frederick Delius, and his music, which is like no other in the world. I have tried here to analyse and understand the differing facets of this cosmopolitanism; and I use the term as defined in its adjectival form by the *Concise Oxford Dictionary*: 'belonging to all parts of the world: free from national limitations.'

A number of people have helped in the preparation of this book. John Bird allowed me to consult the extensive research material on Percy Grainger he has compiled; my father, G. E. Palmer, investigated E. J. Moeran's Norfolk affiliations; and I made copious inroads into Bernard Herrmann's encyclopaedic knowledge of music – and into his extensive library. I am indebted to Colin Scott-Sutherland and John Bishop for supplying many of the illustrations, to Felix Aprahamian for his help and encouragement at all times, and to C. W. Orr, the late Patrick Hadley and Eric Fenby for bringing Frederick Delius and his work so much closer to me – and, I hope, to my readers.

C.P.

London, October 1975

CHAPTER ONE

America

Why did the 22-year-old Delius choose to seek salvation in orange planting in Florida? There is a story that as a small boy he had been especially attracted by the outline of Florida on a map; but it is more probable that, at a time when his refusal to apply himself conscientiously to the business of wool-bartering had rendered his position *vis-à-vis* his parents virtually untenable, he saw in Florida a locality which would preclude any attempts at direct interference on the part of his father, and in orange growing an occupation which would leave him a generous allowance of free time in which to pursue his own interests. However this may be, in March 1884 Delius and his partner set sail on board the Cunard liner Gallia for New York, proceeded, also by sea, to Fernandina in Georgia, and thence by train to Jacksonville. The property which Delius *père* had been cajoled into purchasing was by name Solano Grove, an old Spanish plantation overlooking the St John River, several days' journey upstream from Jacksonville; here the young Delius remained until August 1885 when he moved into Jacksonville itself, setting himself up as a music teacher and supplementing his insubstantial income through (incredibly) singing in a local synagogue. Thence he passed to Danville, Virginia, where his time was spent pleasurably and profitably instructing the daughters of wealthy plantation owners in music. Before sailing home in the midsummer of 1886 Delius had, apparently, been earning his living as an organist in a Manhattan church.

It is annoying, if understandable, that these two years – the most crucial in the composer's life – should be so imperfectly chronicled; there are, for instance, discrepancies between contemporary accounts of his rise to fame and prosperity in Danville, and available evidence provides us with a very incomplete picture of the actual length of time he spent in New York and of his activities during that period. However, these factual minutiae, interesting as they may be in themselves, are not of any real importance; the main outlines of the story are perfectly clear, and there is evidence in

1

abundance for the significance of these years in the later course of his development.

Delius was an exceedingly fortunate man in most respects; in fact in reviewing his career one is almost tempted into believing in the existence of the proverbial Guardian Angel. Among the multifarious favours bestowed by this benevolent personage, the provision of useful people at each critical juncture of his charge's career must be rated especially highly. Caring only for his music and being notably inexpert at organising the practical side of his life, Delius had the uncommon good fortune to meet a woman prepared to devote her all to ensuring that his art could flourish untrammelled by the pettifogging domesticities of everyday existence. Again, no sooner were his first truly representative compositions off the stocks than he chanced upon his ideal interpreter; and the unprecedented privilege of an entire London festival devoted to his music, under this interpreter, was conferred upon him during his lifetime. Finally, in his last years, blind and paralysed but with a brain still teeming with fertile creative ideas, the presence of a dedicated young fellow-Yorkshireman made possible a brief but glorious Indian Summer. But the first link in this chain of opportune relationships was forged in Florida, one day when he had gone to Jacksonville in search of a piano. Entering a music shop, sitting down at a piano and improvising idly, he attracted the attention of another musician in the shop who perceived an excitingly unfamiliar element in the sounds being produced. He introduced himself as one Thomas Ward, a Brooklyn organist on a health visit to the South. The pair took to each other immediately and Delius invited Ward back to his shack at Solano Grove where he stayed for several months, instructing the younger man in the rudiments of musical composition. Delius recalled these months to Eric Fenby in glowing terms:

It was not till I began to attend the harmony and counterpoint classes at the Leipzig Conservatorium that I recognised the sterling worth of Ward as a teacher . . . as far as composing was concerned, Ward's counterpoint lessons were the only lessons from which I derived any benefit. Towards the end of my course with him – and he made me work like a nigger – he showed wonderful insight in helping me to find out just how much in the way of traditional technique would be useful to me . . . and there wasn't much.

Ward was evidently much impressed by the talent and receptivity of his pupil, as well he might be, for the young enthusiast who applied himself so ruthlessly to the mastery of the musical science was by no means the callow dilettante who had arrived in Florida some months earlier in a state of listlessness and dejection. What had happened in the meantime to create so profound a change in him?

1. Percy Grainger (third from right) with Duke Ellington at New York University, c. 1930.

2. Duke Ellington (left) with Billy Strayhorn; Johnny Hodges in the background.

3. Constant Lambert.

The key to Delius's musical personality, to his entire spiritual and emotional constitution, is to be found in the answer to this question. For as Delius himself explained to Fenby, it was in those days before the arrival of Ward, while alone with Nature in the wilderness, that he first experienced the creative urge. For every artist a period of withdrawal from the world is a necessary preliminary to the proper maturation of the creative faculty. Delius found himself in Florida to a large extent cut off from human companionship of the sort to which he had been accustomed, and – a fact the importance of which it is impossible to over-emphasise – in a setting of phenomenal natural splendour. Here for the first time he responded fully to the potency of natural beauty and to the terrible reality of its impermanence. For to Delius the quality of transience was to become far more than a mere preoccupation – it was to prove tantamount to a pathological obsession.

This awareness, which was to seek expression in one form or another in almost everything he was ever to write, was, however, impressed upon him not merely by contemplation of his physical surroundings. Let Cecil Gray take up the tale:

'That which is known to the mystics as "the state of illumination" is a kind of ecstatic revelation which may only last for a split second of time, but which he who has known it spends the rest of his life trying to re-capture. Those who have experienced it always recognise the presence of the peculiar quality of that which appertains to it. The music of Delius is an example, and I was immediately aware of it in the first work of his I heard . . . I knew, too, the exact moment at which that experience must have occurred in Delius's life, and when I asked him if it were so and if I were right, he was surprised and admitted that I was. The occasion was one summer night, when he was sitting out on the verandah of his house on his orange grove in Florida, and the sound came to him from the distance of the voices of the Negroes in the plantation, singing in chorus. It is the rapture of this moment that Delius is perpetually seeking to communicate in all his characteristic work. . . .' (Cecil Gray, *Musical Chairs*, London 1948, p. 191.)

The affinity between Delius and the American Negro, which the former intuitively recognised on that first occasion alluded to by Gray, is a deep-lying one. The American Negroes were a dispossessed minority, strangers in a strange land, bereft of their culture, natural environment and traditions. Behind them lay an appalling history of suffering and privation. Their themes, voiced particularly in the spirituals and blues, were those of the sorrow of parting, insecurity and uprootedness, and they were themes which had already begun to preoccupy Delius even at this early stage; to be brought into daily contact with people on whom awareness of these miseries of the human kind had been so painfully foisted, and who expressed it unselfconsciously in their music, was to leave an indelible imprint upon his mind and to condition his emotional responsiveness in such a way that the same crises, the same facets of human experience and existence would be continually coming to the fore and striking the same primordial chord in his emotions, no matter how outwardly different their manifestations might be. For Delius was one of those composers who never grow past a certain early stage in their development but merely see that stage in different perspectives as they grow older. The result in his case was music that explored with increasing intensity the same areas of feeling: he was never able to take past experiences and achievements for granted and constantly expand his universe. Delius's music is the philosophy of a man who found life brief, bitter but beautiful; the brevity and bitterness – the tragedy – had been revealed instantaneously to him in that split second of illumination on the verandah at Solano Grove. Life as a commodity in itself is intolerable, and can be made meaningful in one of two ways: by surrendering one's soul to God, or to the earth. Delius was sustained by no orthodox faith but subscribed to those late-nineteenth-century dogmas which rejected the concept of God in favour of a materialistic reassessment of the relation of man to the cosmos, man henceforward being responsible for the development of his own aptitudes and capabilities without deference to transcendental sanctions. What Delius evokes is a state of nature in which man is thrown upon his own resources and is unable, by virtue of any long-term policy or prospect, to alleviate the essential tragedy of his short-term existence; his only salvation lies in imbuing the here-and-now with significance and merit.

Now for all Delius's sympathy for the 'black man's burden', nothing could be more misleading than to envisage his work as a social document in anything more than an incidental sense. Delius, as will become abundantly clear later on, was a confirmed egocentric; any problem which lay outside his immediate orbit of reference was of negligible interest to him. His own indomitable will-to-power (Nietzsche's 'Wille zur Macht') and the continuing good fortunes already mentioned made him independent, unbound by the necessity to submit himself to any form of experience he might find uncongenial. So the suffering of the Negroes under the white man's yoke would have left him totally unaffected unless it had for him a symbolic value in relation to some deeply-felt emotional experience of his own, which those strains of improvisatory song being wafted across the plantation had permanently crystallised in a certain point of time; hence his life-long anxiety to recreate and preserve it. What, then, was or could have been this personal experience which Delius saw mirrored in the poignancy of Negro music and which he found himself perpetually trying to renew in *his* music? The Negro opera *Koanga* surely provides us with the clue. For between 1888 and 1896 (the year of Acts 1 and 2 of *Koanga*) little came from Delius's pen that any student composer well-versed in the idiom of Grieg and the later German romantics could not have produced; but from 1897 onwards – from *Koanga* Act 3 – we can sense a gradual deepening and broadening of creative scope and power, culminating in *A Village Romeo and Juliet* (1901) and the revised version of *Appalachia* (1902) with *Paris – The Song of a Great City* (1899) marking a definite transitional stage.

Obviously therefore the period 1896–1900 warrants the closest scrutiny. Unhappily, by one of those ironic quirks of fate of which instances abound in musicology, these very years are the most poorly documented of the composer's life and we have tantalisingly little knowledge of the one event that in all probability is of inestimable importance in their history – Delius's return to Florida in 1897. Were this episode to be satisfactorily accounted for – if we knew why he went back and what he did there – we should probably be in a very much better position to understand the course his creative development was henceforward to take. The avowed pretext for the journey was the putting-in-order of matters relating to the property at Solano Grove which had to a large extent been left to its own devices ever since its owner abandoned it some twelve years previously. It has been stated that Delius found it convenient to effect a speedy departure from Paris at that time, but there is reason to believe that in reality the composer planned a return to his former haunts in an attempt to resume a chapter in his life that had been of necessity broken off when he had left to enrol at the Leipzig conservatory. The attempt was unsuccessful, and thereafter his knowledge of the 'still sad music of humanity' gleaned on his plantation and intensified through personal experience of love and separation, sought expression in his music. The two early years in Florida certainly kindled the creative flame, but immediacy of impact does not necessarily make for valid expression in art. In Delius's case it needed that the emotions then aroused be revivified and recollected in the tranquillity that came with the fullness of maturity (Delius was 35 when he returned to America); only then could they be seen in their true perspective and recreated in a form which, while it retained and projected their burning intensity, refined them and purged them of all irrelevant connotations. In view of the fact that work on *Koanga* was broken off at the time of the composer's journey back to Florida and resumed only on his return to Paris, I believe that the third act of this opera marks the dividing-line between the insipid if charming water-colourist of the *Florida Suite* and the fairy-tale opera *Irmelin*, and the rapt nature mystic we revere today.

Delius himself was under no illusion as to the significance of his self-imposed exile in Florida. Describing the singing of the Negroes to Fenby, he said :

. . . they showed a truly wonderful sense of musicianship and harmonic resource in the instinctive way in which they treated a melody, and, hearing their singing in such romantic surroundings, it was then and there that I first felt the urge to express myself in music.'

Small wonder that Delius so often resorts to voices distant, wordless and unseen, at moments of peak emotion. They may all be traced back to that revelatory experience on Solano Grove, when he first became aware of what was literally the 'still, sad music of humanity'. Like Wordsworth who chanced one day to overhear the singing of a solitary highland lass as she worked in the fields, he might have said :

> I listened, motionless and still;
> And, as I mounted up the hill,
> The music in my heart I bore,
> Long after it was heard no more.

This is the Delian Experience in a nutshell.

In *Appalachia* – that fine set of variations on a Negro slave song in which Delius enshrined most memorably his impressions of the Negro country and its people – are moments when he is attempting directly to reproduce that sound of agony and ecstasy. Like the later *Song of the High Hills*, *Appalachia* is episodic, and as it proceeds wordless voices begin to be heard singing the episodes to their rest (Philip Heseltine described these exquisite codettas as 'doxologies'). Only at the climactic point does the chorus interpose with words – 'After night has gone comes the day' – but the words are of no consequence. What matters is the *sound* of the close-harmony singing; the emotional stuff of the experience Delius is wishing to communicate is in the physical, sensual impact of the voices and in the texture of their harmony.

In its context this variation is probably the closest he ever came to recreating the actual sound of that moment of illumination, although it is echoed time and again in the music of his maturity. In one of the best passages of evocative writing in his early work – the prelude to Act 3 of *Koanga* – distant tenors improvise pentatonically around a sustained chord in the orchestra, foreshadowing a similar procedure in the finale of *Hassan*; the effect is similar to that of the vocal writing in Milhaud's *L'Homme et son désir*, likewise a depiction of a tropical forest by night. The distant 'Heigh ho! Travellers we a-passing by' of the unseen bargemen in the finale of *A Village Romeo and Juliet* is one of the most celebrated moments in all opera, and the end of the second dance song in *A Mass of Life* dissolves magically into silence with the distant wordless voices of the singers re-echoing through the trees. The opening of the second picture of *Fennimore and Gerda* incorporates a wordless tenor vocalise in the distance on the fjörd, and in *The Song of the High Hills* the first appearance of the theme representing 'the wide far distance, the great solitude' is wondrously enhanced through a distant semi-chorus picking out various strands in the harmony. The cataclysmic outburst for the unaccompanied wordless chorus at the climax is directly parallel to the *Appalachia* finale, although the voices *are* wordless here and the harmonic technique is more assured. The context is different, but here probably with even greater accuracy than in *Appalachia* do we hear what Delius heard as he sat on his verandah overlooking the river, enveloped in a haze of cigar smoke and listening to the sound of those voices improvising on the night air. So too in the setting for unaccompanied chorus of Tennyson's *The Splendour Falls*, the two wordless choruses *To be Sung of a Summer Night on the Water*, and the lovely wordless choruses heard behind the scene in *Hassan*.

If we discount those works directly inspired by Walt Whitman (one of Delius's three great literary loves) there are three compositions, none of them a product of the composer's true maturity, which relate directly to the American scene, more particularly to the American Negro. The first is the *Florida Suite*, an expertly-crafted synthesis of Grieg and Negroid Americana. The theme for horn choir at the beginning of the last movement 'At Night' (the first of Delius's many nocturnes) brings to mind the distant sound of a Negro spiritual accompanied by harmonium; the cadential move from seventh degree to tonic is avoided in favour of the jump from *sixth* degree which is an American 'fingerprint'. Additionally, the 'Sunrise' and 'Sunset' movements both incorporate Negro dances. The first has become very popular under the title 'La Calinda' and later found its way into Act 2 of the opera *Koanga*; 'Sunset' catches the sounds of revelry on a nearby plantation in an artless pentatonic melody of the type that later recurs as Porgy's 'I got plenty of nuttin'' in Gershwin's *Porgy and Bess*. The constant ambiguity of the third suggests a blue note, and we may assume that this was Delius's reconstruction of a tune he actually heard somewhere in the vicinity of his orange grove. Another interesting fact relating to this 'Plantation Dance' is that a fragment of pentatonic melody first heard on the oboe at fig. 4 in the score (Ex. 1a) seems to have haunted Delius over a number of years, for it later becomes part of one of the chief Negro themes in *Koanga* ('Come out, niggers, come out to cut the waving cane') (Ex. 1b) and, astonishingly, re-appears some thirty years later in the movement known as 'Late Swallows' in the String Quartet (Ex. 1c).

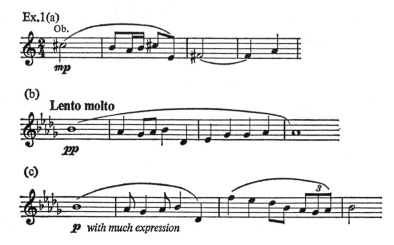

Ex.1(a) Ob.

(b) **Lento molto**

(c)

p with much expression

This elegiac piece, autumnal in mood, was apparently inspired by memories of the swallows darting back and forth in the eaves at Grez; but this unconscious (surely it *is* unconscious) flashback to *le beau temps de jadis* suggests that the waving ostinato which surrounds it may be the waving of the sugar cane in the plantations of Florida. A wistful reminiscence of halcyon days: the String Quartet was written in Norway whither the Deliuses had been driven during the First World War, not knowing whether they would ever see their beloved home again. What more natural than that the remembrance of things past should come to crowd out the evil of the day?

Florida, the most polished (if not the most characteristic) of the composer's early orchestral pieces, betrays an attractive melodic gift and an enviable command of the orchestral palette; an advance on Grieg is noticeable in this respect, if in no other. The Negro folk music elements are limned against a European-oriented harmonic and colouristic background, and incidentally it is interesting that the Viennese naturalised American composer Max Steiner (1888–1971), in the score he wrote for David O. Selznick's film of Margaret Mitchell's epic of old South *Gone with the Wind* (1939),* contrived to hit upon the same kind of Europeanised variant

*Delius in his setting of Dowson's *Cynara* unwittingly draws attention to the fact that Miss Mitchell distorted the meaning of the quotation she appropriated as title for her book. The lines in question run:

> I have forgot much, Cynara! gone with the wind
> Flung roses, roses, riotously with the throng

– where 'gone with the wind' obviously does *not* mean 'dispersed by the wind' which is nevertheless how we are intended to take it in Miss Mitchell's context.

of the Negro vernacular as Delius in the *Florida Suite* – although Steiner cannot have known Delius's work. By this I do not just mean that their respective stylisations of plantation type dances are similar, they could scarcely be otherwise. I mean that there are melodies in both scores which have no specific or surface affinity with the Negro folk-melos but yet resemble one another noticeably, and so coincide simply because, for all their apparently European glamour and sophistication, their roots in fact strike deep into that very folk-melos in which both composers were steeped. (Steiner did many months of research into the folk and traditional music of the South before starting work on the score.)

Koanga itself, though the most 'operatic' of Delius's operas, is of variable musical interest. There are pointers to the composer's mature manner: the dawn which breaks over the plantation on that 'soft May morning' to coincide with the end of Uncle Joe's narrative is the same blinding sunrise which fills the empty streets of Paris with splendour (cf. Ex. 2a and b). Nature-evocation was Delius's *forte*; apart from this oft-performed finale with its graphic depiction of the new sun leaping into the sky (the three interpolated bars of 6/8 after Renée's aria) I have already

mentioned the atmospheric tropical nocturne at the beginning of Act 3 which, though it originated in an even earlier work (the unpublished opera *The Magic Fountain*) is remarkably prophetic of later Delius. The scene is set as follows: 'A glade in the dense forest, at nightfall. Will o' the wisps shine over the marshes. Hills in the background.' An orchestral prelude anticipates in a rudimentary way the mood and substance of *Summer Night on the River*. Then, wordless voices – tenors and basses answering each other – are heard from afar over a sustained chord, anticipating the finale of *Hassan*. This is perhaps the earliest attempt at recapturing that 'revelatory experience', just as the *Hassan* finale is the last.

It is above all in Delius's treatment of the Negro folkmusic element that *Koanga* is significant in the light of later developments. Delius assimilated many facets of the Negro dialect into his own musical speech

9

with an ease and fluency the reasons for which I shall be discussing later in the chapter. Extensive ethnomusicological research alone could determine the measure in which Delius drew on authentic plantation melodies for the Negro choruses and dances, of which there are many; but especially interesting is the way in which he diverts any ready-made material to his own expressive ends, and with such unerring sympathy of style and idea that (as in *Appalachia*) there is no suspicion of conflict or disparity of idiom. As William Randel has shown, the melody of the work-song 'John say you got to reap what you sow' was derived from what was originally a *dance*-song given by G. W. Cable in his novel *The Grandissimes* which C. F. Keary used as the basis of the *Koanga* libretto. Delius modified this tune only slightly before including it in the opera; yet the implications of this 'slight' modification are far-reaching. He dispenses with the square-cut cadence in favour of a final phrase rising through a major third which repeats itself, echo-like, until it seems to be lost in the distance. Evidently the words suggested this poetic treatment to the composer ('ere the sun sinks low in the forest'),* for we can see the sun sinking ever lower in the last four bars. How neatly, and how typically, are thus dovetailed the twin themes of human sorrow and the sweet gradual passing of things in nature – the 'dying fall'! There is too a lovely unaccompanied chorus which sounds as the curtain goes up on Act 2 ('He will meet her when the sun goes down') which is very similar in its character to the *Appalachia* unaccompanied chorus although its harmonic substance is of course a great deal less elaborate (later in the act it is deftly combined with the sprightly melody of 'La Calinda' – a contrapuntal sleight-of-hand very untypical of Delius). There and in the case of Ex. 1b, the other Negro melody prominent in *Koanga*, the harmonic technique is of more than passing interest (this melody – first heard in the Prologue and later set to the words 'O Lawd, I'm goin' away and I won't be back till fall' – is apparently Delius's own invention, though he has given it the outline and imprint of Negro folk-music).** The harmonisation of this melody on its penultimate appearance (vocal score, p. 153, at *Lento molto*) is more lustrous than on its first appearance and it clearly indicates the direction in which Delius's harmonic thought was progressing: how much surer is his grasp of expressive chromatic harmony in Act 3 of *Koanga* than in Act 1! Here we see him anticipating the work of an erratic genius born in the very year that he was putting the finishing touches to the opera, for the harmonic settings of the Negro songs and spirituals in George Gershwin's *Porgy and Bess* are,

*The revised libretto alters this phrase to 'Oh John say reap in the harvest.'

**A. G. Lovgreen has pointed out that the melodic line of Ex. 1 is identical with that of 'Marching through Georgia', a song which contains a number of references to Negro slavery.

as we shall see, a natural outcome of these moments in *Koanga* and the unaccompanied *Appalachia* chorus.

Finally, *Appalachia* finds Delius on the verge of creative maturity. 'Nostalgia' is too misleading a term for the Delian Experience as it is here communicated: it has too many overtones of sentimentality and invertebrate self-indulgence, a vague, mildly masochistic revelling in misery. I prefer to think of it as a tragic awareness of the human condition: Delius was deeply saddened by the knowledge that all our finest and strongest and most meaningful joys are fleeting and impermanent. Vain and insubstantial no, but 'all good things come to an end'. There is nothing in this world so fair that it cannot be taken from us. In the best parts of *Appalachia* this tragedy, this awareness, is effortlessly dissolved along with the 'scented woods', the orange trees, the magnolias, the sinister everglades, the grey-beard and giant-spider-webbing of Spanish moss, the vast, silent and empty river – all are exquisitely transmuted into that luxuriantly brooding kind of sonority, that sensuous sweetness, that we have come to accept as the quintessential Delius sound.

Appalachia in fact constitutes a plethora of sound-impression of the Negro country. The opening is magical – an early morning on the banks of the misty river with re-echoing horn calls and the upward-reaching triplet which is Delius's most durable fingerprint (Ex. 6). Pizzicato strings and harps establish a rhythmic pattern suggesting the strumming of Negro banjoes (for which the composer had actually scored in *Koanga*) and then a majestic brass motif (derived from the theme of the variations which has yet to be presented) invokes the mighty river itself in a magnificent passage of descriptive writing. Several of the later variations may bear a direct relation to Delius's own experiences in the locality, probably Danville. A waltz (p. 88 of the miniature score), graceful if rather over-civilised, could perhaps be an echo of dance-parties enjoyed amid the upper strata of Danville society – although the cry of the distant voices at the end is most strangely moving, a true 'call of the wild'. There soon follows a reminiscence of a Jacksonville or Danville street-parade (p. 106) as the theme is turned into a jaunty, almost Sousa-like march (in 6/8) with raucous brass-band-type scoring complete with snare-drum, big drum and cymbals. In complete contrast comes the following variation, also a march, but this time a grief-stricken funeral procession with a solo trumpet sounding a kind of poetic last post at the very end (herein are sown the seeds of the opening movement of the *Requiem* and of the 'Procession of Protracted Death' in *Hassan*). Those who profess to find even *Appalachia* quintessentially 'English' are advised to compare this variation first with, say, the funeral march in Elgar's E flat Symphony, and then with the dirge at the beginning of Act 2 of *Porgy and Bess*. The closing stages of the work enact the tragedy of a male slave being shipped down river and forced to leave his loved ones behind. A *Misterioso lento* variation suggests the heavy drag of oars, and a solo baritone in the chorus assumes the role of spokesman as if from the helm of a boat, following the Negro call-and-response pattern. The choir seizes on the promise of reunion and the theme swells to a mighty peroration, only to die away as the boat disappears round a bend in the river, returning the scene to the horn calls and solitude of the opening.

Delius's readiness to use authentic Negro material in all these works is typical of his approach to folk and popular music and the fascination it exerted over him, especially in those early days. We tend to overlook this, too mindful as we are of the irascible old invalid of Grez-sur-Loing with the proud, finely chiselled Graeco-Roman features, the disdain, the aloofness, the Olympian standards of refinement and discrimination, the utter rejection of anything or anybody regarded as contaminated by Nietzsche's *Menge* or *Pöbel*. He was not always thus, though doubtless the patrician in him was always latent. But in his younger days he was 'throwing roses, roses riotously with the throng' as well as any man, and *Paris* and the fair scene in *A Village Romeo and Juliet* both in their different ways testify to the appeal of popular music to the unbridled, more extrovert side of Delius's nature. We should also remember that his first published composition was, incredibly, a polka entitled *Zum Carnival* (the German title remains a mystery, since the piece was issued in Jacksonville in 1892). As a polka it is well enough, if in no way distinctively Delian; and there is also the strange fact that *Appalachia* when it started life was little more than a lively fantasy on *Yankee Doodle* and *Dixie*, bearing little or no intimation of the dramatic *dénouement* or the haunting evocative nature-music that we admire in it today. All of which suggests that there was a part of Delius's musical personality which, given the right encouragement, might well have turned him into a kind of superior-grade Louis-Moreau Gottschalk or even a Scott Joplin. In the same way, perhaps, the music of Lehár and the entire school of Viennese operetta meant far more to Mahler than he ever cared openly to admit; and while it would obviously be an exaggeration to speak of split personalities in this connection, it is arguable that the positive response elicited from a composer such as Delius by folk, traditional and pop music proved a salutory stimulus to the process of creative maturation. Freedom from inhibitions, breadth and diversity of experience leading to a well-rounded personality, a fuller, deeper awareness – just as these come in everyday life from exposure to the world, so in music too a continual awareness of the musical pulse of the time, whatever its levels of manifestation cannot but result in a richer and more vital range of creative expression and fulfilment.

2

Although after *Appalachia* none of Delius's compositions were specifically connected with North America, from the purely *technical* point of view the influence of that early plantation singing was more thoroughgoing than he himself probably realised. We can do little more than hazard a guess as to the exact nature and actual sound of the music he heard from his Negroes, but it is evident that what appealed to him above all else was its *harmonic* unfamiliarity. Although by the 1880s orthodox part-singing among Negroes was becoming widespread (largely as a result of increasing emancipation and conscious efforts on the Negroes' part to adapt themselves to white civilisation) it seems reasonably certain that the harmony Delius heard had little in common with that of the Methodist hymn book. Text-book harmonisation of Negro spirituals, academically sound and un-exceptionable by European standards, has tended to obscure the fact that, before the dissemination of such arrangements either in printed form or through the singing of trained Negro choirs abroad, harmony in the sense we understand it was virtually unknown in original Afro-American music. Early accounts of Negro singing almost uniformly stress the fact that there was no singing in parts; yet it is equally certain that this singing was no mere communal unison chorus. In the first book on Negro spirituals ever to be published, *Slave Songs of the United States*, editor W. F. Allen describes Negro singing in the Port Royal Islands (Georgia) thus:[1]

'There is no singing in *parts*, as we understand it, and yet no two appear to be singing the same thing; the leader starts the words of each verse, often improvising, and the others, who "base" him, as it is called, strike in with the refrain, or even join in the solo when the words are familiar. When the base begins the leader often stops, leaving the rest of the words to be guessed at, or it may be that they are taken up by one of the other singers. And the "basers" themselves seem to follow their own whims, beginning where they please striking an octave below or above (in case they have pitched the tune too high) or hitting some other note that "chords", so as to produce the effect of a marvellous complication and variety and yet with the most perfect time and rarely with any discord . . .'

In such a performance the concept of functional diatonic harmony would of course play no part whatsoever, but it is easy to see from this description how the co-incidence of disjunct lines, the blending of different tessitura,

[1] Quoted in Gilbert Chase, *America's Music*, New York 1955, p. 238.

scalic peculiarities and melismatic embellishments would together form this 'marvellous complication and variety' which might in itself give the impression of a strange, untutored but haunting harmony. Even more revealing are accounts of the Negroes' idiosyncratic approach to 'white' harmony before it became over-sophisticated. The essential harmonic originality of the Negro is also vouched for by Natalie Curtis Burlin in an article published in the *Musical Quarterly* in 1919. She tells of hearing a group of Negro workers in a tobacco factory and of being impressed by 'their brilliant unmodulated grouping of diatonic chords, their sudden interlocking of unrelated majors and minors and their unconscious defiance of all man-made laws of voice-progression'.

So it is clear that however the trend to quasi-functional harmony may have started in Negro music – whether the impetus came from instrumental accompaniments to songs (i.e. on the banjo or the guitar) or from the part-singing in 'white' spirituals (the religious folk-songs of the Southern white population) the Negro soon showed an instinctive flair for manipulating it. He proved himself early capable of abstracting only those elements of European harmony which were not at variance with his own melodic and textural inclinations, and of subjecting them to an idiosyncratic manner of treatment which contemporary Europeans would have been at a loss to understand. We may safely assume that it was music of this kind which held Delius entranced during those long summer evenings on Solano Grove, and which caused him to describe to Fenby the 'subtle improvisation in harmony' he had heard, and the Negroes' 'truly wonderful sense of musicianship and harmonic resource in the instinctive way in which they treated a melody'. When elsewhere he remarked that this music had borne remarkably little resemblance to the standard spiritual, he was evidently comparing his recollections with those 'concert' spirituals known to him, in which the number of genuinely Negroid elements would have been drastically reduced.

Technically speaking, this Afro-American music which made such an impression on Delius may be related to later music – his own and other people's – in a number of interesting ways. We have seen that he was attracted to this music primarily through its harmonic inventiveness and unorthodoxy, Delius who was later to develop into an original harmonist in his own right. If we are to understand the true nature of one of the most widely commented-on phenomena of all – the affinity between Delius's harmonic technique and that of the typical mid-century jazzband – a change of perspective is necessary. We need to view him within the broader context of American folk music as it developed in the *fin-de-siècle* period.

In the early '30s Percy Grainger, lecturing in New York, called attention to the affinity between Delius and Duke Ellington, and in 1934 Constant

14

Lambert published his *Music Ho!*, a trenchant analysis of the contemporary scene which included the first serious attempt by an Englishman to evaluate the intrinsic musical merit of jazz and to speculate on its future. In the chapter entitled 'The Spirit of Jazz' he makes a number of pertinent observations on the origin of jazz harmony, maintaining that Afro-American harmony originated above all in the religious music of the Anglo-Saxon which naturally had a powerful effect on the *déraciné* Negroes of America, bereft as they were of their language and cultural traditions. 'We find it hard to realise now not only the emotional effect but the full sensual effect of the hymns of John Bacchus Dykes and his followers. They were however the first real popularisation of what is known as "juicy" harmony, and the force of their influence can be judged by the fact that the modern English composer brought up in their tradition often hits upon the same type of variant of their harmonic style as does the Negro composer – possibly Delius, who has been subjected to the influence of Anglo-Saxon church music and its Negro variants, provides the link.'

This is very true. In connection with Alfred Ewing's tune for *Jerusalem the Golden*, Ethel Smythe once spoke of 'a kind of groping ecstasy contained within Ancient and Modern fetters', and 'groping ecstasy' is really a very good phrase by which to describe the character of Dr Dykes's harmony (how appropriate that his second name was 'Bacchus' – a rare instance of parental foresight). The entire body of Victorian hymnody (some of it poetry, most mere poetasting) is saturated through and through in a spirit of repressed romantic yearning and nostalgia; this would have sanctioned the Rev. Dr Dykes in his ventures in chromatic harmony, its natural musical equivalent (as the American Negro discovered). Many of Dykes's hymn-tunes are extraordinarily fine, his harmony sometimes maudlin but more often genuinely expressive – e.g. the daring last line of *Strength and Stay* (the original harmonisation in the Old A & M, not the expurgated version in the Revised), *Pax Dei, Commendatio, Gerontius, Rivaulx, Dominus Regit Me* (the thirteenth on *fail*-eth), *Veni Cito* (a particular favourite of Lambert's, with three consecutive phrases each beginning on a dominant seventh on a different degree of the scale – primitive Delius, absolutely), *Alford* which gropes in ecstasy indeed throughout its third, fourth and fifth lines, *Lux Benigna, Melita* with its almost Franckian enharmonies in the refrain, *Sanctuary* (an added sixth on the first note of the last phrase, a startling enharmonic change on the second), *Beatitudo* with its sumptuous added sixth and dominant ninth ('*Whence* all their *white* array'). In all these tunes, whether they actually make prominent use of lush chromatic discords or not (and most of them do), the emotional feel of the melodic-harmonic amalgam is heated, succulent and sensual in a way which carries more than a vague hint of

'After night has gone comes the day' in *Appalachia*. And if we examine Sir John Goss's tune for 'Praise, my soul, the King of Heaven' in this light, we even find a rudimentary anticipation of Delius's harmonic procedure in *Brigg Fair* and the *First Dance Rhapsody*; for Goss harmonises each verse specifically to accord with the varying sentiments of the text, though, of course, the melody remains unchanged throughout. In other words contrasting nuances of harmony are employed to lend flexibility of expression and emotive power to an essentially neutral melody, and Goss's grasp of chromatic harmony, however basic, is assured – especially in the third verse with its wither-wringing diminished seventh-type 'scrunch' on '*Widely* as His mercy flows'. Delius may well have had such music thrust upon him in his Bradford days, but surely it must have made an impression, however unconscious: Eric Fenby was one day astonished to hear him ask for Barnby's *Sweet and Low* which he considered a very good piece. Obviously something registered at the right time.

However the really important fact to which the Lambert quotation draws attention is that the nostalgia common to the religious Victorians, Delius and the American Negro sought expression in what grew into a basically identical harmonic language. Lambert later refers to the 'Impressionist harmony of the Debussy-Delius era' as forming the harmonic stock-in-trade of the jazz composer, but the issue is complicated. Was Delius consciously plundered by jazz composers? If so, what was the extent of his contribution compared with that of the true 'Impressionists', Debussy and Ravel? Alternatively, could it be that jazz harmony developed independently of contemporary European procedures, any similarity between the two being purely fortuitous and not indicative of influence either way? In the evolution of jazz harmony it is possible, without running the risk of excessive simplification, to isolate the three main indigenous tributaries which gradually converged to form, during the second decade of the century, a single harmonic current which was to carry all future developments on the crest of its wave. These three tributaries are:

(i) The harmony of the spiritual (derived basically from Anglo-Saxon church music).

(ii) 'barbershop' harmony.

(iii) the harmony of American popular music or 'Tin Pan Alley'.

The problem with which we have to contend in attempting a reasoned survey of this particular *genre* of harmony from its disparate sources, is that a certain point is reached whereat it becomes almost impossible to distinguish between direct or acknowledged European influence, unconscious borrowing, intuitive affinity and the purest coincidence. The issue becomes even cloudier as we note that while Debussy and Delius were busy at their respective keyboards widening the scope of European harmonic thought, similar ventures of a more primitive variety were in progress in America. The popularisation of the guitar, and to a lesser extent the banjo, was an important factor in the growth of harmonic sense in the white American as well as in the American Negro, for it gave rise to novel concepts of harmony familiarly classed as 'barbershop'. It is said that it originated in the barbershops of the South where, to while away the time on hot afternoons, the waiting customers would take it in turns to vamp upon the instrument which belonged to the establishment and by a process of trial and error experiment with unfamiliar chord combinations in a way exactly parallel with their more sophisticated European contemporaries at their pianos. These stringed instruments are so constructed as to allow combinations of three or more notes produced by a specific arrangement of the fingers of the left hand. Now once the fingering of a particularly attractive chord had been established, the player would naturally be drawn to using the same arrangement at other points along the fingerboard. It is easy to see in such procedures the characteristics of jazz harmony in embryonic form – the close-textured chromaticism, the love of parallel motion, the unselfconscious merging of one chord into another without regard to traditional norms of consonance and dissonance. 'Barbershop' harmony is not of course associated exclusively with the Negro; in fact it is more commonly thought of in connection with hillbilly, cowboy and other types of American rural folksong. None the less it was left to the impressionable, ever-fertile mind of the Negro to exploit most fully the innate potentialities of these methods and to introduce thereby highly personal permutations into the acquired harmonic content of his music.

The third of the chief contributory factors in the formation of jazz harmony is the American popular music industry, commonly known as 'Tin Pan Alley'. The names of Debussy, Ravel and Delius are frequently bandied about indiscriminately in connection with the harmony of the standard American pop song, but the key figure here, as in other facets of the development of early twentieth-century music, is undoubtedly Debussy. Debussy was the first to focus attention on the chord *per se* as a sonic entity freed from vassalage to a melodic line; his revolutionary status as a harmonist consists in his depriving chromatic harmonies of the need or even the desire for resolution. Debussy did not in fact invent new chords; it was his novel treatment of old ones – whether ordinary common chords or higher chromatic discords – that radically altered the entire Western concept of harmony. Debussy's methods necessarily brought into prominence the strikingly emotive qualities of ninths, elevenths and thirteenths, chords which, though present in the work of composers of the mid-nineteenth century and earlier, had by virtue of their assimilation into the

17

traditional harmonic context drawn little more attention to themselves than their more familiar confrères the common chord and its inversions and the seventh, dominant or diminished. It was inevitable that the surface appeal of these chords would sooner or later be exploited through attempts to revitalise the jaded harmonic palette of *fin-de-siècle* commercial music, and America was first in the field, partly because there was there a far greater influx of classically-trained musicians into the popular music industry than in other countries (the dividing-line between 'pop' and 'art' has always been much less rigidly observed in America than elsewhere). The harmonic innovations of Debussy were therefore ruthlessly pillaged, a process no doubt accelerated by the fact that he wrote small piano pieces which could be easily ransacked. The superficial trappings of Impressionism (needless to say the subtleties of Debussy's actual harmonic technique were disregarded completely; it was the blatantly sensuous appeal of his chords which were the centre of attraction) soon passed into the common-or-garden vernacular of the Tin Pan Alley song plugger, Broadway arranger or vaudeville pianist and from here into the *lingua franca* of the jazz band. The ground had after all been tilled beforehand; the harmonic experiments of Debussy and those of the barbershop string-pluckers differed only in the degree of sophistication and knowledge aforethought with which they were carried out, and when the harmonic idiosyncrasies of Impressionism crossed the Atlantic they became readily assimilated into an idiom which had been preparing itself quite unconsciously to receive them. There has always been a measure of cross-fertilisation between the parallel streams of American popular music and jazz, and if the rhythmic and melodic peculiarities of jazz gave a kind of strychnine injection to popular song-writing and musical theatre, jazz in reciprocation drew heavily on the harmonic bricks-and-mortar of Broadway commercialism in its endeavour to increase and develop its expressive scope.

The specific role played by Delius in this process is a curious one and difficult to define. During the period under discussion Delius's music was being played with tolerable frequency in England but practically nowhere else. In Germany, where many of his early successes had been scored, he was regarded as having failed to fulfil his early promise, and in France and America he was almost completely unknown. There can thus be little question of his exerting any direct form of influence on either jazz or Tin Pan Alley at this time. That his name is often mentioned in connection with one of the most distinguished jazz composers, Duke Ellington (of whom more anon), is due to a rather peculiar brand of coincidence.

The common denominator (again) is Debussy. The musical relationship of Debussy and Delius will be discussed in detail in a later chapter; it is sufficient to note here that none of the music of Delius's maturity came

into being in the years *preceding* his sojourn in Paris and eventual settle-
ment in rural France. In other words it is arguable that exposure to the
Impressionist aesthetic played a large part in the crystallisation of his
individual style, above all with regard to his concept of harmony. Debussy
and Delius may have differed greatly in their respective harmonic techniques, but the principle of emancipated discord, with unconditional repeal
of all laws relating to preparation and resolution, formed the *point de
départ* for both of them. Delius would have been receptive to such procedures both as a result of his own practical experiments at the keyboard
and through his great love of Grieg. It is obvious that when these rich
emancipated chords were prostituted by commercial hacks, they would be
reduced to the level of raw harmonic material and be capable of sounding
like rough, untutored Delius, rough untutored Debussy or like anybody
else who happened to be working in that particular brand of post-romantic
chromatic harmony; so that if a random harmonic sequence in a typical
pop song of this period sounds vaguely Delian, the resemblance is predictable but coincidental.

More specifically, certain *melodic* traits regularly observable in the mature
Delius are almost certainly Negroid in origin, for these melodic traits are
those which bear a distinctive profile of folk-music.

Despite the chauvinistic apologia of those who would couple Delius with
Elgar in the vanguard of the English Revival, nowhere in the entire Delian
oeuvre is there the remotest incidental suggestion of *English* folksong.
Rather is it *Scottish* folk-music that his melody often calls to mind. In this
connection Cecil Gray again provides the clue; in an earlier chapter of
Musical Chairs he describes the profound impact made upon him when he
first came across a collection of Majorie Kennedy Fraser's *Songs of the
Hebrides* which he regarded as the most important single musical influence
in his life. Later, speaking of his own music and its general dissimilarity to
that of Delius, he has one important exception to make:

'. . . There is one striking and curious affinity between us, namely a common
predilection for similar melodic formulas—curious, because this element, as far
as I am concerned, derives unmistakably from Hebridean folksong, which I
came to know before I ever heard a note of Delius, and which Delius never
heard at all. There is, for example, a melodic progression in the finale of his
music to *Hassan* which is almost note for note identical with one of the themes in
my *Deirdre*; yet there can be no question of any direct influence one way or the
other, since my melody existed on paper long before Delius wrote his incidental
music to Flecker's play, and he did not see my opera until after he had completed
his score . . .'

Gray is mistaken in thinking Delius entirely unacquainted with Hebridean folksong, for Fenby tells us that he enjoyed listening to records of this music from the very Kennedy-Fraser collection that Gray had earlier spoken of in such glowing terms. However there is no evidence that he was familiar with the songs when they first appeared in 1908, nor that Scotland occupied any higher place in his affections than England. The two factors which link his melody with Scottish folk-music are the pentatonic scale* and the Scotch Snap, a little syncopated rhythmic figure frequently noted in Hungarian folk-music as well. In fact both are regular constituents of countless folk-cultures throughout the world, but they are particularly prominent in both Scottish and Negro music.

When discussing the role of the pentatonic scale in Delius's music we must be careful to distinguish between pentatonic melody *per se* and what we may conveniently term pentatonic *figuration*. The latter in all probability has no generic connection with the pentatonic scale as such. If the triad of F major is played, and the second and sixth struck with it, we have, admittedly, a verticalisation of the pentatonic scale : but the practice of adding 'pimples' to chords, especially the second and the sixth, became widespread among composers of the post-impressionist period in France and England in an attempt to widen their vocabulary of euphony, and the fact that this particular chord and the pentatonic scale were one and the same thing was purely fortuitous (although no doubt the discovery of this particular added-note *trouvaille* was the result of some pianist's idle toying with the black keys of the pianoforte). The temptation to linger lovingly over the sensuous beauty of these sounds and to weave a kaleidoscope of textures out of pentatonic patterns was frequently succumbed to, not so much by Delius and Vaughan Williams as by their acolytes – E. J. Moeran, John Ireland and Herbert Howells. In Delius's music the use of this figuration rarely descends to the level of purposeless doodling. The little motivic fragments of which he is so fond (e.g. Ex. 6) have sufficient intervallic and rhythmic distinction to assert themselves wherever they may appear; elsewhere a pentatonic wreath of arabesque may enhance the movement of a chord sequence (e.g. the violin solo at the end of 'Pale amber sunlight' in *Songs of Sunset* or at the baritone's 'Yes, my brother, I know, for I have treasured every note' in *Sea-Drift*), or a short repetitive ostinato-like pentatonic pattern may support either the entire textural structure (as in the finale of *Songs of Farewell*) or a long-breathed melodic span as in the central section of *In a Summer Garden*. Pentatonic melodies *per se* are not infrequent in Delius's music. We have noted an early instance in the third movement of the *Florida Suite*, which is akin to

* Here and subsequently this term implies the most familiar of the five forms of this scale – F G A C D.

the 'Banjo Song' in Gershwin's *Porgy and Bess*. The theme of *Appalachia* is pentatonic, and so is the leader's cry from the helm of the boat, from which the beautiful cello cantilena in the slow section of the Double Concerto is in a direct line of descent. The tenor solo in the finale of *Hassan* (Ex. 4a) is of similar lineage. Since the 'missing' notes of the pentatonic scale are the fourth and seventh, pentatonic melodies will naturally dispense with the familiar rise from seventh degree to tonic at a cadence and will substitute the sixth. This is a marked characteristic of all Negro music (two well-known examples are the spirituals *Bye and Bye* and *Deep River*). Although the *Appalachia* theme itself uses a more expanded, though still utterly Negroid, form of cadence (one which is to be found earlier in the central portion of *Over the Hills and Far Away* and later in the theme of the First Dance Rhapsody) Delius instinctively incorporates the sixth degree-tonic formula in the variation which introduces the voices for the first time (p. 76 of the miniature score) so familiar was he with it in Negro vocal music. Thereafter it recurs in a number of different contexts – for instance at the end of the violin solo in *Songs of Sunset* which sings 'Pale amber sunlight' to its rest, and at the luminous cadence 'with bright eyes' in the first part of *Sea-Drift*.

The so-called 'Scotch Snap' is in Negro music a rudimentary form of anticipative syncopation and in Delius makes an early appearance in 'Near the plantation'; it is naturally prominent in the Negro melodies of *Koanga* and *Appalachia* but is also an occasional feature of the mature Delius. It occurs in the slow section of the Violin Concerto, in the 'March of Spring' in the *North Country Sketches*, and in the haunting tune in the second movement of the Third Violin Sonata. The fact that it is very prominent in the setting of Fiona MacLeod's *Hy Brasil* (the western isles of Celtic legend where sea and stars meet, and where light and life are eternal) is indicative merely of Delius's capacity for donning the national garb of whatever country he happens to be visiting in terms of literary texts; but the inclination to pentatonic melody and the Scotch Snap was already present. A final example is given as Ex. 3 which combines pentatonic melody with Scotch Snap and includes the characteristic cadential rise from sixth degree to tonic. The quotation is from *A Song of Summer*.

There is no accurate method of gauging the extent to which Negro melody drew on antecedents in the form of Anglo-Celtic folk-song or of estimating the proportion of indigenous to borrowed material in Negro music.

Ex.3

Both the Scotch Snap and the pentatonic scale are recognisable ingredients of both folk-cultures in their primordial state, and the fusion of the latter in the form of Afro-American music makes the drawing of hard-and-fast conclusions a hazardous business. The most likely explanation is that the American Negro found in Anglo-Celtic music certain elements which coincided with rhythmic and melodic tendencies of his own, and thus assimilated them quite effortlessly into the mainstream of his musical thought while preserving, to a certain extent, the flavour of their original context. What more natural than that Delius, retaining in his unconscious memory certain distinctive characteristics of music indissolubly associated with momentous events in his spiritual and emotional development, should automatically reproduce them in his own music which, as we have seen, was generated, in whole or in part, by recollection of those events? It is interesting that Delius in later life was apparently very fond of listening to records of Jerome Kern's *Ol' Man River* and other music of that nature, for obvious reasons: *Ol' Man River* is itself a stylised representation of a Negro worksong and is entirely pentatonic with a Scotch Snap in every phrase. Delius would have been heedless of any possible ambiguity of ethnological connotation, and a public attuned to the concept of him as a European, more specifically as an English composer as opposed to an American, will naturally seek in the first instance to relate any folkish traits to the British Isles rather than to America. Nevertheless there is every reason to suppose that America rather than Scotland was the progenitor of these idiosyncrasies as they occur in Delius's music, whatever their indirect relation to Hebridean folk-music may be.

3

If, then, as we have seen, so much in the sculpting of Delius's musical personality was the prerogative of America, it follows that there may well be *echt*-American composers exposed to similar influences and experiences whose music will show more than a superficial or coincidental *rapport* with Delius's. There certainly are, and two in particular whose musical relationship with Delius was complex and consisted in far more than a mere passing similarity of inflection.

The fundamental bond of sympathy between Delius and the Negro was that of sorrow and isolation. If Delius found in chromatic harmony of the post-Wagnerian variety the ideal agent for the expression of his nostalgia, what more natural than that an intelligent and sensitive Negro musician, similarly oppressed and with a similar stockpot of ripely expressive chromatic harmony at his disposal, should employ similar means to similar ends? Bix Beiderbecke was probably the first to become consciously aware of how chromatic harmony was permeating the atmosphere and being filtered down into pop (cf. *In a Mist* and other piano pieces of his), not that 'conscious awareness' in these matters is of any great importance. But it is worth trying to establish exactly why it is that Delius's name has so often been mentioned in conjunction with that of Duke Ellington; the fact that Ellington inherited his chromatics strained through the sieve of Broadway commercialism, whereas Delius's were evolved instinctively out of the varied influences at work upon him in his formative years, in no way colours the issue. Despite marked stylistic divergencies the underlying ethos is similar, and Ellington was able to forge his own personal idiom in the years when the very name of Delius was unknown to him. Later, after Percy Grainger had acquainted him with Delius's music, he was known to number *In a Summer Garden* among his favourite concert pieces, a list which also included Debussy's *La Mer* and Ravel's *Daphnis et Chloë*. Significantly, both these Impressionist works were honoured with a place in Delius's music library; 'honoured' is scarcely too exaggerated a term in the light of his notorious attitude to his fellow composers, and the number of full scores in his library could literally be counted on the fingers of both hands.

It is significant that Ellington started his life as a student of painting, and by all accounts his progress in this direction was not inconsiderable; he would thus be naturally drawn to the musical counterpart of Impressionism and in particular to the scope and potentialities of its novel harmonic techniques. The titles of his compositions frequently betray the preoccupation with colours and sensations *per se* so characteristic of the Impressionists – *Black and Tan Fantasy, In a Magenta Haze, Mood Indigo, On a Turquoise Cloud, Sepia Panorama, Black, Brown and Beige, Lady of the Lavender Mist, Perfume Suite* – and we constantly find, transformed into the Negro vernacular, echoes of the type of dreamy sensuous mood-evocation which Delius made peculiarly his own – as in *New York City Blues* (a nocturne), *Swanee River Rhapsody* (an aquarelle), *Sultry Sunset, Sultry Serenade, In a Mellotone, Warm Valley, In a Blue Summer Garden* (sic), *Night Time, Dusk* . . . and so the list goes on. Some of the titles even carry explicit Impressionist overtones, for instance *Misty Morning* (the title of a painting by Sisley), *Fontainebleau Forest* (see pp. 103–4) and Billy Strayhorn's Whistler-inspired *Chelsea Bridge*. What links these exquisitely beautiful, sensitively modulated mood-pieces with Delius's Impressionism rather than with Debussy's is the strong vein of personal melancholy which rises to the surface as for example in *Reminiscing in Tempo, Solitude, Awful Sad, Lonesome Lullaby, In a Sentimental Mood.*

23

Again the closely related themes of transience, nostalgia and spiritual isolation in Ellington's Impressionism, as in Delius's, cause abstract pictorialism to yield its monopoly to the contemplation of natural phenomena under the aspect of mutability.

One technical feature – Impressionist-derived – which Ellington shares with Delius is his use of the wordless human voice as an extra colour resource. In the 1927 recording of *Creole Love Call* it quickly becomes apparent that if Ellington is equating Adelaide Hall's wordless voice with the instruments in his band, he is no less equating the instruments with the voice. Miss Hall imitates a growl trumpet, but once Bubber Miley (trumpet) and Rudy Jackson (clarinet) have had their say it becomes almost difficult to determine who has been imitating whom – who has been singing and who has been playing. The studied ambiguity here and elsewhere is a legitimate musical variation on the familiar Impressionist theme of vagueness and imprecision. Perhaps Ellington's two masterpieces in this respect are *On a Turquoise Cloud* and the closely-related *Transblucency* ('A blue fog you can almost see through' – there is often poetry in Ellington's titles as well as in the music they embrace). These were both recorded in the mid '40s with Kay Davies, whose voice possessed a natural ability to blend and coalesce with the instruments in the band. In *Transblucency* it is virtually impossible to distinguish between her soft-grained vocalise and Lawrence Brown's trombone when he takes over from her. Then she does a duet with Brown and later with Jimmy Hamilton's clarinet; and we ask ourselves: Are we listening to two voices – or two trombones – or two clarinets? In *Heaven* (in the Second Sacred Concert) Johnny Hodges's alto saxophone with its feline voluptuousness of tone-quality and phrasing seems every bit as eloquently expressive as Alice Babs's preceding soprano solo, even though on this occasion she has the advantage of a lyric to sing. *T. G. T. T.* (in the same programme) is however a piece of pure vocalise (like *Minnehaha*) conceived more as a virtuoso vehicle for the voice than is the case with *Turquoise Cloud* or *Transblucency* where the voice is a component strand in the overall instrumental texture.

It is only comparatively recently, in the context of the Sacred Concerts, that Ellington has been drawn to examining the expressive potential of the chorus. Here, as occasionally elsewhere, we are reminded that if Ellington and Delius start together, there may not be any guarantee that they will finish together, but at least there will have been certain places *en route* where their paths will have crossed. In the Third Sacred Concert, given in Westminster Abbey on United Nations Day, October 24, 1973, there was a lovely solo for Alice Babs entitled *Is Love a Four-Letter Word for God?* The vocal sections were bisected by a monologue for Toney Watkins who declaimed his text to a soft background of wordless close-harmony choral singing. From where I was sitting in the nave I could not see the choir; I could only hear this floating turquoise cloud of ravishing choral sound. I suddenly realised that I was here participating in the Delian Experience. This was probably something approximating in a sophisticated manner to what Delius heard that evening 90 years ago on the verandah by the river. No wonder that the music bore so marked a resemblance to those wordless choruses behind the scenes in *Hassan*, and, now as then, brought before the mind's eye that vision of a better world where all is 'luxe, calme et volupté'. I understood the Delian Experience in that flash of revelation as I had never quite perceived it before.

Though there is a genuine analogy between what happens in Delius's harmony and colour-schemes and in Ellington's, for reasons we have already noted there can be no question of any *direct* Delian influence (at least insofar as Ellington's early mature work is concerned). Ellington would have assimilated the rudiments of Impressionist harmony chiefly through Will Vodery, chief arranger for the Ziegfeld follies, who advised him on matters of commercial harmonisation and scoring. In actual fact there is no real comparison between the way in which Delius and Ellington employ their chromatics, and this is closely bound up with their widely divergent approaches to form. Despite misleading titles such as *Creole Rhapsody*, Ellington is not, like Delius, fundamentally a rhapsodist; whereas Delius thinks naturally in long paragraphs, Ellington's pieces have the terseness and concentration of a Debussy prelude. Correspondingly Ellington's harmony is much less amply proportioned than Delius's; chromatic discipline is more severe, with tonal schemes sharply etched and rigidly adhered to – there is no drifting endlessly in chains of unresolved modulations, and while the norm of dissonance is more pronounced than in Delius, inversions of chords are generally avoided with a resultant increase in linear stability. The repercussions of Impressionism were certainly widespread, but, harmonically as in every other sphere, Ellington's music is as highly personal as Delius's and as subtly different from the latter's as Delius's is from Debussy's or Debussy's from Ravel's.

There is, of course, one vital difference between Delius and Ellington – the one is white, the other black. Delius's reactions to the Negro and his life and music were essentially those of an onlooker, however great the emotional affinity between them. *Koanga* and *Appalachia* are essentially stylised representations of Negro life and in this sense are far removed from the authentic spirit of Negro music. Yet the spiritual identification remains, and in this respect there are a number of remarkable similarities between Delius and another American composer, a white man whose obsession with Negro idioms oriented his entire creative career – George Gershwin.

Gershwin was born in Brooklyn in 1898 of Jewish parents, both Russian naturalised Americans, and that simple factual statement both throws light on his subsequent development and suggests an immediate parallel with Delius. For Delius was similarly born in a foreign land of emigré parents and lived a peculiarly stateless existence throughout his life. We noted when examining the various types of late-nineteenth-century Negro music that the themes which prompted them – the sorrow of parting, insecurity, uprootedness – were precisely those which preoccupied Delius even at a very early stage in his career. For though he might find temporary comfort and security in any one of a number of parts of the world – England, America, Scandinavia, Germany or France – he did not really seem to *belong* to any of them; he was fundamentally incapable of identifying himself with any one land or culture. Rural France proved sufficiently congenial to induce him to regard it as his base, but even in his younger days he was never absorbed into the mainstream of Parisian life and letters as were so many of his European and American contemporaries, and the older he grew the more unassailable became the barriers he erected between himself and the outside world. Now Gershwin never suffered from physical rootlessness in quite the same way, but psychologically his Jewish origin forms an exact counterpart to Delius's self-imposed cosmopolitanism. Constant Lambert in 'Music Ho!' draws attention to the increasing preponderance of Jews in the fields of jazz and popular music, remarking that '. . . the nostalgia of the Negro who wants to go home has given place to the infinitely more weary nostalgia of the cosmopolitan Jew with no home to go to.' Wilfrid Mellers also writes with special relevance to this point in *Music in a New Found Land*:

'This minority (the Negroes) could imbue its awareness of dispossession with a universal significance, making its melancholy serve as symbol of the alienation of modern, urban man. D. H. Lawrence said that humanity today is 'like a great uprooted tree'' and James Joyce made the hero of his modern Odyssey a Jew. The American Negro was literally uprooted from his home : the American Jew was a polyglot whose traditions had become so confused as to be inapprehensible. So, in the early days of jazz, the American Negro stood for the reality which the commercial world of the American Jew denied. Both asserted the vitality of low life as against the vested interests of "culture"; this may be why they had to seek, in Tin Pan Alley, a partial *rapprochement* – as in the case of George Gershwin.'

Gershwin's musical awakening had taken the form not of a Chopin waltz (as in Delius's case) but of Dvořák's *Humoresque* which he overheard played by a schoolfriend. But an event of equal, if not greater, significance had taken place some three or four years earlier. One day while roller-skating in Harlem, he heard jazz being played inside a club. He was quite transfixed by what he heard, and from then on often skated back to listen on the pavement outside. He later admitted that his lifelong attraction to Negro rags, blues and spirituals undoubtedly began at this time. Now this experience offers a quasi-parallel to Delius's first encounter with the Negro folk-idiom on Solano Grove which made such a lasting impression upon him.

Gershwin's predilection for Negro music revealed itself at an early stage in his work; his first instrumental composition was a piano rag entitled *Rialto Ripples*, and before long his popular songs began to bear the unmistakable imprint of the blues – the magnificent *Stairway to Paradise* and *Somebody Loves Me* were both products of the early 1920s. Then in 1922 Gershwin first conceived the idea of a Negro folk-opera, an apparently novel concept at that time (evidently no-one knew anything about *Koanga*, written some thirty years before). In the event a twenty-five minute long concoction of popular songs, jazz-like recitatives and other evocative effects entitled *Blue Monday* was incorporated in the George White *Scandals* of 1922. Although the score failed both to sustain its original run and to stand the test of revivals in 1936 and 1953, it represented a new departure in American musical theatre and a serious attempt by Gershwin to widen his scope in an unorthodox way; before long he was trying to effect a fusion of jazz traits and traditional classical idioms, with the results that all the world knows. The blues are prominently featured in Gershwin's first ambitious orchestral work, a rhapsodic evocation of Paris (*An American in Paris*) and here we may resume the parallel with Delius. For Delius's *Paris – A Nocturne (The Song of a Great City)* was the first work in which he revealed his skill at manipulating an orchestra of Straussian proportions, and, as in Gershwin's *Paris*, moods of unbridled gaiety and gnawing nostalgia are set side by side. The fine central B flat blues in *An American in Paris* is the counterpart of the quiet introspective episode in Delius's *Paris* (figure 13 in the Universal Edition score) which recurs, lyrically expanded, at figure 27 (*Molto lento*). There are no Negroid elements in Delius's *Paris*, but the sense of nostalgia and oppression – that of the homesick innocent lost in the big city – is identical with that of Gershwin, as is its expression within the form and context of an episodically-designed orchestral tone-poem.

As time went by it became a matter of increasing concern to those who believed in Gershwin that for all the admirable qualities of his music there was as yet no sign of any real personal involvement, no great emotional depth or conviction. There were isolated instances – odd moments in the Concerto and the more introspective Piano Preludes – which had fleetingly revealed the presence of a more searching insight, but his work as a whole lacked the strength of purpose and the blood-and-toil, sweat-and-tears commitment sought by those who looked to Gershwin for a contribution of lasting validity to American music. After the first performance of *An American in Paris*, Gershwin's friend and patron Jules Glaenzer gave a party at which Otto H. Kahn made a speech that must have sounded an oddly hollow note under the circumstances, saying in part that for the sake of Gershwin's art he could wish for the composer '. . . an experience, not too prolonged, of that driving storm and stress of the emotions, of that solitary wrestling with your own soul, of that aloofness . . . which are the most effective ingredients for the deepening and mellowing . . . of an artist's inner being and spiritual powers'.

By the early '30s it seemed that Kahn's wishes were going to be gratified. In 1931, with *Of Thee I Sing*, Gershwin scored his last great Broadway hit; the two shows he produced in 1933 were complete box-office failures, and at the same time his private life began to deteriorate. He became aware of an inner hollowness, a spiritual isolation. He began to suffer more chronically than ever from the digestive disorders which had assailed him all his life, and his sense of aloneness and insecurity can scarcely have been alleviated by reports from Europe of the rise of Nazism and persecution of the Jews.

It was in such a frame of mind that Gershwin in October 1933 finally decided to collaborate with DuBose Heyward on an operatic version of his novel *Porgy*, although the project had been mooted as long ago as 1926. The story was set in a Negro community in Charlestown, South Carolina, and during the summer of 1934 Gershwin went for an extended stay on Folly Island, a small barrier island some ten miles from Charlestown. Existence there was primitive in the extreme, but Gershwin was prepared to impose such privation on himself.

Evidently he felt instinctively that the time to realise his full creative potential was at hand, and his quest for authenticity took no account of any cost to himself. He visited numerous plantations, churches and other Negro haunts in his search for *materia musica*. His first real encounter with the raw taste of Negro living made an extraordinary impact on him. When he visited James Island with its primitive population of Gullah Negroes, DuBose Heyward noted that for Gershwin the visit seemed more like a homecoming than an exploration. 'The Gullah Negro . . . prides himself on what he calls "shouting". This is a complicated rhythmic pattern beaten out by feet and hands as an accompaniment to the spirituals, and is undoubtedly of African origin. I shall never forget the night when, at a Negro meeting on a remote sea-island, George started "shouting" with them, and eventually to their huge delight stole the show from their champion "shouter" . . .'

We cannot fail to be struck by the analogy with Delius here. In his case also, a period of withdrawal from the world was a necessary preliminary to the burgeoning of his creative powers, and, as with Gershwin, this withdrawal was into the ambience of the American Negro and involved exposure to a music which sang continuously of the great sorrows of life. For Delius the gestation period was abnormally long, and it needed a return to the scene of his self-imposed exile to goad the creative spirit into positive action; Gershwin's period of apprenticeship was already over, however, and creative fulfilment was the immediate outcome of his retreat from the world. Both Delius's *Appalachia* and Gershwin's *Porgy and Bess* interpret the Negro's sorrow in terms of the white man's nostalgia, and it is irrelevant that the music offers a highly personal evocation of the Negro country in the one case, and a synthetic picture of Negro life in the other. The main difference is that while Gershwin identifies himself so completely with the Negroes and their 'singing of the Lord's song in a strange land' that the application of the theme in a wider context evolves almost incidentally, in *Appalachia* the directly personal participation of the Negroes is reduced to a minimum. We may appreciate this the more fully if we compare Delius's use of a Negro folksong in the variations and finale of *Appalachia* with Tippett's incorporation of spirituals in his oratorio *A Child of Our Time*.

Tippett's preoccupation with Negro music had begun well before the Second World War; the earliest manifestation is probably the exhilarating pentatonic swing of the coda melody in the last movement of his 1939 *Concerto for Double String Orchestra*. Wishing in his wartime oratorio to put Nazi persecutions of the Jews into a musico-dramatic perspective, he turned naturally to the spirituals for their symbolic relevance to the contemporary scene: the perfect musical expression of the theme of man's inhumanity to man. Within the framework of the oratorio they function as a 'distancing' element, pointing the universal significance of the topical events recounted; and they offer an appropriate stylistic contrast, the composer skilfully integrating the two *genres* of expression through certain rhythmic, melodic and harmonic formulae common to both. In the highly-strung, emotionally-charged recitatives, set pieces and choruses, and no less in the cool, reasoned dignified sadness of the spirituals, Tippett embodies a selfless compassion both for the victims of the tragic history he chronicles and for suffering humanity in general. Now 'selflessness' and 'compassion' are qualities one hesitates to refer to in connection with Delius's philosophy of life. This is why we sense that when he built the climax of *Appalachia* round that trivial but strangely haunting fragment of Negro doggerel, his thoughts were as far from the plight of a Negro family being broken up through one of its members being transferred to a distant plantation down river as from suffering humanity in general. He was moved solely by personal application to himself and his experiences; he 'identified' with them in a personally-oriented context only.

Porgy and Bess is Gershwin's finest achievement. Predictably it is this work which offers the most striking parallels with Delius's music though not necessarily with his *Florida Suite*, *Koanga* and *Appalachia*. The first solo aria in *Porgy* – Clara's lullaby 'Summertime' – provokes in fact a comparison with *A Mass of Life*:

> Summertime
> And the livin' is easy
> Fish are jumpin'
> And the cotton is high;
> O your daddy's rich
> An' yo' ma is good-lookin',
> So hush little baby
> Don't you cry.
>
> One of these mornin's
> Your gonna rise up singin'
> Then you'll spread yo' wings
> An' you'll take the sky.
> But till that mornin'
> There's a-nothin can harm you
> With daddy and mamma
> Standin' by.

We may compare this passage to the alto solo in Part 1, Section 3 of the *Mass*:

'O Zarathustra! Beyond Good and Evil we found our own island and our green pastures. But when you hear that midnight bell striking the hour, you remember, Zarathustra, that you will soon have to leave me.'

The theme is identical: the rapture of the moment overshadowed by the imminence of loss. The mother knows that one day the baby *will* 'spread its wings', 'take the sky', leave its home and its parents, and in the conversation between life and Zarathustra, Life anticipates the moment when the Midnight Bell, Nietzsche's symbol of Death, will summon Zarathustra to take his leave of her. In each case the tragedy is underlined by a pentatonically-oriented vocal line supported harmonically over a bitter-sweet chromatic flux. Harmonically speaking, Gershwin was merely writing in the popular idiom of the day; but having followed the evolution of this harmony, noting that Duke Ellington was able to respond to its inherent poignancy and to some extent re-instate it upon its former pedestal, we can see how Gershwin, working within the same 'commercial' framework but bringing a new nobility and depth of sentiment to his task, likewise succeeds in re-investing this harmony with much of the poetry and emotive power of its prototype. Gershwin apparently had no great opinion of Delius's music – 'wet' music was how he described it to Bernard Herrmann – yet one of the many links between them is their feeling for the expressive range and flexibility of rich chromatic harmony. Witness not only 'Summertime' but also the lovely verse of the Boatmen's Chorus ('I'm a goin' out to the Blackfish banks'), Serena's superb lament over her dead husband ('My man's gone now'), and spirituals such as the tender, consolatory 'Clara! Clara! don't you be downhearted' or the exciting 'Oh the train is at the station an' you'd better get on board'. (Several of these, notably 'Summertime' and 'My man's gone now', weave the wordless chorus (singing to 'ah' or 'oo') into the accompanying orchestral texture in true Delian fashion.) Many of Gershwin's individual songs repay close study from the harmonic point of view, and so does the marvellous beginning and end of the slow movement of the *Piano Concerto*, and the *I Got Rhythm* variations. Few popular song composers were really Gershwin's equal in this respect, although many worked in a debased form of Delian harmonic currency. An exception is Harold Arlen in such songs as *One for my Baby* and other blues. The themes are ever-constant – the death of love, the yearning towards some distant haven of fulfilment.

Bearing in mind the probable connection between Delius's pentatonic melody and Negro folk-music, it is interesting to find that in both Delius and Gershwin pentatonic phraseology often occurs in contexts where some state of pristine innocence or unclouded happiness is involved (e.g. the 'easy summertime' and 'island beyond good and evil' of the above). No better example of this can be found than in the similarity between the tenor soloist's beautiful wordless melismata in the closing scene of *Hassan* and the street-cries in Act 2 of *Porgy*. In *Hassan* Ishak, the minstrel of Caliph Haroun-al-Raschid, revolted by his master's cruelty to the two lovers Rafi and Pervaneh, persuades Hassan, the poor confectioner who has been an unwitting instrument in their downfall, to join with him the great summer caravan to the cities of the far North East, divine Bokhara and happy Samarkand: 'It is a desert path as yellow as the bright seashore, therefore pilgrims call it the golden journey.' This theme of going on a journey is a typically romantic notion and a virtual *leitmotif* in Delius. The mysterious Negro minstrel in *Appalachia* is 'going down the river in the morning', the Dark Fiddler and his companions in *A Village Romeo and Juliet* are 'ever journeying onward, towards the setting sun', and in the final scene the barge with the two lovers in it drifts down the river, slowly sinking, to the 'Heigh ho! Travellers we a-passing by' of the distant boat-men. In Ishak the minstrel's own words:

> 'We are the pilgrims, master: we shall go
> Always a little further: it may be
> Beyond that last blue mountain barred with snow
> Across that angry or that glimmering sea,
> White on a throne or guarded in a cave
> There lives a prophet who can understand
> Why men were born: but surely we are brave
> Who take the Golden Road to Samarkand.'

This entire concept is wonderfully conveyed by a few bars of pentatonic vocalise: a sense of golden infinities of desert, 'the wide far distance, the great solitude'* and beckoning from beyond the horizon Samarkand, the oriental *Hy Brasil*, where all is peace, order and contentment. Time is suspended: there is no harmonic movement, merely a drone with added sixth, the voice in pentatonic quasi-improvisation, thrice interrupted by the sound of camel bells, and thrice returning ever closer (Ex. 4a).

Now there is an evident affinity here with the grief-stricken craving for the 'Promis' Land' so persistent a feature of Negro folklore. In Act 2 of *Porgy and Bess* Bess is recovering from her maltreatment in the hands of Crown, her ex-lover, and Peter, the simple-minded honey-man, has just returned from prison after being arrested in connection with Crown's murder of Robbins in Act 1. The air is oppressive, heavy with tragedy and foreboding, and into this atmosphere the street-vendors cry as if from another world, again a world of peace, order and contentment (Ex. 4b).

The coincidence in technique and mood between these two passages is extraordinary; in Ex. 4b we find the same loss of harmonic movement, the same vocal pentatonic quasi-improvisation, even identity of key – and the impact of each within their respective dramatic contexts is identical.

In this connection there is a distinct kinship between Porgy's final aria 'Oh where's my Bess' and the epilogue to Delius's *Sea-Drift*, 'O past, O happy life'. Both are in E major, there is the same yearning upward leap at the beginning, and the same obsessive tendency of the harmonic move-ment to revert to the tonic, as if in search of some elusive emotional equilibrium. In that marvellous ensemble – the finest in the opera, with Serena's and Maria's lines blossoming against Porgy's in curves of infinite grace and loveliness – Porgy sings of his grief at finding Bess gone upon his return home, and his aria is shot through with remembrance of past happiness as well as awareness of loss; while the bereaved sea-bird recalls

* Delius, *The Song of the High Hills*, UE score p. 23.

Ex.4(a)

 = blue note

the idyllic day-to-day existence he had once shared with his mate and accepts the permanency of his bereavement. Significantly Porgy's closing spiritual reverts to the theme of searching for the 'Promis' Land' and remains in E major; the pentatonic ostinato-like figuration with which the opera had opened (a lazy, aimlessly happy Saturday afternoon before Crown's arrival) here returns as a counterpoint in the orchestra – a schematic resemblance to *Sea-Drift* in that 'O past, O happy life' muses upon material earlier presented in the opening E major section which represented the love-happy life of the two 'feathered guests from Alabama'. The opera ends in a blaze of glory, with the falling blue thirds of Porgy's theme defiant rather than anguished as he drives out of Catfish Row on his search for his lost Bess and New York. The implications are that he will never find either (in the final stanza of the spiritual, muted trumpets slyly interject the theme of 'What you want wi' Bess?') and though Gershwin radically altered DuBose Heyward's original ending which left Porgy 'alone in an irony of morning sunlight', the conventional 'happy ending' is equally remote. Gershwin contends that abandoning oneself to one's grief is reprehensible and only by making a stand against circumstances can one learn to come to terms with them – just as the sea-bird eventually accepts the reality of his bereavement but only after long nights of solitary vigil taunted and mocked by the wind and the waves. 'Acceptance' rather than 'resignation' is the appropriate term in this context; Delius was an instinctive 'yea-sayer' to life, and the recurrent themes of spring and re-birth which permeate his music colour even his most poignant expressions of grief with an optimistic ray.

Constant Lambert's name has been invoked on more than one occasion concerning Delius's relationship with jazz; in fact it was he who first mooted the possibility of a direct link between them. To view the situation from the vantage-point of his own activity as a composer yields some interesting results. For Lambert's attitude to jazz and the widespread infiltration of jazz elements into his music had little in common with the procedures of other European composers of the period, who dallied with the subject in varying degrees of committal, only to drop it like a red-hot coal when it had passed the peak of its notoriety. Lambert's response, like Gershwin's, was altogether more positive, and both his personality and his music were profoundly affected by his intuitive sympathy with the American Negro.

Lambert's most revealing musical experience occurred in 1923, when C. B. Cochran brought from the USA a troupe of coloured singers and players for one of his revues at the London Pavilion. Lambert was particularly struck by the opening fanfare-like fantasia on 'Carry me back to old Virginny' played by the Negro orchestra, and in an article written for *New Statesman and Nation* in 1932 he recalled his experience as part of a protest against the 'emasculated gaucherie' of the typical English jazz band of the day:

'After the humdrum playing of the English orchestra in the first part (of the revue) it was an electrifying experience to hear Will Vodery's* band playing the Delius-like fanfare which preluded the second. It definitely opened up a whole new world of sound.'

* The same Will Vodery who had been Duke Ellington's tutor (see p. 25).

From that day Lambert's enthusiasm for American Negro music never deserted him. He was among the first to foster a serious appreciation of jazz in general in this country and of the work of Duke Ellington in particular, whose talents as a creative musician were being recognised simultaneously by Percy Grainger in New York. With Grainger, also, Lambert perceived the technical and spiritual affinity between Ellington and Delius. We have seen how in *'Music Ho!'* he pointed out that their respective harmonic idioms had evolved, not only from the debris of Wagnerian chromaticism filtered through Debussy, but also from the hymn-tunes of J. B. Dykes and his contemporaries, Delius having been exposed to these hymns not only in the pristine state in Victorian Bradford but also in their actual Negro transmutations on his orange plantation in Florida. Lambert was also aware of the joint indebtedness of Delius and Ellington to the techniques of French Impressionism – though in either case Impressionism of the subjective variety.

Although in his own music Lambert was not to any appreciable extent affected either by Delius or by Ellington, there are certain correspondences in the work of all three which may be directly attributed to their common sympathy with the Negro ethos and its expression in music. The most striking is the use of the upward-thrusting pentatonic triplet at x in Ex. 5, which is a reconstruction from memory by Angus Morrison of the fanfare by which Lambert was so enthralled in 1923. This figure seems to have haunted Lambert for a number of years, for while it is introduced fairly unobtrusively into the *Elegiac Blues* (written, as was Ellington's *Black Beauty*, in memory of Florence Mills, the black singer), it so

Ex.5

Ex.6

and any number of variants all producing the pentatonic/added 6th sonority - c.f. Ex. 2a and b, 9, 16, 23b, 28, 31, 32.

permeates *The Rio Grande* as to give pulse and incandescence to the entire score; the first choral entry is a case in point.

This very motif is also one of Delius's most easily recognisable finger-prints (Ex. 6). From the early Björnson setting of *Twilight Fancies* (1889) to the final *Song of Summer*, reconstituted by Fenby some forty years later, there is hardly a single important composition in which it is not to be found; significantly, it first appears in readily recognisable form in the prologue to *Appalachia*. The phrase is also to be found in Ellington's *Black and Tan Fantasy* and is evidently an example of what Wordsworth called 'these arbitrary connections of feelings and ideas with particular words and phrases from which no man can altogether protect himself', though here we have an instance of similar ideas and emotions prompting a similar musical reaction in not one but four composers (if we include the anonymous author of Ex. 5). Again, Lambert mentions Delius specifically in connection with the *Plantation* fanfare in that *New Statesman* article; his experience at the Cochran revue corresponded exactly to that of Delius at Solano Grove and of Gershwin in Harlem and, later, on Folly Island; in each case the music of the American Negro struck a vibrantly sympathetic chord in an imagination which had previously been searching in vain for a satisfactory mode of self-expression. No wonder that Lambert in later life was so taken by the 'Dance of Deliverance' in Arthur Bliss' ballet *Miracle in the Gorbals*, one of the scores whose premiere he directed in his capacity as chief conductor of the Sadler's Wells Ballet. *Miracle in the Gorbals* was an allegory of the passion set in the Glasgow slumland whose turning-point is reached when a young girl suicide is brought back to life by a mysterious stranger. The girl starts a dance to express her new-found faith in life, and the crowd encircling her gradually becomes infected with her enthusiasm. They begin to dance with her 'showing something of the religious ecstasy and fervour of a Negro congregation'. The music takes its kindling power of fire from the Negro-Delian conventions of harmonic syntax it perforce adopts – a syntax normally quite alien to Bliss – and the result is a miracle (Ex. 7).

Another name which could be mentioned in this connection is that of Darius Milhaud, a Jew born and reared in the heart of Provence, of whose jazz ballet *La Création du monde* both Lambert and Gershwin were fond admirers. A wonderfully fresh note of pastoral lyricism and a receptivity to a wide variety of folk-cultures have always been two of the most attractive features of his work; yet surely, as in Gershwin's case, the fact that he was a Jew decisively influenced his response to Negro music. He first became interested in jazz in the summer of 1920 at the Hammersmith Palais de Danse in London, where Billy Arnold and his band were playing. He was fascinated by the subtleties of timbre and the wide range of ex-

4. J. P. Jacobsen.

5. Percy Aldridge Grainger
(photo inscribed to
Bernard Herrmann).

6. Left to right: Grieg (the last photo); Grainger; Nina Grieg; Julius Röntgen, Troldhaugen, 1907.

7. Delius and Percy Grainger in Frankfurt, c. 1923.

Ex.7

pressive nuance extracted from saxophone, clarinet, trumpet and trombone. Then came his discovery of Harlem. 'The music I heard there was absolutely different from anything I had heard before, and was a revelation to me. This was authentic music which had its roots in the darkest corners of the Negro soul, the vestigial traces of Africa no doubt . . .' As a result of these experiences Milhaud composed what is universally regarded as one of the best of his works, *La Création du monde*. Milhaud was nurtured on Impressionist harmony – the harmonic base of jazz – and, again, the Negroid inflections superimposed upon it bring the result on occasions quite close to Delius; particularly the closing bars, dissolving as they do with infinite sweetness and tenderness in the fresh mists of a Provençal spring.

So the re-creation of that 'whole new world of sound' became Lambert's over-riding preoccupation, just as some thirty years earlier it had become Delius's. The 'sound' was that of the American Negro, the music of a dispossessed race. In Will Vodery's fanfare (Ex. 5) he glimpsed a vision of far horizons, exotic climes and a respite from the drabness and disillusion of the contemporary scene; and these were qualities which attracted him to Sacheverell Sitwell's poem *The Rio Grande*.

Eric Fenby has said that *The Rio Grande* was one of the few 'modern' works for which Delius had a special regard. No wonder. Lambert, reciprocally, was a sympathetic and discerning admirer of Delius's music, and *The Rio Grande* is the work in which the two draw closest together; there are a number of subtle correspondences.

There is no apparent justification for the jazz element in *The Rio Grande*, and in fact the South American setting of the poem is reflected in appropriate dance-rhythms and local melodic colour. However, Lambert was less concerned with topographical niceties than with the fact that the poem was a virtual transliteration of that mood of feverish activity suffused with desperate melancholy which accorded so well with his own temperament and outlook, and which he had found reflected in the music of Ellington. He found a jazz idiom fully equipped to express the nostalgia and weariness through which the riotous, effervescent, kaleidoscopic sequence of images is put into true perspective. Delius's *Paris – The Song of a Great City* is similarly conceived, a frenetic whirl of activity being contrasted with slow lyrical passages of an intimate, deeply personal nature. As we noted earlier when discussing Gershwin's *American in Paris*, the core of Delius's *Paris* is the haunting theme first heard on the violas and later eloquently developed, which indicates a withdrawal for contemplation, an introspective brooding on the sights and sounds of Parisian night-life and their significance in terms of the onlooker's own experience. This episode and its emotional overtones correspond exactly to the central section of *The Rio Grande* – 'the noisy streets are empty and hushed is the crowd' – an impression enhanced by the very Delian sound of the unaccompanied chorus. Braced by a slow tango, the fine passage which follows evokes the awesomeness and poignancy of the great city of Rio deserted by night; there is 'such a space of silence through the town to the river/that the water murmurs loud, above the band and crowd together', and then the music launches abruptly into the saga of river and waterfall 'as the great Rio Grande rolls down to the sea', resuming the ebullience of the opening. In the same way Delius, his nostalgia temporarily forgotten, hurls himself even more recklessly into the bustle and revelry which this time threatens to exceed all bounds (fig. 28 in the UE score). Three climactic gong strokes, and the spirits of night vanish into thin air; 'the noisy streets are empty and hushed is the crowd'. The scene remains to be flooded momentously by the rising sun, finally dissolving in a Technicolor haze of added sixth sonority; but the epilogue of *The Rio Grande*, after the climactic augmented eleventh chord (also heralded by a massive gong stroke) which carries a second piano cadenza in its wake, subsides peacefully into a quiet commentary on earlier motifs, and evoking a strange calm of ships at anchor, noiseless in a sunset harbour:

> Till the ships at anchor there
> Hear this enchantment
> Of the soft Brazilian air
> By those Southern winds wafted

Slow and gentle,
Their fierceness tempered
By the air that flows
between.

It is here that the most striking parallel to Delius occurs, though this time *Appalachia* not *Paris* is involved. After the alto soloist has sung of 'the soft Brazilian air by those Southern winds wafted', these words are echoed in turn by a solo soprano and tenor *from the chorus*, stepping anonymously out of the massed wordless murmur with spellbinding effect. This is notably reminiscent of the baritone soloist's 'O Honey I am going down the river in the morning' in *Appalachia*, similarly a voice from the crowd – the soloist must sing from within the chorus, not beside the conductor, as Delius is at pains to make explicit. The voices call from the dim distance, a mystic summons from 'leagues beyond the sunset bar'. That Lambert in this instance was unconsciously mindful of *Appalachia* is virtually attested in an article on Delius he wrote for *Apollo* in which he claims:

[In his work] human passion and its background of elemental nature are inextricably interwoven. I am thinking of *Sea-Drift* and *Appalachia* where to my mind his art reaches its greatest height, and in particular of passages like the outburst of the chorus to the words 'Shine! Shine! Shine!' in *Sea-Drift* and the entry of the solo voice in *Appalachia*. Such moments strike too deeply to bear analysis.

In an interview given in 1930 Lambert expressed a wish to perform *The Rio Grande* with a Negro choir, and admitted that he had conceived the vocal writing in terms of Negro voices. It is possible that, if such a treatment were accorded not only *The Rio Grande* but also *Appalachia* (a Paul Robeson would be wonderfully idiomatic as soloist) the result would come in the nature of a revelation.

CHAPTER TWO

Scandinavia

1

Of all the countries to which Delius was instinctively drawn, Scandinavia held him the most permanently in thrall. This is understandable, when we remember that Sweden, Denmark and particularly Norway were initially responsible for liberating in him the artistic, if not actually the creative, impulse. Pitchforked by his father into a career of industry and commerce in the highest degree repugnant to him, Delius was first sent to Scandinavia in 1882 on a business trip.

All notions of business fled, however, as, upon arrival in Stockholm, he abandoned himself for the first time to the type of sybaritic indulgence which was thenceforward to colour his entire life and personality. The atmosphere of the capital, cultured, bracing and exuberant, contrasted tellingly with the pettifogging sordidness of his own home town of Bradford; and then came the revelation of the Norwegian mountains and fjörds. The effect of the scenic wonders of Norway was little short of cataclysmic on a youth who had first felt intuitively, in the vastness and remoteness of the West Riding moors, that he might do 'something unusual' with his life. Here for the first time his affinity with high, wild and lonely places, 'the wide far distance, the great solitude' (as he was later to label one of the salient themes in *The Song of the High Hills*), was made manifest.

Men like Delius who love hills find in them something more than a medium whereby they may express themselves in terms of physical force; for hills have the power not only to draw out the best from within a man, but to interpret his inmost thoughts in terms of an even greater awareness, an awareness that height somehow brings exhilaration, enhances life, quickens it to a finer rhythm. It is the unchanging quality in mountains which makes them so valuable to man : they are steadfast, they are perfectly in tune with the universal rhythms and harmonies of nature, they bring man into touch with those forces which mean happiness, and they are a medium whereby beauty can be experienced in its freshest, purest, freest form. In

40

the high hills Delius found the beauty he craved above all else; and throughout his life they were a constant and quickening source of inspiration to him. In the most wonderful music he ever wrote – *The Song of the High Hills* – he is alone with the mountains of Scandinavia, just as Sibelius in *Tapiola* is alone with its vast forests.

The year following his first visit (1883) Delius went on another business trip to Norway, and became well enough acquainted with the language to understand the plays of Ibsen and Björnson; in due course he also acquired enough Danish to be able to read in the original language the works of the man who became one of his three favourite authors – Jens Peter Jacobsen. But it was first and foremost Norway which attracted him, not only by its scenery but by its general atmosphere, climate, culture and people. He contrived whenever possible to spend a part of each year in Norway, a practice discontinued only in the 1920s when the onset of his disease severely restricted the range of his physical capabilities; it was his habit to ponder his works in the mountains of Norway during the summer and commit them to paper on his return to his home in France, and during the 1914–18 war he acquired the permanent lease of a home in Romsdal.

The early years in particular brought Delius many memorable experiences in Norway. In 1887 he visited it for the first time since 1883 and stayed in the region of the Sogn Fjörd. He carried a notebook with him in which he even tried his hand – with little success – at notating songs in the fields; but the notebook accompanied him on mountain holidays for many years. Two years later he, Grieg and Christian Sinding went for a walking tour in North Norway which Delius later declared to have been the most memorable of all; he was taken for the first time into the Jotunheim, and as he explored the country round, the subject of his first opera *Irmelin*, based on an amalgamation of two Scandinavian folk-tales, took root in his mind. So did the overture *Paa Vidderne* ('On the Heights') based on Ibsen's poem – one that Delius had earlier set in the form of a melodrama for speaker and orchestra. (Rachel Lowe-Dugmore discovered that the *Paa Vidderne* overture was the first orchestral work of Delius to be publicly performed; it was given by Ivor Holter in Christiania in 1891.) Another orchestral piece inspired by the Norwegian mountain country – more frequently performed than *Paa Vidderne* – is *Over the Hills and Far Away*, written in 1894. Two years later we find Delius working on the opera *Koanga* on his mountain holiday. He writes to Jelka in June 1896: 'I am living on a big farm in Valders on the mountainside of a lovely valley and work at my opera – the air is delicious and I live very well. The nights are *grand*: light all night, and the atmosphere, the colours of the hills, the woods and the vales are really beautiful. The sun sets at about 8.30 behind the mountains and huge shadows begin to creep across the valley: at 10.30

41

only the tops of the hills covered with fir trees are lighted by the sun's rays and stand out as if in gold. Then everything disappears in a mystic half-light, all very dreamy and mysterious – it is light enough to read and to distinguish every detail at the other end of the valley and on the mountain tops. Only one drawback – I cannot sleep! It is quite day at 2.30 a.m. and my room has four windows looking out over the valley. The inside of the room is painted a faint pink and the blinds are only bits of pink cloth. The result is that all through the night I have a wonderful sunrise effect in my room . . .' Later: 'I've been out in the wilds – went with a knapsack into the Jotunheim, that very wild group of mountains with wonderful glaciers and snow-topped and jagged peaks. My guide and I tramped for several days in the delicious air and most of the time over snow and reindeer-moss – a sort of pale green light moss which covers the hills when there is no snow and which the reindeer eats. What a wonderful feeling being up so high, tramping twelve or fourteen hours a day in this invigorating air – how I enjoyed it! I then went across to Taaga, a lovely and smiling valley on the other side of the Jotunheim and thence to Gudbransdalen where I went up into another wild range of hills, the Rondane, and tramped for several days over to Foldalen on the other side, staying the night at *saeters* in a very primitive style. On top of the Rondane we were overtaken by a tremendous thunderstorm – in fact we were up so high that we were literally in the thick of it, lightning flashing all about us. It looked awfully dangerous but I don't suppose it really was. We lay down in the drenching rain and waited till the lightning calmed down a bit; a few scared reindeer rushed by a short distance from us at a tremendous pace – quite a rare thing, as I believe you rarely see them closer than a mile or two away. However, after the storm the sun came out and dried us and we had a lovely walk to the nearest *saeter*.'

In later years Jelka sometimes accompanied her husband on his Norwegian mountaineering trips, but in the summer of 1908 his companion was none other than the 29-year-old 'Mr' Thomas Beecham (Delius was by then 46, and it is obvious from the foregoing that he must still have been in the peak of physical condition). He writes from Molde to Jelka on 4 August 1908: 'This is a place where you would like to stay sometime and paint. The sun sets just opposite a wonderful range of mountains and throws its rays straight upon them just as in Grez with the trees.' On 22nd he writes from Geiranger: 'We have just arrived here from Grotlien where we stayed last night. Grotlien is well situated: from there to Merok is the finest scenery I have ever seen. It is really fantastic; you must see it. We passed one lake hemmed in by a gigantic black, blue and green cliff of solid rock with patches of snow on the sides which were quite perpendicular – perhaps a clear thousand feet from the lake. The sides were reflected in the entirely dark blue water to extraordinary effect – all purple, green, blue and white.'

An earlier letter from Jendesboden speaks eloquently for Delius's physical stamina. I reproduce it in its entirety:

Dearest Jelka,

We arrived here yesterday evening at 6 after a glorious walk thro' Uladalen from Spiterstulen. The weather since Sunday is blazing hot and not a cloud in the sky. Gjendin looks lovely. We left Skaare in Stryn on Wednesday midday and walked up to Sundalsaeter. We found there only a dirty little hut and nothing to eat and we had to sleep on some dry twigs with only a dirty cover. Of course we were eaten up by fleas and neither of us slept at all. Next day we left at 6 p.m. for our big walk over the Jostedal brae to Nysahytten – we could only get a cup of coffee and a few pieces of bread and butter but the weather was fine and sunny. It had rained all night and our hut was swimming – it was a frightfully tough walk up to the glacier. 5 hours almost as steep as a house – Beecham seemed quite done up and faint and I thought we should have to turn back – he pulled together however very pluckily. I carried his knapsack and the guide carried mine. The walk over the glacier was grand and nothing but snow in sight and snow-covered peaks. After we crossed the glacier we descended gradually to Mysahytten-Saeter which was a frightful distance. We were 14 hours walking with only a couple of sandwiches each. B. could scarcely walk any more – we had to wade a stream which took me almost up to my waist, the man carried B. across. We got within 50 yards of 4 wild reindeer and a splendid 'Storbock'. At Mysahytte we found a somewhat better saeter, but just as many fleas – our food was fladbroed and cheese only with a few slices of fat bacon. Next day we walked to Sota Saeter where we arrived at 1 p.m. and could get nothing but goats cheese and fladbroed. We then walked to Dyring Saeter and there we got a horse and haycart to carry us to Mork and a stolkjaerre from there to Flekhoi. There we behaved like pigs over a wonderfully good supper: we had had nothing but cheese and fladbroed ever since leaving Slaare. We went on to Roesheim and arrived at the same time as you and I did on our memorable journey. We got a guide to carry the heaviest knapsack and trudged along up towards Gjuvas-hytten. On the way it began to pour and kept it up for an hour – just enough to wet us all thoroughly – it then stopped and we arrived at Gjuvas-hytten at 10.30 p.m.; they were all in bed, but got up and made us tea and supper. Next day sunny and glorious again and we went up Galdhoepig together with 2 other Englishmen. The view was again splendid – In the afternoon we took it easy down to Spiteratulen, where we arrived in time for supper. The other guests were 4 German women of the ugliest kind – even the guides began to laugh as they came in; something fearful to look at – Next day, Monday we started at 9 a.m. for Gjendeboden and had a most glorious trip thro' one of the wildest valleys of Jotunheimen – we got an excellent meal with fresh trout and clean beds; we are staying a day over here as it is so nice and clean. Today, Tuesday, not a cloud in the sky and very warm. I went out to fish and caught

one, missed a very big one as I have no landing net; at 4 I am going again with
B. to help me to land the fish – we are enjoying ourselves splendidly and feel in
wonderful health and spirits.

I have quoted extensively from this correspondence (previously unpublished) to allow the reader to experience at first hand something of the
rapture to which Delius was ever moved by the beauty and grandeur of
mountain scenery. The seeds of *The Song of the High Hills* were actually
sown when Delius was in Norway in 1907 whither he had travelled with
his wife to attend Grieg's funeral. After Grieg's death, and in proportion
as he grew older and the first tokens of his fatal illness began to sap his
bodily strength, Delius found himself turning more and more to the North-
lands for inspiration: *The Song of the High Hills*, big pieces inspired by
the writings of J. P. Jacobsen (*Fennimore and Gerda* and *Arabesk*), the
orchestral suite *North Country Sketches* and the orchestral ballad *Eventyr*
(an evocation of Scandinavian folk-lore as represented by the *Norske
folkeeventyr* of Asbjörnsen and Moe) – these are all typical of the trend.
Although his actual visits to Norway necessarily decreased in number, he
continued to go even after losing the use of his legs, and Eric Fenby
movingly relates the story of the last of these visits when the composer, still
retaining some sight, was carried up the mountainside by his wife and
Percy Grainger, on an improvised chair on poles, for one final glimpse of
the sunset over the great hills in the distance.

Delius's circle of friends both in Leipzig and in Paris was composed predominantly of Scandinavians. He made the acquaintance of Christian
Sinding and Johan Halvorsen, and at Christmastide 1887 Eduard and Nina
Grieg arrived for the first performance of Grieg's C minor Violin Sonata.
Their friendship continued unbroken to the end of Grieg's life, and its
importance can hardly be over-estimated. Most of Delius's early compositions
were submitted either to Sinding or to Grieg for inspection and criticism,
and he certainly declared much later that the sole benefit he had
derived from his three-year sojourn in Leipzig had been his meeting with
Grieg – but for whose kindly intervention the years immediately following
upon his departure from Germany might have been more fraught with
difficulties than they actually were. For when his Leipzig studies were over,
Delius was faced with the problem of dunning a recalcitrant father for
further financial assistance which would have indubitably been refused had
not Grieg, dining Delius senior at the Hotel Metropole in London, affirmed
his belief in the young man's creative talent and urged paternal indulgence.
Unstinted praise from a musician of Grieg's eminence had the desired
effect, and the allowance was continued, though reduced to the barest
minimum. A benevolent uncle living in Paris agreed to subsidise the young

Delius who made his home in or around *la ville lumière* for the next eight or nine years.

Upon arrival in Paris Delius soon began to attract a small but select entourage of Scandinavian musicians, writers and painters. His chief companion was a violinist from Hamar, Arve Arvesen. The painters Eyolf Soort and Gudmund Stenersen were both studying in Paris at this time and visited Delius in his little house in Ville d'Avray and later in Croissy, and he also knew Bergliot Björnson, daughter of the patriot poet, through whose invitation he stayed with the Björnsons at Aulestad in the summer of 1891. The start of his friendship with the mysterious itinerant Norwegian violinist Halfdan Jebe (dedicatee of *Arabesk*) also dates from this period. Jebe, Delius and the novelist Knut Hamsun all embarked on an extraordinary kind of mock-musical Norwegian tour in the summer of 1896, and Jebe also accompanied Delius on his fateful return journey to Florida later that same year. Jebe springs up at various intervals during Delius's life but he later seems to have disappeared into thin air, and no legal heir has so far been traced (a pity, for there must have been a prolific correspondence between the two musicians).

A favourite rallying-point for Scandinavian artists in Paris was the household of William Molard (a musician-cum-civil servant married to Ida Erikson, the Swedish sculptress) into which Delius was introduced early in his Paris days. Through Molard and his wife he came to know Gauguin, Strindberg, Munch, Gunnar Heiberg, Johan Selmer, Jappe Nilssen, Helge Rode. Delius wrote music for Heiberg's play *Folkeraadet*, produced at Christiania in 1897, and Rachel Lowe-Dugmore has shown that although this satire on the Norwegian parliamentary government and the political tension existing at that time between Norway and Sweden seems an unlikely subject to inspire Delius, the politics of Scandinavia interested him intensely throughout the period 1891–7.* When the Norwegian consular question hit the headlines in 1892 Delius corresponded with Mrs Otto Blehr, wife of the Norwegian Prime Minister from 1891–3, with whom he sometimes stayed on his visits to Norway. This correspondence reveals that the plot of *Folkeraadet* parallels in certain respects Delius's convictions

---

* The *Folkeraadet* music has now been revived and performed in the form of a four-movement *Norwegian Suite* for orchestra. It reveals indebtedness to Grieg and also to Wagner – but, oddly, to the Wagner not of *Tristan* but of *Meistersinger*: the textures have that unmistakable neo-Bachian crispness and crackle. There are many foreshadowings of the later Delius, most notably in the lovely oboe melody which forms the second subject of the Overture, parent to the celebrated solo in the *Fennimore and Gerda* intermezzo. The third movement, a scherzo, is first cousin to the *Appalachia* brass-band variation which must have been composed at much the same time; as trio it contains one of those powerfully tender melodies which in the mature Delius are always affianced to nature in her calmness and stillness.

about the division of humanity into three distinct groups, the 'All or Nothing People', the 'Something People' and the 'Nothing People'.

A large proportion of Delius's apprentice compositions are Scandinavian in flavour, notably the opera *Irmelin*, the orchestral pieces *Paa Vidderne*, *Summer Eve*, *Marche caprice* and *Sleigh Ride*, the *Florida Suite*, the *Legend* for violin and piano (or orchestra), and nearly all the early songs. Delius was a prolific song-writer at this stage of his career, and he chose his texts primarily from the works of Scandinavian poets – Vinje, Welhaven, Björnsen, Holger Drachmann, Paulsen, Munck, Ibsen and particularly J. P. Jacobsen. In this respect he resembled and, in his choice of individual poems, often vied with, the composer who exerted more musical influence over him than any other. This was Grieg.

2

Delius's first contact with Grieg's music and his later meeting with the composer himself were among the most momentous events in his formative years, comparable only with his early experience of the Negroes and their music in Florida. Grieg's influence would have been invaluable enough had it been merely a matter of constant help, encouragement and advice bestowed by a composer of distinction and attainment upon an immature young artist; from a purely practical point of view, Delius's debt to Grieg was considerable. However, in the technical sphere as well, Grieg's influence reigned paramount and supreme over Delius's early work; and despite the numerous extraneous elements which came in due course to contribute to its distinctive identity, in tone and temper Delius's music remained fundamentally Scandinavian to the end of his life, with Grieg as its primary source. To understand the reason we need to recognise one fact above all – that Grieg was to all intents and purposes the first nature mystic in music. And, like all mystics, he was primarily a poet. Delius once told C. W. Orr 'Grieg's music is so fresh, poetic and original – in fact, just like Norway.'

Norwegian music came of age in the wake of a great wave of national sentiment framed historically by the move for national independence which gathered momentum in the latter half of the nineteenth century and won its ultimate victory in 1905. When the earliest investigators, imbued with the fervour of national romanticism, began systematically to collect Norway's folk-music, they discovered an astonishingly rich fund of material which was immediately requisitioned in the quest for an authentically Norwegian national musical idiom. This was the professed aim of the three most prominent figures in Norwegian music before Grieg – Ole Bull, L. M. Lindemann and Rikard Nordraak. It was Nordraak who finally convinced Grieg of the true stature and merit of folk-music, but Grieg found therein far more than a welcome and opportune alternative to the Germanic symphonic tradition with which he had failed to come to terms at Leipzig – he glimpsed in the melodic, rhythmic and potentially harmonic unfamiliarities of folk-music the technical means of adding an entirely new dimension to the expressive orbit of music in general.

Grieg was one of the first composers to perceive the latent possibilities of music as an agent of evocation and suggestion; he cultivated the properties of atmosphere and colour as opposed to form and dialectic. He was prompted by his desire to reproduce something of the essential spirit of his country, not only of its people but also – and in this respect Grieg was a pioneer – of its *landscape*. He was the first composer to draw inspiration *directly* from nature and in folk-music with its origins in, and redolence of, rural as opposed to urban communities; he found it the natural and inevitable *materia musica* he was seeking. In this respect Delius was one of Grieg's legitimate sons and heirs, for nature throughout his life was his prime source of inspiration – and historically he was in a position to utilise the novel techniques of expression patented by Grieg without having first to develop these techniques from the raw materials of folk-song. For Grieg had intuitively realised that, for the next half-century at least and possibly longer, the folk-song held the key to the future. If the natural evolution of the musical language was not to be arbitrarily impeded, new influences had to be assimilated without regard to technical convention or academic rectitude. The new melodic principles rooted in folk-music necessitated a re-orientation of accompanying harmonic texture, and Grieg's preference for line and colour as opposed to form led him to far-reaching experimentation in an urge to exploit the coloristic and atmospheric potential of harmony. The first palpable signs of originality came with the *Humoresques* Op. 6 although unorthodox peasant elements are present even in the *Poetic Tone Pictures* Op. 3. Predictably, the most enterprising harmonically of his early works are those in which he is treating original folk-material, the *Nordic Songs and Peasant Dances* Op. 17 and the *Pictures of Norwegian Life* Op. 19,* but the definitive break with classical harmony does not come until the 1880s, and subsequently, with the *Lyric Pieces* Ops 54, 68 and 71, the *Six Songs* Op. 60, the harmonisations of Norwegian folk-songs Op. 66

---

*One of which, the well-known 'Norwegian bridal procession passing by', Delius transcribed for orchestra in 1889.

and the *Slätter* Op. 72. Grieg was a born harmonist, a lover of beautiful sounds for whom the *ear* alone was the infallible touchstone.

The recent re-assessment of Debussy's previously much-underrated contribution to the development of twentieth-century music has focused attention on the various catalysts to his individual style, and one of the most obvious forerunners of Impressionism is seen to be Grieg: for although the formation of Impressionistic techniques necessitated a thorough overhaul of the machinery of music down to its tiniest component part, the revolution was first and foremost *harmonic*. The doors were thrown wide on a new uncharted world of harmonic experience where no fruit was automatically forbidden: instinct and the ear were the sole means of discrimination between right and wrong. The resulting harmonic innovations consisted chiefly of chains of unresolved dissonances; triads embellished with all manner of added notes; consonances and dissonances moving in parallel motion; free use of the whole-tone scale or part thereof; modal influences (whether of popular or ecclesiastical origin); avoidance of the leading note and conventional cadential formulae involving tonal ambiguity or indefiniteness.

Now Grieg's avowed aims – nature-worship, colour and fragrance, mood and atmosphere evocation, suggestion or intimation in preference to literal depiction – were identical with those of the Impressionists, and Delius also has been classed as a 'romantic of the Impressionist school'. His acknowledged indebtedness to Grieg, however, inclines one to the view that his particular brand of Impressionism, and the harmony for which he was to gain such renown, were less a result of exposure to the musical Impressionist ambience in Paris than a logical outcome of Grieg's innovations – to which Delius stood in obviously greater proximity than Debussy. A fundamental bond of sympathy between all three composers was their admiration for Chopin, the Chopin of the mazurkas, glowing with harmonic colour and alive with the rhythms of the Polish peasantry. They were all harmonists in that they concentrated on the idea of the chord as an entity, adjusting not only its essential intervals but also its balance and distribution of notes to obtain an effect of pure and beautiful sonority. Chopin and Grieg were two of the few composers whom Delius admired consistently throughout his life; in fact it was hearing Chopin's posthumous *Valse in A minor* that initially stimulated his interest in music. When he first came upon Grieg's songs and piano lyrics he would have recognised in him a true disciple of Chopin.

Delius's personal approach to harmony was as fearless and unacademic as that of Grieg himself. He both enlarged Grieg's chord vocabulary and applied the principles the older man had evolved in the service of piano miniatures and songs to larger-scale canvases and broader designs; but he built firmly on the foundations of Griegian harmonic techniques. This is particularly true in the matter of chromaticism. For Delius, like Grieg but significantly unlike Wagner, was unable to sustain a chromatically-biased melodic line purposefully for any length of time. The essential quality of Delius's chromaticism is that the *harmony* is chromatic, the melody not; wherever he does project a chromatic melody line he generally does so for colouristic purposes (for instance at the words 'The wind of the North doth blow' in the first of *Songs of Sunset*). This is also typical of Grieg, whose melody retains a diatonic cast from its origins in Norwegian folk-song. The abiding interest of Op. 66 and other works treating the folk-song at first hand lies in the way in which straightforward diatonic melodies are subject to, yet never subjugated by, kaleidoscopic sequences of chromatic harmony. The chromatics never flounder helplessly but are given rock-like diatonic support by the melody. Speaking of Wagner's *Ring* which he heard in Bayreuth in 1876, Grieg complains of '. . . the numerous chromatic transitions, the ceaseless changes of harmony which result in one's being gradually overcome by nervous irritability and finally by complete apathy'. In his attitude to tonality Grieg looked backwards to Chopin and Schumann rather than forwards to Mahler and Schoenberg, and Delius's approach is frequently similar. Tonal chromaticisation of harmony could scarcely be carried much further than in the entry of the *a capella* wordless chorus in *The Song of the High Hills*; yet its restless ebb and flow is effectively counteracted by the sturdy melodic backbone with its symmetrical phrase-lengths. Earlier in the same work chromatic figuration in the upper strings is offset by a cleanly-etched, generously-proportioned bass line although bass-ic melody is rare in Delius; more frequently a sturdy diatonic top line enables the middle parts to move and intersect freely in semitones (e.g. the cello melody which passes to the upper strings and dominates the main part of *Summer Night on the River*). Grieg's other favourite method of stabilising chromaticism, the folk-music-derived drone-bass, is also found occasionally in Delius, in modified form. In the seventh picture of *Fennimore and Gerda* a beech forest in autumn is evoked by chromatic sequences in thirds over drone-basses; and in the autumnal movement of the *North Country Sketches*, 'The wind soughs in the trees', swaying branches, drifting clouds and an all-pervasive greyness are suggested by long serpentine lines of muted string chromatics over near-static, drone-like basses. Pedal points also function prominently in the 'cités lointaines'* of *Paris* (introduction and coda) and the *Idyll* (introduction).

The fact that Delius in his *On Hearing the First Cuckoo in Spring* incorporated a folk-melody which had already been harmonised by Grieg

*See p. 132.

in his Op. 66 (No. 14, 'In Ola Valley') provides us with a unique opportunity to examine and compare their respective harmonic techniques at close range. Grieg presents the melody complete three times in his setting; on its first and second appearances it is enclosed within pedal points and in each case the harmony within the pedal points is basically diatonic. The final verse, however, the third, brings a complete change of technique. The melody again appears in the top line as before, but is this time subject to chromatic treatment in the manner typical of Grieg, upper and lower parts defining progression and holding in check the tortuous movements of the inner voices. In other words chromatic harmony is introduced with subtle discrimination only at the very end of the setting, the harmonic norm remaining diatonic.

With Delius the reverse is the case. The *First Cuckoo* is no modest essay in folk-song-like ingenuous freshness; on the contrary it is considerably sophisticated. The 'Ola Valley' theme is interwoven with another (uncredited but noticeably redolent of the 'Student's Serenade' in the piano *Moods*, Op. 73) which appears at the beginning and in a short element of recapitulation and conditions the rhythmic substance and general atmosphere of the piece. 'In Ola Valley' is actually introduced unobtrusively by the flute at the eighteenth bar, and evolves so naturally out of the melodic flow that its personality and significance as an extraneous element pass altogether unnoticed. Thereafter it dominates the scene, but Delius treats it with the utmost freedom (unlike Grieg who preserved it intact): now he presents it complete, now repeats phrases at random, now develops them. At one point the folk-song serves to crown a climax, at another to launch a new self-generating stream of song, at another to accompany the cuckoo-call, discreetly simulated by a clarinet. Tune thus grows unceasingly out of a gently persistent liquefaction of harmony, chromaticism here being the norm – in contradistinction to Grieg's setting where, as we have seen, its function is more specialised. As Percy Grainger remarked, Grieg's setting is concentrated, pristine, miniature and drastic; Delius's has the opulent richness of an almost over-ripe fruit and the luxurious long decline of a sunset.

If in the matter of harmony Delius thus built steadily on foundations laid by Grieg, this was no less true with respect to form and orchestration. Grieg's one great weakness – a weakness common to many composers whose style is founded on folk-idioms – was an inability to sustain any but the simplest small-scale structures. Although he renounced symphonic writing at an early stage in his career, he continued to 'fight his way through the larger forms' of sonata, concerto and string quartet; but the standardised ritual of nineteenth-century Germanic formal discourse proved incompatible with his new concepts of harmony and texture. Eventually he learned to accept the fact that songs and piano lyrics were for him the most congenial expressive outlets. It is in the ten books of *Lyric Pieces*, the substantial corpus of songs and the original folk-music settings that we look for Grieg's most characteristic utterances; in other words he was essentially a miniaturist. Now Delius, having inherited and developed Grieg's novel concepts of harmony and colour, found himself able to evolve a formal mould of suitable scope and flexibility in which they could be cast; unlike Grieg he was not confined, formally speaking, to a restricted area but could think spontaneously in terms of longer-spanned structures and more spacious conceptions. Although a master of the lyric miniature (e.g. the *Irmelin* prelude, a late reworking of material from the early opera, and the *Two Pieces for Small Orchestra*) he found no difficulty in filling a large canvas; for him in fact this was the most natural and idiomatic form of self-expression.

In the earliest of his larger orchestral ventures, *Paris*, a quasi-sonata substructure is made a vehicle for a swift-moving sequence of scene changes in which motifs rely more on variety of orchestral colour and plasticity of context than on organic self-propagation and cumulative growth; and this variation-type treatment is featured more explicitly in three major works – *Appalachia*, *Brigg Fair* and the *First Dance Rhapsody* (also, in miniature form, in *On Hearing the First Cuckoo in Spring* already discussed). Grieg too had found variation form to his liking, not only in those works specifically cast in that form, but also in his folk-music settings which very frequently ('In Ola Valley' is a case in point) preserve the melody virtually intact within an ever-changing harmonic framework; the form also suited his liking for short, self-contained, well-contrasted sections each exploiting a different harmonic or rhythmic device. Similarly for Delius the principle of one melody repeated over and over again reduced or at least drastically modified the architectural problem while offering abundant scope to his lyric-harmonic resourcefulness. In *Appalachia* (the earliest of the series) each variation is self-contained and sharply characterised in the manner of Grieg; but *Brigg Fair*, as its subtitle 'An English Rhapsody' implies, is altogether more fluid in structure, the component sections are less clearly differentiated; in this case the twofold interjection of the preludial woodwind arabesque (the first time surrounding a warm *cantabile* string line of great beauty with fetching folk-song-like repetitions and echoes) provides in highly unorthodox manner the necessary points of repose. The *First Dance Rhapsody*, a type of extended orchestral scherzo sporting a curious vein of pseudo-orientalism, makes much less pretence at studiously 'varying' its tune, and (with the exception of the lachrymose, almost Chaplinesque transfiguration of the theme on a solo violin immediately before the coda) contents itself with varying the orchestral and

51

harmonic background. Of character variation, such as *Appalachia* and *Brigg Fair* had afforded in rich measure, there is little, and Delius is really at his best in the languidly evocative introduction.

Delius defined form as the 'imparting of spiritual unity to one's thought' and his most personal answers to the question of form are to be found in *Sea-Drift, In a Summer Garden* and *Songs of Sunset* all of which, apart from a tripartite ground-plan in *Summer Garden* and an element of re-capitulation in *Sea-Drift*, owe little or nothing to traditional principles of structure, and evolve their own 'spiritual unity' in a way which scarcely lends itself to black-and-white analysis. Nor do Delius's concertos and sonatas betray much affinity with established modes of practice, although all are cast in tri-sectional form whether as three separate movements or one continuous movement. His early works, however, conform to the mosaic-like, highly sectionalised patterns of construction which Grieg had been obliged to adopt – short unpretentious pieces such as *Summer Eve, Sleigh-ride*, and *Marche Caprice*, the *Florida Suite*, and more ambitious orchestral projects such as *On the Heights* and *Over the Hills and Far Away*, both of which have obvious conceptional affinities with the great masterpiece of Delius's maturity, *The Song of the High Hills*. It is significant that in the latter and its near-contemporary, the opera *Fennimore and Gerda*, Delius returns to these piecemeal methods of formal design – and both stand at the head of the already-designated phase in which Scandinavia once again played a prominent role.

In an interview given nine years after the completion of *Fennimore*, Delius expressed his opinions on the question of opera and its future as an art form. 'Length and cumbrousness', he claimed, would have to go; the ends to which he was working were 'brevity and conciseness', 'long dia-logues and wearisome narrations' would be replaced by 'short, strong emotional impressions given in a series of terse scenes'. Delius had in fact planned *Fennimore* along such lines, and it is therefore not surprising that we find therein an anticipation of certain contemporary trends in opera, notably the chamber operas of Benjamin Britten. Cast in the form of eleven short tableaux, each separated by an orchestral interlude of variable length, the opera can in no sense be thought of in terms of traditional acts and scenes, and in its compact, deftly-chiselled workmanship certainly reflects Grieg's preference for neatness, freshness and clarity of design. This tendency is even more marked in *The Song of the High Hills* where the division into sections with a distinct line of demarcation between each recalls the formal scheme of the earlier hill-piece, *Over the Hills and Far Away*. There is none of the constant process of fusion and regeneration of short, pregnant thematic fragments so typical of *In a Summer Garden* or *On Hearing the First Cuckoo*; contours are drawn more pragmatically and

8. Percy Grainger rowing on the Loing.

9. Edvard Munch, *Melancholy: the Yellow Boat.*

10. Munch, *The Mountain of Man and Zarathustra's Sunrise.*

firmly, the harmony is pared of excess flesh, and the creative imagination seems to have opened out on to an entirely new vista. It is as if, as
Delius approached the autumn and winter of his days, the early influence
of Scandinavia (where, for the composer, autumn and winter reigned
supreme) gradually regained its hold over the creative processes, cleansing
them of accumulated impurities, and applying to them the sharper, more
penetrating edge of a bracing North Wind. *The Song of the High Hills*
falls readily into nine sections, all palpably distinct yet subtly interrelated
and plotted with a sure eye for gradation of tension, sequence of meaningful incident, and inevitability of dramatic growth. At the mid-point of
the work, Delius introduces a theme which he has been careful to hold
back until a suitably critical juncture and which proves to be the focal
point of the entire composition – it represents, as the composer tells us in
the score, 'the wide far distance – the great solitude'. This forms the sole
subject of development for a period, but – a telling move – the peroration
is delayed by a thick blanket of wraith-like string ostinati which descends as
a backcloth to a series of eloquent wood-wind solos, eventually letting
through fragmentary derivatives of 'the wide far distance' like shafts of
sunlight glinting at intervals through a mist. A thousand voices sound from
afar deploying the mystic melody in an elaborate chromatic context – the
Delian Experience, and one of the great moments in music. They are
joined little by little by the enormous orchestra and eventually achieve a
climax of overpowering hymnic splendour at the height of which the very
first theme, yearning with appoggiaturas, peremptorily re-appears – a
compellingly dramatic stroke. As the vision fades all the themes from
earlier sections are passed in review, the voices are lost in the far distance,
and the hills are left to their re-echoing horns until these too dissolve in an
awe-inspiring nothingness.

So we can see that while nothing could be further from the truth than
to describe *The Song of the High Hills* as a series of disconnected, incon-
sequent episodes, its form is very much less diffuse and rhapsodic than
many of Delius's earlier compositions, and the same may be said of
Fennimore and Gerda. But, if the latter also glances back nostalgically at
Brigg Fair and *To be Sung of a Summer Night on the Water*, *The Song of
the High Hills* anticipates, texturally and harmonically, the lofty Scandinavian masterpieces of later years. *The Song of the High Hills* is an
epic nature-drama, but its antecedents are the tiny crystalline impressions
of the Norwegian countryside which formed part of the legacy of
Grieg.

The two folk-songs brought to Delius's notice by Grainger had far-
reaching consequences. But what connection, if any, have they with the
very many other folk-song elements in Delius's music? There were in

fact two main sources: Norwegian folk-music (acquired through Grieg), and American Negro folk-song of the pre-jazz era. Delius remained by temperament and inclination utterly uninterested in the cult of peasant music and therefore would have assimilated most elements of this kind quite unknowingly.

First and foremost there is the question of modality. The most common modal scale in Norwegian folk-music is the Lydian with its striking sharpened fourth, and consequently this is extremely prominent in Grieg's music. Not only does it appear in the numerous 'hallings' and 'springdans' scattered throughout his *oeuvre* (especially in the *Slätter* Op. 72) but also occurs frequently without the immediate context of folk-music. It exercised a peculiar fascination over Delius. The theme of the *First Dance Rhapsody* might almost be described as Negro-Norwegian, since the persistent sharpened fourth is as distinctly Norwegian as the final cadence is distinctly Negroid; another Scandinavian opus in which this cadence suddenly appears is *Over the Hills and Far Away* (the penultimate variation in the central section). This mode is very prominent in the orchestral prelude to the third scene of *A Village Romeo and Juliet,* and in the *Mass of Life* (Part II, the 'Second Dance Song'). It is beautifully worked into the closing pages of the *Requiem* as a cuckoo-call above the bell-like chimings of horns and harps and distant bitonal brass fanfares; the scoring is instinct with a marvellous Norwegian freshness and the tang of the Lydian fourth has already been skilfully built into the third movement of the work, 'A la grande amoureuse', where it gives a pleasantly dissonant bite to one of the salient orchestral motifs. Finally, the Lydian mode recurs in the new introduction to *A Song of Summer* dictated by the composer to Fenby in 1929 (the 'seagull' motif, Ex. 8). Dorian and Aeolian modes are employed quite ordinarily by both composers, but the mildly exotic colouring of the Phrygian mode is reserved by Grieg for special effect, and similarly is used in only one context by Delius – that of the distant call of the unseen bargemen in *A Village Romeo.* Likewise the quasi-oriental permutations employed by Grieg in 'Shepherd Boy' (*Lyric Pieces* Op. 54 no. 1) or 'Evening in the Mountains' (*Lyric Pieces* Op. 68 no. 4), consisting chiefly of the augmented second and the sharpened fourth in the minor scale, are used by Delius exceptionally in the *First Dance Rhapsody* and *Hassan.* The fact that the proportions in which these modes are employed coincide in the works of the two composers certainly suggest that Grieg's music served as a model for Delius's in this respect.

In the matter of melodic patterns Delius was indebted to Grieg on a number of counts. The triplet-headed phrase with which the *First Cuckoo* opens is one of Delius's most easily recognisable 'fingerprints', and its prototype is to be found in Grieg's Ibsen setting, *The Swan.*

Ex.8

Ex.9

Similarly the ascending pentatonic triplet motif which threads its way through Delius's life-work – *the* Delian fingerprint *par excellence* (Ex. 6) – is prefigured in the central section of Grieg's *Symphonic Dance No. 4* (Ex. 9). Triplet figuration, frequently pentatonic and evidently folk-song derived, is very familiar in Delius, and again the model was undoubtedly Grieg, whose 'Evening in the Mountains' shows the type of triplet propulsion which in a context such as Ex. 10 from *The Song of the High Hills* becomes a textural constituent rather than a self-sufficient linear entity. Once the origin of this and many another like passage is appreciated it becomes easier to understand why Delius's music has been superficially associated with that of the English 'Pastoral' School: Grieg and Vaughan Williams, and Delius at second hand via Grieg, all extracted nourishment from the common stockpot of folk-monody. Compare, for instance, the pastoral piping of *Evening in the Mountains* with the haunting evocation of desolate mountain country implicit in the opening and closing paragraphs of Vaughan Williams's *Flos Campi*; here the connection lies in the triplet-patterned approximation to herdsmen's calls. This figure, sometimes varied in interval but not in general shape or contour, forms an integral part of Delius's melodic phraseology. *Repetition* is of its essence, because it is grounded in folkmusic, folkmusic is the music of nature, and there is a certain repetition, an unmonotonous monotony in nature – the monotony of the sea, vast plains, the sky, and smaller manifestations such as rustling leaves, rippling brooks, soughing winds. Yet we can stand transfixed for hours watching water flowing under a bridge. Therefore the musical symbols of nature tend to this same 'unmonotonous monotony', an everchanging sameness, a non-repetitive repetition. The triplet figuration in Ex. 10 from the *Song of the High Hills* could almost be described as an ostinato, and the same principle can be seen at work in other nature-pieces – in the icy harp and woodwind motif in 'Winter Landscape' (*North Country Sketches*) which again is virtually an ostinato; and the rising and falling wave-like ostinato in 'Now Finale to the Shore' (*Songs of Farewell*) is one

Ex.10

of Delius's most potent sea-symbols. There is also fine sea-music in the earlier 'I stand as on some mighty eagle's beak' piloted throughout by the one deep-delving little phrase first heard on the horns in bar 10.*

There are many variations on the repetition principle, all connected with Grieg and nature – the ascending phrase first given in *The Song of the High Hills* to wordless tenors and basses to evoke a first glimpse of the snowy peaks shimmering way above relies on the folksong-like device of repeated notes within a phrase, and it also lends much weight and accumulated strength to the ultimate choral-orchestral apotheosis. Very common also in Grieg, and again a variation on the folksong principle, is the use of an echo-like repeat of a phrase, cadential or otherwise. When this occurs

* This motif was earlier used by Delius in the Prelude to Act V of *Hassan.*

in Delius it is often as an inevitable outcome of his Grieg-like love of horn fanfares and characteristic figures (a particularly poetic instance being the concluding bars of the *Brigg Fair* interlude with its trance-like echo effects and folksong-like variable third) but there are contexts where it is featured less self-consciously – the many answering echo-like phrases in the *First Cuckoo*, for example, or the cuckoo-calls in the closing bars of the *Requiem* which become more and more fragmented until they are lost completely in the distance. In the expectantly throbbing 'March of Spring' (*North Country Sketches*) much of the woodwind writing is stylised imitation of birdsong, just as we can hear the chirruping of all manner of nocturnal insect life in *Summer Night on the River*, a piece of unusually strong visual suggestiveness. The Lydian upward skirl on the flute in *A Song of Summer* is supposed to represent a seagull flying by. 'Imagine', said Delius to Fenby as he prepared to dictate the new opening to a piece originally known as *A Poem of Life and Love*, 'that we are sitting in the heather on the cliffs by the sea.' Cliffs . . . there must be a horn somewhere. And indeed there is, a single horn-call, a triplet figure clearly belonging to the family of Ex. 10. Delius's range of mountain-moods will be discussed more fully in Chapter 3.

How is Delius related to Grieg in the matters of texture and sonority? For all Grieg's pioneer work in the exploitation of harmony and melody as colouristic media, his favourite instrument was the piano and his best work was conceived in terms of that medium – although even here he extended but negligibly the range of contemporary piano technique, and there is little to prefigure the developments of the Impressionists. He may have caught a glimpse of the colouristic possibilities latent in the orchestral palette but he remained unable to harness them in the service of his own experiments in beautiful sounds. This task he bequeathed to his spiritual heir, Delius. Delius, as we have seen, was fundamentally not a miniaturist and thought in large time-spans; this, added to the fact that he was singularly untalented as a pianist, spurred him thoroughly to investigate the allurements of the modern orchestra, which feat he largely accomplished through study of the scores of Richard Strauss. (Significantly, those few scores in his library with their pages actually cut were works by Strauss, Debussy and Ravel.) Although Delius habitually *worked* at the piano and settled any questions of chord structure or disposition there, he always *thought* directly in terms of orchestral colour and wrote immediately into full score without a preliminary piano draft. Delius's original compositions for the piano, although for the most part competently laid-out, often give the impression of a much-compressed full score in need of an orchestra for proper realisation. This applies not only to the original piano music and sonatas for violin and cello, but also to the songs, the accompaniments of which were in many cases orchestrated by the composer. The one exception lies in the piano part of the Piano Concerto, but aside from the fact that this work is essentially an apprentice work the writing is of a stereotyped, derivative, latter-day Lisztian order.

Nor, with one important exception, is such individuality as Grieg did show in his handling of the orchestra necessarily reproduced in Delius. Grieg wrote beautifully for strings, viz. the *Holberg Suite* and the string version of the *Two Elegiac Melodies*, though not a violinist; Delius, a sufficiently competent player to be able to number among his youthful indiscretions a performance of the solo part of the Mendelssohn Concerto in Danville, Virginia, was rarely conspicuously successful in his manipulation of the string body: his chordal conception of line obviated the sense of polyphonic tension and interaction which generally makes for a satisfactory string sonority, and he preferred to cultivate the more immediately colourful properties of woodwind and brass. His use of the latter frequently corresponds to that of Grieg, i.e. as a means of consolidating and enriching the texture. There are however many instances of assertive and peremptory brass writing – the opening choruses of Parts 1 and 2 of *A Mass of Life*, moments in the first and last sections of the Violin Concerto, the striking series of block chords leading into the final D major epilogue of the *Requiem* – and at such times the ruthlessness, arrogance and fanatical intolerance of Delius the man seems to be obtruding for a split second upon the finely-attuned sensibilities of Delius the musician. It is an odd fact that whereas the *Florida Suite* of 1888 is beautifully and unexceptionably scored in the manner of Grieg's *Peer Gynt* and the *Symphonic Dances* the orchestral works which follow (particularly *Paa Vidderne* and *Over the Hills and Far Away*) show a distinct falling-off, a tendency to use the brass and woodwind stridently and coarsely. There is little of the polish and refinement so promisingly demonstrated in *Florida*. Eric Fenby is inclined to attribute this to the influence of Johan Svendsen, whose orchestral technique, while admirably suited to his own purposes – the four *Norwegian Rhapsodies*, the *Carnival in Paris*, the *Norwegian Carnival of the Arts* (all excellent works, unfairly neglected today) – was essentially at variance with the inner texture of Delius's poetic thought. Paradoxically, *Over the Hills*, for all its crudities of scoring, is a piece which contains a maximum of pointers to Delius's mature manner – the mountain mood set by horns re-echoing with the same short phrase (Ex. 11b); a characteristic horn fanfare-like figure (just before the first *Allegro ma non troppo* section); the salty, masculine, tramping energy of the latter which re-appears in *The Song of the High Hills* and in the Double Concerto; the miniature set of variations comprised in the central section, and the intimations here provided of an individual approach to chromatic harmony.

Ex.11(a)　　　　　　　　　(b)

Most personal of all is the quiet, introspective passage marked 'tranquillo' taken twice, its characteristically Delian theme of yearning given first to the violas (as in *Paris*: see p. 13) and later, beautifully, to a solo horn. This passage is echoed in the 1902 Holger Drachmann setting *Summer Landscape* (the epilogue of which, incidentally, *pre*-echoes the lengthening horn-shadows in sixths in the fourth movement of the *Requiem*). Here too, to open and close the 'variation' section of *Over the Hills*, is the pastoral swaying 6/8 rhythm to which Delius was later to become so addicted; and the music is saturated through and through in the modal atmosphere of folksong. Orchestrally, however, (with the exception of the horn solo passage mentioned above) *Over the Hills* is below par, and Svendsen may be held partially responsible. Yet Delius *did* learn from Grieg's poetic feeling for the woodwind, and here once more it was a question of the younger man receiving an initial impetus from the older and pushing a line of development to its ultimate conclusion. Few composers can have written more gratefully for the woodwind than Delius; he exploited to the utmost its capacity for haunting, wayward melodic lines, delicate tracery of figuration or fleet interplay of arabesque. His especial fondness for the sharper, more astringent qualities of the oboe family resulted in that acidulous bite which his characteristic orchestral sonorities always have about them – 'quelque chose de fort et salubre', as one early French critic once put it – and contributed in no small degree to the impression of clarity, freshness and firmly sculpted outline whereby we identify an essentially Nordic inspiration – an especially beautiful example is the *Fennimore and Gerda* intermezzo. Now this fondness was shared by Grieg, whose wholly idiomatic use of the woodwind no doubt influenced Delius's attitude to this family: e.g. the lovely oboe solos which open the *Symphonic Dance No. 2* and the slow section of the *Symphonic Dance No. 4*, and the flute solo hovering above tremolo strings in the finale of the Piano Concerto. One cannot open a single orchestral score of Delius without remarking a wealth of wood-wind detail, exquisitely pointed. It is worth noting that Delius extended Grieg's partiality for the oboe in that on several occasions he wrote for the rare heckelphone or bass oboe – in the introduction to the *First Dance Rhapsody*, and in various parts of the *Requiem* and the *Mass of Life* ('Heisser Mittag schläft noch auf den Fluren'). There is no doubt that

Delius's especial sympathy for the woodwind family is responsible above all else for the distinctive sound of his scoring.

So far we have been considering Grieg's influence mainly with regard to its bearing upon Delius's mature style, i.e. with reference mainly to those works composed after the turn of the century – from *Paris* and *A Village Romeo* on. In this music Delius revealed himself as the true successor of Grieg, working exhaustively the ground which the 'miniature Viking' had already begun to till. Yet in those works produced before 1900 – the fruits of an abnormally long apprenticeship – Delius is far more of an imitator of Grieg than a collaborator. Grieg's influence on these early works vies only with that of Strauss and above all Wagner. We can thus sense a conflict between two antithetical modes of musical expressions – the Nordic, characterised by clarity, neatness, precision; and the Teutonic, implying a preoccupation with breadth, voluminousness, even hyperbole, and un-inhibited directness of emotional expression. Delius's mature style effects a fruitful reconciliation between these two rival claims. The workings of Grieg's pictorial technique can be observed at close hand in the *Florida Suite* and *Irmelin*; Wagner's influence counters in *Paa Vidderne, Summer Eve, Over the Hills and Far Away* and *Koanga*, but the slow section of the Piano Concerto is evidently modelled in texture, mood and dynamic after the D flat major episode in Grieg's own. However, Delius's Scandinavian sympathies are most pronounced in his early songs, in as much as many were set to Scandinavian texts in the original language.

The early Norwegian songs are particularly interesting by way of the opportunities they offer for direct comparison with Grieg, since on a number of occasions the two composers set the same text. In addition to *Two Brown Eyes* and *The Homeward Way* already mentioned, Björnsen's *Twilight Fancies* (Grieg's better title: *The Princess*) and *Hidden Love*, Ibsen's *The Bird's Song* and *The Minstrel's Song*, Paulsen's *Summer Eve* and Munck's *Sunset* attracted the attention of both composers. Comparison reveals, rather surprisingly, that in none of these cases would it be possible to mistake Delius's version for a second setting of the same poem by Grieg; the stylistic discrepancies are greater than they superficially appear. This is particularly true with regard to *Twilight Fancies*. I quote the Björnsen poem (in mood and theme not unlike the Tennyson of *Mariana* and *The Lady of Shalott*) – in F. S. Copeland's translation:

> The Princess looked forth from her maiden bower
> The horn of a herd boy rang up from below.
> 'Oh, cease from thy playing, and haunt me no more,
> Nor fetter my fancy that freely would soar,
> When the sun goes down.'

The Princess looked forth from her maiden bower,
But mute was the horn that called from below.
'Oh why art thou silent? Beguile me once more.
Give wings to my fancy that freely would soar
When the sun goes down.'

The Princess looked forth from her maiden bower
The call of the horn rose again from below.
She wept in the twilight and bitterly sighed :
'What is it I long for, what is it I long for?
God help me!' she cried.
And the sun went down.

Grieg sets the poem strophically. There is only one musical discrepancy between the three stanzas : in stanza 2 the horn figure is obediently silent. The setting in its ballad-like simplicity is engagingly typical of Grieg. Tonally it is orthodox, being safely poised between the C minor tonic and its dominant – a perfect complement to the Björnsen poem, we might be tempted to say. Yet to turn to Delius's setting is to be made aware of a completely new emotional dimension, of a breadth and range of vision to which Grieg's music could not aspire. Delius's music is steeped in the *Weltschmerz* implied in the final stanza, that terrible despair-inducing sense of world-weariness which necessitates a continual impassioned reaching-out beyond oneself for some dimly perceived, imperfectly imagined instrument of self-fulfilment. Delius was German, and he inherited the means of expressing in music this Tristanesque condition of emotional turmoil from Wagner; we are thus drawn out of the sequestered nostalgia of medieval Norway into the turbulent maelstrom of nine-teenth-century Western Europe. Grieg illustrates, Delius illuminates.

As so often in Delius the horn is the *agent provocateur* of the emotional temperature. Here the horns (there appear to be two of them) actually do rouse the Princess from her apathy, they do not wait to be invoked in the second line. The unrelated fifths of these fanfares are followed by the semi-diminished chord, thus negating any sense of immediate tonal and therefore of emotional stability; but as the Princess voices her longing there is an unexpected and beautiful irradiance of D major with the characteristic Delian upward-thrusting pentatonic triplet (Ex. 6) echoed, Grieg-like, by the piano.

In the second stanza the horns are absent, but the general pattern of the first stanza is repeated. The horns again introduce the third stanza but this time they prompt the Princess to a heart-rending outburst of despon-dency and unappeased longing. Therefore the music sideslips the exhil-arating D major modulation of the first stanza and passes instead to an

anguished series of descending sequences. With true poetic insight, however, Delius now brings back his original horn-calls, and at the repetition
of the words 'and the sun went down' fashions a final cadence in a minor
key to impart an air of gloomy finality.

Despite its retention of a number of Griegian characteristics (a simple
diatonic melody with repeated notes, and the echoing of certain vocal
phrases by the piano) Delius's setting is notably Wagnerian in its greater
richness of illustrative detail, its greater depth of emotional involvement
and its greater range of expression; out of its palatable blend of Nordic
and Teutonic technical ingredients a clearly-defined personality is beginning
to emerge. It is particularly surprising to discover that this strong, fine
song was written as early as 1889, so characteristic of the mature Delius is
its musical symbolism. For the yearning to be free, to 'speed where there
is space enough and air enough at last' – the Lady of Shalott's laconic 'I am
half sick of shadows' – is associated, as so often later, with horns beckoning
into the distance and the upward-struggling, bursting triplet, Ex. 6. The
song, in embryonic form, is already quintessential Delius.*

This is an appropriate moment at which to consider Delius's relationship
to the American composer Edward MacDowell since, like Delius, he sat
first at the feet of the German romantics and refreshed himself at the
fountain of Grieg. Like Grieg, he wrote a large number of short and fairly
easy piano pieces, the majority of them modest nature-impressions; and,
born as he was a year earlier than Delius (1861) it is predictable that the
character of his own ventures in chromatic harmony for the purpose of
quasi-impressionistic nature-evocation should to some extent coincide with
Delius's own. Much of his more accomplished piano music could easily
be mistaken for early Delius, vintage early Delius at that. Delius's sea-
music is among the finest ever written, and there is body and impulse
behind MacDowell's own *Sea Pieces* which, as in the significantly-named
Eroica, *Norse* and *Keltic* Sonatas, look forward to the rugged lyricism of
Bax (this is particularly true of 'To the Sea', 'From the Depths' and 'In
Mid-Ocean'). On the other hand the chromatic drifts of harmony in 'To a
Wandering Iceberg', 'Starlight' and the exquisitely fragile 'Nautilus' –
and the Grieg-like poising on chords of the dominant seventh and ninth –
are very close to the manner of Delius. In the *New England Idylls* 'Mid-
Summer' recaptures something of the dreamy lyrical manner of 'Nautilus';
'In Deep Woods' the diatonic added-note grandeur of the chords which
evoke the 'long slender shafts of opal flame' is the Nordic imperiousness
of 'To the Sea' all over again with all its strong pictorial magniloquence.

*Here the horns are impersonated by a piano. In the thrilling Tennyson choral setting *The
splendour falls on castle walls* the voices do duty, thus creating a composite symbol -
horns and distant unaccompanied singing.

But in 'From a Log Cabin' there is one of these moments of pure sweetness and clarity so dear to the heart of Delius, Norwegian folk-poetry rather than saga-esque prose (Ex. 12). So too in turns of phrase as in 'From a German Forest' (the cream of the collection entitled *Fireside Tales*) with its exhilarating climax merging into a distant chorale, so distant as to be

Ex.12

barely articulate, 'like men's voices'. There is here chromatic arabesque in the manner of the forest pictures in the *Mass of Life*, and the temper and feeling of the two pieces is notably similar, even allowing for the fact that the one is a pristine miniature for piano, the other a choral-orchestral dance-poem on a large and fine scale. The *Woodland Sketches* too offer food for thought. The first bars of 'To a Water Lily' melt and sway over a Delian added sixth chord (Grieg never opened a piece so daringly); at the end of 'By a Meadow Brook' there is a very Delian fade-out to a characteristic 'dying fall' repeated over and over again, as in a trance, until lost in the distance; and 'To a Wild Rose' closes with the cadential formula beloved of Delius – the rise from sixth degree to tonic – which, as we know, is probably derived from Negro music. MacDowell was more interested in the music of the American Indian than the American Negro; and in view of the possibility or probability that Delius acquired elements of Scottish folkmusic through exposure to its Negro variants, it is interesting that when the 'Negroid' Scotch Snap occurs in MacDowell, as it occasionally does (e.g. the second movement of the *Second Indian Suite*) it is in this case more readily associable with Scotland via MacDowell's Scottish

Ex.13

ancestry.* The second of the *Six Poems* for piano (after poems by Heine) is explicit enough, since the setting of the poem in question is a grey castle on the rocky cliff of Scotland, and the song sung by the transparent, marble-pale woman is both pentatonic and features the Snap. There is a devious kinship here; it is worth listening with this in mind to the beautiful theme of the slow movement of Delius's Piano Concerto (also pentatonic) which is pure MacDowell (Ex. 13).

*Part of Grieg's ancestry was of eighteenth-century Scottish origin, and Percy Grainger suggested that a certain downward phrase occurring in the Scottish folksong *The Two Sisters O' Binnorie* is echoed several times in Grieg's music; he cites the trio of the slow movement of the C minor Violin Sonata, and the close of the first section of the 'tranquillo' movement in the fourth of the *Symphonic Dances*. Grainger also claimed a close kinship between the *pianissimo* passage just before the *crescendo* leading into the recapitulation of the main theme of the *Norwegian Bridal Procession* and the Scottish reel *Tullochgorum*. These various Scottish overtones in the work of Grieg, MacDowell and Delius speak well for the staying power of Scottish folkmusic.

The comparison with MacDowell also highlights one essential feature of Delius's personality burnt ineffaceably into his music, one which cannot be too firmly impressed on those who persist associating Delius with the 'soft lights and sweet music' escapism of an Ethelbert Nevin or Ketèlbey. The piano pieces singled out for mention are those which have survived; MacDowell's humorous pieces, too, are worth playing – 'Of Brer Rabbit', 'From Uncle Remus' and 'Will o' the Wisp'. But others – 'An Old Love Story', 'By Smouldering Embers', 'An Old Garden', not to mention the greater proportion of the songs – now sound hopelessly dated. The reason is their ruinous sentimentality; they mourn for a 'land of lost content', but are in actual fact content with their loss, and that is fatal. The very titles of those pieces which bear the taint are significant; the synthetic emotion which they are pleased to categorise as 'love' is very different from the experience of love which saturates the music of Delius. Here there is none of this vague revelling in misery and precious little of the romantic pessimist. Delius rarely permitted himself the kind of morbid self-laceration he voiced in his settings of Ernest Dowson's *Songs of Sunset*; and he never set such lines as the same poet's *Villanelle of the Poet's Road*:

> Wine and women and song
> These things garnish our way,
> Yet is day overlong. . . .

This is Zarathustra's old arch-enemy, the 'Geist der Schwere', the 'spirit of heaviness' whom Delius had early met, grappled with and conquered. All of his music may be instinct with the reality of someone loved and lost, but this was the love of someone who loved and lived life with every fibre of his being. Never for him was 'day overlong'. Even in the latter years of his life, blind and a helpless cripple, he astonished those who saw him by his tingling aliveness – how could somebody who was physically in a state of such extreme and distressing decrepitude yet be so intensely alive and aware? And only people who are thoroughly alive in this way find a great love, as Delius found his. They find it at least once in their lives; it usually fails to last because all the other important issues of life are confounded by it, and the intensity with which those involved feel for one another finally exhausts them. There are perhaps basically two categories of people in the world – those who never find a perfect love and learn to live without one, and those who do find one and spend the rest of their lives remembering it. Delius spent the rest of his life remembering his. We do not know who she was or how he lost her, nor is it of any real consequence; the important thing is that this was the personal, localised experience which complemented the vicarious, generalised experience of Solano Grove. There dawned at this moment of contact a consciousness which thenceforward sought expression in a music the like of which had never been heard before; nor has it since. It is essentially a positive, yea-saying music, a continual thanksgiving for what has been – inextricably interwoven with regret at its passing, of course, but imbued with that electricity, that fine zest and relish for life which is the antithesis of sentimentality. There is a richness, a fullness and a masculinity too deep-seated in Delius's best pages to be mistaken for facile emotionalism or synthetic self-indulgence. Consider the full-hearted Second Violin Sonata, the golden euphony of the Cello Sonata, the magnificent approach to the first climax of *A Song of Summer*. These, and countless other passages in which Delius is reliving his tremendous adventures of the human spirit, reveal him as a man of exceptional physical and moral stamina. The melodic outlines so strong, firm and bold, the harmony red-bloodedly vital (no mere wash or haze of titillating sonorities), the scoring amply proportioned yet clean and forceful – all suggest the man who said to his amanuensis, 'I have seen the best of the earth and done everything that was worth doing. I am content. I have had a wonderful life.'

3

If Grieg's was the principal Scandinavian *musical* influence upon Delius, his favourite Scandinavian author was the Dane, J. P. Jacobsen (1847–1885) one of the few Danish writers whose works have become standard reading for students of comparative literature in the Western world. (He commanded a particularly large following in Germany, and we shall encounter him again in the next chapter.) Jacobsen's canon is small: two novels, some short stories, a few poems: and his life-story is soon told. He was born in the little town of Thisted in Jutland and from earliest childhood his interests were twofold: poetry and botany, and when faced with the problem of deciding upon a career found himself torn between the two. For a time he applied himself to both; he was one of the first in Scandinavia to realise the importance of Darwin, and translated both *The Origin of Species* and *The Descent of Man*. But after the attention attracted by his first short story *Mogens*, he devoted himself to literature and published first the novel *Maria Grubbe* which cost him four years of labour (he was a stylist of Flaubertian scrupulousness and precision), then his masterpiece *Niels Lyhne*. This he managed to complete while warding off the advances of TB, but he eventually succumbed and died quietly in his home town of Thisted at the age of 38.

One of Jacobsen's special preoccupations being with intrinsic beauty of style and language, we find in his prose and verse that paradoxical blend of precision and vague dreaminess which also occurs for instance in the Arthurian romances of the Middle Ages, in Coleridge, in De Quincey, in Poe, the progenitor of Symbolism, and also in the French Impressionist painters. Jacobsen's 'professional' interest in the natural world – his botanical studies – tended not only to determine his choice of imagery but also to enhance his sensitive response to scents and particularly to colours. In his ability to weave his impressions of these phenomena into the warp and woof of his writing he approaches very nearly the stylistic tenets of Impressionism, and it is significant that almost all the composers who have responded to Jacobsen's work have been in some way affiliated to the musical Impressionist movement. (The one major exception is Jacobsen's countryman Carl Nielsen who set two groups of five poems as Ops 4 and 6.*) *Niels Lyhne* played an important part in the spiritual development of the American Impressionist Charles Tomlinson Griffes (the composer of *The White Peacock* and *The Pleasure Dome of Kubla Khan*, after Coleridge) although he never made any actual settings of Jacobsen. Bax on the other hand, who was probably introduced to Jacobsen by his brother Clifford, made at least five settings, three of which, composed in 1927, are much more familiar in Delius's versions – *Irmelin Rose*, *Let Springtime Come* and *Little Venevil*. Delius set a total of eight Jacobsen lyrics to music, most of them in 1897, and they are the most distinguished of his early efforts in that medium. Something in Jacobsen evidently touched a nerve in Delius, but whereas with Nietzsche and Whitman he was stimulated musically by both philosophy and poetry, Jacobsen appealed to him essentially as a poet. To be sure, Jacobsen was also an atheist; he abandoned his faith after the revelation of Darwin and, as in Hardy's case, the result was a protracted struggle against mental and spiritual chaos. *Niels Lyhne*, the novel from which Delius extracted the libretto for his last opera *Fennimore and Gerda*, is a reflection of this moral upheaval. It is concerned not so much with the individual's relationship to society as with the individual's relationship to himself. It recounts Lyhne's attempts to arrive at a workable philosophy of life and his ultimate failure to do so. Now Delius did evolve a satisfactory philosophy of life. He was an optimist, fulfilled in love, whereas Jacobsen was essentially a pessimist, unfulfilled; and it quickly becomes apparent, if we compare the opera libretto with the original, that Delius has precious little interest in the conflict of ideologies which lies at the core of the latter. All the basic issues are ruthlessly simplified; layer after layer is pared away until all that remains is a skinny broken-backed story-line such as might have been lifted straight out of any

*But even in Nielsen's case there are points of contact : see p. 149.

number of *Woman's Own*: romantic fiction at its cheapest and most commonplace. Delius picks up the threads of the narrative at the point where Niels realises he is in love with Fennimore, his friend Erik's wife. Erik is killed in a road accident, whereupon Fennimore rejects Niels. Spring comes back into his broken life in the form of the sweet innocent Gerda to whom he eventually becomes engaged. At this point the opera comes to an end. In the novel Niels marries Gerda, but her premature death is followed by that of her child, and Niels himself dies of wounds received in the Dano-Prussian war. Delius opted for a quasi-conventional 'happy ending', less from theatrical expediency than in accordance with his own preoccupation with spring and re-birth, his unfailing consciousness of

> How many times the rose
> Returned after the snows.

Two things impelled Delius to attempt to turn *Niels Lyhne* into an opera, unsuited as it was to operatic translation: his affection for the novel *per se* and its Scandinavian setting, and the ever-present backdrop of nature before which it unfolds. We noted that Jacobsen's 'professional' interest in nature informs much of his poetic writing, and it was to the sensuousness of his poetic style that Delius warmed. As in *A Village Romeo and Juliet* the music is at its happiest when commenting upon either the lovers' rapture (as in the big lyrical duet at the end of the seventh picture) or the beauties of the changing seasons. Here Delius, as is his custom, wins the hearts of all. The opening of the second picture, however, perhaps takes us rather deeper into the nature of Delius's response to Jacobsen. I quote the stage directions: 'The lower end of the Claudis' garden which reaches down to the fjörd: at the far end there is a small landing-stage surrounded by large old trees, where lies a boat in which Erik and Fennimore are sitting. It is dark and the sea sparkles with phosphorescence . . . From the fjörd comes the sound of singing, though no boat is visible.'

In Jacobsen's short story *Mogens* there is a wonderful moment in which the hero, stung with remorse for his dissipations following upon the death of his beloved, and regretting the loss of his faith, suddenly hears in the moonlight the sound of a girl's voice singing:

> O flower in the dew,
> O flower in the dew,
> in the whispering dreams you know
> does the same tune reach your ear
> that strange elfland air that I always hear

murmuring and low?
Is it a sigh that comes to you, a lament
That stirs the twilight, or a fading scent,
or has any song found
that awakening sound?
I live in longing,
in longing.

'Then silence reigned once more. Mogens breathed deeply and listened intently; but the song was ended. He laid his head on his arm and wept . . .'

(trs. Ursula Vaughan Williams)

Now is this not the quintessential Delian Experience – the sound of the human voice floating on the night air from an unseen source bringing with it a sudden blinding flash of illumination? Is this not the kind of extra-sensory perception in which the unseen wordless voices of the High Hills enable us to share? Erich Heller in *The Disinherited Mind* tells the Rilke story of a rowing boat which sets out on a difficult passage. The oarsmen labour in synchronised rhythm; there is no sign yet of the destination. Suddenly a man, seemingly idle, bursts into song. And if the labour of the oarsmen meaninglessly defeats the real resistance of the real waves, it is the idle singer who magically conquers the despair of apparent aimlessness. While the people next to him try to come to grips with the element that is next to them, his voice seems to bind the boat to the farthest distance, so that the farthest distance draws it towards itself. It is the 'farthest distance' to which Delius is bound, like all poets, and the 'farthest distance' to which the voices of the High Hills call him, conquering his plain-induced aimlessness. The woman's voice conquers the aimlessness of Mogen's blind grief, like the nightingale and King David in de la Mare's poem; and it was perhaps a recollection of this moment in *Mogens* which prompted Delius to give the unseen singer from across the fjörd one of his loveliest vocalises (Ex. 14). 'How beautiful it sounds upon the water', Fennimore aptly comments in the scene which follows. So too in the 'pictures' which follow; and everywhere in the music we encounter the signs and wonders of a Northerly airstream. The orchestral interlude which links pictures 6 and 7 is very much counterpart of the *Brigg Fair* interlude, with a similar undulating ostinato of added-note chords and a similar cast of passionate song spun thereupon; but the one is all bright green and gold and warm sun-flooded fulfilment, the other is bleaker, the gold has turned to yellow, the green to russet and brown, the warmth is that of an autumn sun. This forms an appropriate prelude to the seventh picture, set in an autumn beech forest: here is musical symbolism later associated with *North Country Sketches*, with sad processions of chords moving restlessly over long-held pedal-points, an image which persists in many varied forms through virtually all the remainder of this part of the opera as we progress ever deeper into winter cold and snow. Then the celebrated Interlude which is really the turning point, the emotional peak of the entire opera, just like 'The walk to the Paradise Garden' in *A Village Romeo and Juliet*. Delius

Ex.14

speaks the more eloquently for having dispensed with the banalities of text. The distant voice on the fjörd has no need of words; nor do the farm-people harvesting in the fields who open the final picture with a dewy-fresh wordless chorus, a-tingle with the Lydian sharp fourth. Spring awakens and interest is centred on Councillor Skinnerup's garden with apple trees in blossom and beds of flowers full of tulips, turk's hats and yellow narcissi. Delius's woodwind writing is without peer: the clear-singing, Nordic oboe and a flute which brings to mind the words of Helen

Waddell's Peter Abelard 'How is it that a flute can play no air but it makes it sorrowful?'

> Mere breath of flutes at eve
> Mere seaweed on the shore.

This is the passage usually tacked on to the main interlude when the latter is extracted for concert performance. And so with the last of the miniature nature-poems on which the musical action largely depends the wheel has turned full circle, as it does in other products of a singularly long and glorious Scandinavian sunset – *North Country Sketches*, the *Requiem*; but not in the most singular of all, the setting for baritone solo, chorus and orchestra of Jacobsen's *Arabesk*.

Arabesk comes from the same collection of poems and short stories which was later to yield Schoenberg the *Songs of Gurre – A Flowering Cactus*, written in 1868 but not published until 1886, after the poet's death. This is a rather odd conceit involving a group of young people who gather to await the long-expected flowering of their host's cactus plant. Each contributes a poem or short story to beguile the time, and in addition to *Arabesk* and *Songs of Gurre* the collection includes two short lyric poems *Autumn* and *Moods*, a short story *Foreigners*, and *Kormak and Stengerde*, a narrative interspersed with songs in the style of the Icelandic sagas. Like Jacobsen's two other poems of the same name, this *Arabesk* represents his poetic craft at its finest. In a programme-note for the 1929 Delius Festival, Peter Warlock summarised it perfectly as 'a strange half-symbolic poem dealing with the darker aspect of the God Pan, who here represents the object of a sensual passion which leads to madness and death. It is at once a lover's rhapsody of long-lost love and a paean in prose of the brilliant, all-too-fleeting Scandinavian summer. In each case the passionate moment is exalted and a short spell of bliss breeds dissolution and decay.' The English text is a version by Peter Warlock of Jelka Delius's German translation. Delius, of course, set *Arabesk* in the original Danish and it was so recorded by Einar Nørby, baritone, with Sir Thomas Beecham and the Royal Philharmonic Orchestra and Chorus, imparting thereby an edge and presence utterly lacking in the English recording. Here is the poem via Jelka Delius and Warlock:

> Hast thou in gloomy forests wandered?
> Knowst thou Pan?
> I too have known him,
> Not in gloomy forests,
> When all the silence spoke;
> No, no, him never have I known,

Delius

Only the Pan of Love have I endured,
Then hushed all that speaketh.

In a sunbathed meadow grows a wondrous herb ·
Only in deepest stillness
Under the beams of the burning sun
Its blossom unfolds itself
For a fleeting moment.
It gleams like the frenzied eye
Of the one enchanted,
Like the glow of a dead bride's blushes.
It is this flow'r I have gazed on
As a lover.

She was like the jasmin's sweet-scented snow,
Red blood of poppies circled in her veins,
Her hands so cold and white as marble
In her lap reposed
Like waterlilies in deepest lake.
And her words they fell as softly
As petals of appleblossom
On the dewladen grass.

But there were hours,
When they rose upleaping cold and clear
As the jet of a silvery fountain.
Sighing was in her laughter,
Gladness was in her pain;
By her were all things vanquished,
And nought there was to gainsay her
But the spell of her own two eyes.

From the poisonous lilies' dazzling chalice
Drank she to me,
To one too that hath perished
And to him who now at her feet is kneeling,
With us all she drank,
Yea she drank and her glance then obeyed her,
From the bowl of troth to eternal plighting
From the poisonous lilies' dazzling chalice!

Now all is past!
In the ground all snow-bestrewn
In the bare brown wood
Stands a lonely thornbush,
The black winds they scatter its leaves!

Scandinavia

One after another,
One after another
Shedding its bloodreddened berries
In the white, cold snow,
Its glowing red berries in the cold white snow.

Knowst thou Pan?

Warlock conveys much of the atmosphere and enigmatic beauty of the poem; but 'from the bowl of troth to eternal plighting' in stanza 5 rather verges on the unnecessarily nonsensical, when all that is meant is that 'she drank from the goblet which pledged us all to never-wavering fidelity'. The poem is a kaleidoscope of sharp antitheses: 'silence spoke', 'the glow of a dead Bride's blushes', 'snow . . . red blood of poppies . . . cold and white as marble', 'sighing . . . laughter, gladness . . . pain', 'blood-reddened berries . . . cold white snow', this final stanza effectively recapitulating the symbolist imagery of the third. These antitheses are the very nut and kernel of the poem, whence its lyrical astringency, its unique atmosphere; and it is Delius's attempt to mirror these antitheses in his music which places *Arabesk* in a category of its own devising. In point of fact it bears little resemblance to anything else in music. The orchestral colour-scheme, the rhapsodic arc-like formal span, the way baritone and chorus complement each other in interpreting the poems on its two levels – the non-human, natural, elemental, and human, all-too-human – all are conditioned by sensitive response to every nuance and inflexion of the poetic text. The two predominant colours in the poem are red and white – can we not hear the red in the splashing and spurting of the celesta (given greater prominence here than in any other Delius score), the white in the frosty glitter of the harp? The orchestral textures are charged with colour and incident; yet there is paradoxically an almost monochrome austerity, a continuous revolving about the polarities of red and white, heat and cold, life and death, orgasmic intensity of passion and the seeds of corruption and putrefaction therein contained. That Delius was able to respond so keenly to the peculiar mood and theme of the poem is perhaps not so surprising when we realise that by the time he came to compose this music (1911–15) the malady he had acquired in the throes of passion, after lying dormant for many years, was now beginning to stir and betray its presence in the form of physical symptoms. *Arabesk* is therefore in the fullest sense a personal autobiographical document wherein is fulfilled the quasi-prophecy of Jacobsen's *Wine Roses* which Delius had set in 1897 –

73

Through long, long years we must atone
For what seemed a trifling pleasure

the tragic irony of which would have completely escaped Delius at the time, though doubtless by then he had already contracted the disease.

Like much else in this fine score the opening has no parallel in Delius; a passage in the finale of the First Violin Sonata perhaps peers momentarily into its depths and shadows, but there is no exploration. Here is conveyed, through a stalking, brooding succession of crotchets rising from the abyss, something of the lurking terror of Scandinavian forest as caught in the relentless pedal-points and *ostinati* of *Tapiola*; this is certainly Delius's most Sibelian score, with an epilogue as desolate as anything in the Fourth Symphony. We are drawn immediately into a pagan, pantheistic world, and then comes one moment when we are transfixed in the primordial sunlight of the midsummer wood, *antiqua silva* ('Then hushed all that speaketh').

And now the spell begins to work: 'In a sunbathed meadow grows a wondrous herb', pagan mysticism and Pan bringing to the surface long-buried memories of Debussy's pagan faun in his afternoon sunlight. Something of the same aura of sylvan enchantment is captured in the orchestral piece *Eventyr*, written in 1917 shortly after the completion of *Arabesk*; Delius sought therein to reflect the spirit of that collection of Norwegian folk tales collected by Cristen Asbjörnsen and Jorgen Engebretsen Moë over a period of years and published under the title *Eventyr* in 1841. There are moments here which belong to the twilit world of *Arabesk*, with Sibelius's 'wood-sprites in the gloom weaving magic secrets' – an oboe glinting and falling through a haze of flickering tremolo strings, a weird ritual enacted on consecutive unrelated common chords (celesta and harp) with syncopated tubular bells mingling their overtones as from a great distance; and two 'wild shouts' from a men's chorus behind the scenes, shouts of unearthly forces exactly parallel with those of Valdemar's men on their 'wild hunt' in Jacobsen's *Gurrelieder* as realised by Schoenberg some sixteen years before *Eventyr*. But physical passion is left out in *Eventyr*, and it is the moving force behind *Arabesk*. The chorus enters at a crucial point – to a long-drawn chromatic sigh ('Ah!') at the first mention of the blossom unfolding itself in the burning beams of the sun; but almost immediately the dawn of love is identified with the finality of death ('like the glow of a dead bride's blushes') in a flash-forward to the bare brown heath and lonely thorn of the epilogue (Ex. 15a) – the hollowness of open fifth-chords with xylophone, chill *ponticello* strings, brass frozen *con sordini*. The flute at 'It is this flow'r I have gazed on as a lover' transports us back to the woodland glade with its bevy of nymphs dancing and singing in the *Mass of Life*; then as the poem calls for madder music and stronger

74

wine ('Red blood of poppies circled in her veins') the chorus advances the narrative, invoking a great girder-like melodic span heard originally high in the strings at the beginning, and destined once more to re-appear. A note of inexorability begins to invade the music as it now surges forward on a powerful lyrical impulse, but there is pause for one more intimation of a *ventura ira*. The text reads 'Her words they fell as softly as petals of appleblossom' but the music runs counter, for the woodwind in their chromatic triplets seem almost to have picked up pre-echoes of the howling winds in Bax's *November Woods*. Antithesis subtly contrived, too, in the harmony: the dissonances at 'cold and clear', hard, glittering, transparent but also incandescent, white-hot as well as ice-cold (Ex. 15b). Now the

Ex. 15 (b)

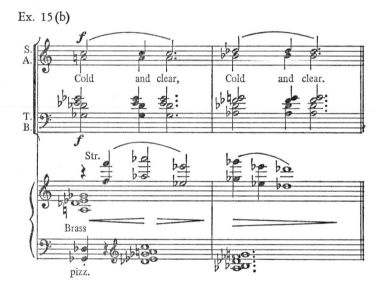

climax is at hand: and biding its time is that memorable, familiar phrase (Ex. 6) in which Delius seems to have distilled the emotional experience of a lifetime. At the climactic point – not before – it dominates the orchestra and explodes, first on horns and then shatteringly, on trumpets ('by her were all things vanquished').* The heat of the blaze is intense but of devastatingly brief duration.

A curious parallel to *Arabesk* up to this point is to be found in Arthur Machen's account of Lucian Taylor's sexual awakening in *The Hill of Dreams*, in the old Roman fort above Caermaen in rural Wales:

*Horns and trumpets really need to play *pavillons en l'air* for these four bars to ensure maximum prominence.

'Within the fort it was all dusky and cool and hollow . . . beyond the ditch there was an undergrowth, a dense thicket of trees, stunted and old, crooked and withered by the winds into awkward and ugly forms . . . their roots gripped the foot-high relic of a wall, and a round heap of fallen stones nourished rank, unknown herbs, that smelt poisonous. From it, in the darkest places where the shadow was thickest, swelled the growth of an abominable fungus, making the still air sick with its corrupt odour. Then there was a gleam of sunlight, and as he thrust the last boughs apart, Lucian stumbled into the open space in the heart of the camp . . .

'Suddenly, he knew that he was alone. Not merely solitary; that he had often been amongst the woods and deep in the lanes; but now it was a wholly different and a very strange sensation . . . and then he began to dream, to let his fancies stray over half-imagined, delicious things, indulging a virgin mind in its wanderings. Slowly and timidly he began to untie his boots . . . glancing all the while at the ugly misshapen trees that hedged the lawn. Suddenly, it seemed, he lay in the sunlight, beautiful with his olive skin, dark haired, dark eyed, the gleaming bodily vision of a strayed faun.

'Quick flames now quivered in the substance of his nerves, hints of mysteries, secrets of life passed trembling through his brain, unknown desires stung him. As he gazed across the turf and into the thicket, the sunshine seemed really to become green, and the contrast between the bright glow poured on the lawn and the black shadow of the brake made an odd flickering light, in which all the grotesque postures of stem and root began to stir; the wood was alive. The turf beneath him heaved and sank as with the deep swell of the sea. He fell asleep, and lay still on the grass, in the midst of the thicket.

'He found out afterwards that he must have slept for nearly an hour. The shadows had changed when he awoke; his senses came to him with a sudden shock, and he sat up and stared at his bare limbs in stupid amazement. Then, with electric heat, sudden remembering possessed him. A flaming blush shone red on his cheeks, and glowed and thrilled through his limbs. As he awoke, a brief and slight breeze had stirred in a nook of the matted boughs, and there was a glinting that might have been the flash of sudden sunlight across shadow, and the branches rustled and murmured for a moment, perhaps at the wind's passage.

'He stretched out his hands, and cried to his visitant to return; he entreated the dark eyes that had shone over him, and the scarlet lips that had kissed him. And then panic fear rushed into his heart, and he ran blindly, dashing through the wood.'

Here, as in *Arabesk*, the pagan ecstasy of physical passion is rendered as a pantheistic experience with strong overtones of fear-inducing corruption. These overtones, and the intensity which derives from them, are what give *Arabesk* its special flavour, its peculiarly sweet acridity. After the climax there is a lovely interlude, strange odours of paradise in strings, harp and celesta, before a ravaged landscape is glimpsed again (the *November Woods*-like woodwind triplets) and the high clinching theme from the beginning is heard for the last time as the inscrutable goddess, whoever she may be, drains the goblet and pledges all her lovers to never-ending thraldom. Then, finally, the infinity of winter in one of Delius's most admired pieces of landscape-portraiture. This cold bare infinity is reflected in the regular, even textured, smooth-flowing movement of this music, as opposed to the straggling, almost painfully rhapsodic quest for articulation in the main body of the score: it is the calm unbroken sleep of death *vis-à-vis* the fitful tortuous efforts of life (Ex. 15a). There is still a piquancy in the harmonic diction which accords with the higher norm of discord earlier established (again the blood-redness of the celesta), but soon the syncopated *pizzicati* of violas and 'celli (the falling leaves and berries) are the only points of sensation in a featureless void, all else being lost in the driving snow. In the final bars all vocal and instrumental timbres are dissolved in a long-drawn chromatic moan of 'Knowst thou Pan?' in which the music seems less an agent of evocation and suggestion than the very sound of snowbound earth and air itself.

Arabesk is a masterpiece; yet in the sixty years or so since it was completed it is performed little and understood less. The Ancients had a term for the lifting of the veil to disclose the real world of spirit beyond the imagined world of matter, the glowing inner core that lies beyond life and outside of time. They called it seeing the god Pan. Hundreds of fine musicians, otherwise well and fluently versed in the music of this century, have lived and died and have never known Pan, as did Eric Fenby, in the music of Frederick Delius.

4

No more interesting perspective is afforded on the complex question of Delius's Scandinavian affiliations than by viewing the extraordinary liaison, both personal and musical, between Grieg, Delius and the man who knew and loved them both. Percy Aldridge Grainger was twenty years Delius's junior and in many ways seemed the very antithesis of the older man in character and temperament; yet there were many factors to unite them: chiefly a passionate love of Scandinavia and a great attachment to the person and music of Grieg. Grainger's sense of positive identity with the spirit and music of Scandinavia was almost uncanny.

Grainger was one of the most remarkably individual artists of his day. He infuriated those whom he termed the 'prigs and snobs of music' by his refusal to conform to stereotyped formulas and to conventional notions of propriety and sobriety in musical conduct; and he endeared himself to those who, like Delius, enjoyed seeing stuffiness, pretentiousness and vulgar respectability held up to ridicule. He strove always for an uninhibited naturalness in music as in life, and it was this above all which was responsible for his life-long interest in folksong and which led him to make substantial contributions to ethno-musical research.

Neither of Grainger's parents was a native Scandinavian. He was born in Melbourne in 1882 and even as a boy was dreaming of a 'free music' with rhythms wayward like those of ocean waves, melodies which swooped like the flight of a bird, harmonies melting into each other like sunset colours, and many melodies all shining together in free polyphony like planets and spheres. Then he came across Longfellow's *The Saga of King Olaf* – and the Scandinavian in him stood revealed. The immediate fruits of this discovery were *The Crew of the Long Serpent*, originally for piano duet, and the song *I am the God Thor*, both dating from 1898 when Grainger was 16. (Manuscript fragments of a *Norse Dirge* dating from 1897 suggest a folk-oriented music without making overt use of folk material.) Thenceforward he steeped himself in all things Scandinavian. He quickly assimilated *Beowulf*, the Icelandic sagas and the Anglo-Saxon Chronicles which he grew to regard as the pinnacle of human achievement in narrative prose. He adored J. P. Jacobsen. He spoke fluent Norwegian, Icelandic and Faroese. He was startlingly Nordic in appearance, with a magnificent crop of blond hair and clear steel-blue eyes. In 1928 he married the Swedish poet and artist Ella Viola Strom, dubbing her his 'Nordic Princess' and waxing lyrical about her thus: 'Now and then in Scandinavia may be met a Nordic type of womanhood, half-boyish yet wholly womanly, whose soft flawless loveliness is like that of a fairy-tale princess; whose broad shoulders, amazon limbs, fearless glance, and freedom of deed and bearing recall the Viking chieftainesses of the sagas . . . whose graceful ease in rhyming, painting, singing, dancing, swimming, is the all-life-embracing giftedness of an unspoiled native-race. Such an uncrowned princess may be found in castle or cottage, in town or countryside, amongst high-born or low-born alike, for hers is bed-rock aristocraticness of race, not mere top-layer aristocraticness of class, culture and breeding. Such a one is my sweet wife-to-be.'

Most important of all, the great musical influence on Grainger's life was that of Grieg. That he should respond keenly to Grieg's music was predictable. He had learned the Piano Concerto while studying at Frankfurt and in 1898 had orchestrated three of the *Lyric Pieces*. By 1902 he was playing the Op. 72 *Slätter*, which came in the nature of a revelation to him. Grieg's admiration for Grainger's interpretation of his music (after they had first met in London in May 1906) knew no bounds. 'Why in the world', he said in October of the same year, 'does Percy Grainger, an Australian, play my music perfectly in rhythm and modulation while a Norwegian cannot grasp either?' Grainger for his part saw in Grieg's music 'the general human tendencies of the heroic, active, poetic, excitably emotional Norwegian race from which he sprang . . . no less, the characteristics of the hillscapes and fiordscapes of his native land, the brilliant colouring and striking clarity of the scenes, and the almost indescribable exhilaration of the Northern atmosphere.' He also sensed in Grieg what he termed a 'North Sea mood' which, he claimed, informed the work of other composers 'hailing from the North Sea girding lands – Brahms, Franck, Delius, Herman Sandby. There seems to be some climatic influence at work here – some Rembrandtian fog of the sea, the soil and the soul – that continually and uniquely, in these composers, produces a soaring ecstasy of yearning wistfulness . . . we discern this North Sea mood strongly at the root of such creations as Brahms's *Alto Rhapsody*, Franck's Symphony, Grieg's *Den Bergtekne*, Delius's *Song of the High Hills* and Sandby's *Sea-Mood*.' Grainger became one of the foremost exponents of Grieg's Piano Concerto after studying it with the composer at Troldhaugen in 1907. Although he was a comparatively experienced folklorist before he met Grieg, the older man greatly stimulated and encouraged him in his enterprises, particularly in the matter of folksong collecting in Britain. In recognition of this all Grainger's British folk-music settings are 'lovingly and reverently dedicated to the memory of Edvard Grieg'.

The passion for the Scandinavian landscape shared by Delius and Grainger, and for the literature and music to which it had given rise, is symptomatic of their intoxication with nature, particularly with the sea, mountains and wide open country. Both loved freedom, space, air, wild beauty and the mystic solitude endemic in untrammelled contact with nature – hence a yearning for high and lonely places, discovered by Delius during his tramping of the Yorkshire Moors in youth and of the Norwegian mountains in early manhood, and by Grainger through his indefatigable hikings in the Scottish Highlands, the Canadian Rockies, the Jotunheim and elsewhere. The familiar title of Delius's early fantasy-overture *Over the Hills and Far Away* was used by Grainger for his 'Children's March' for wind band (enigmatically dedicated to 'my playmate beyond the hills'), and Delius's *Song of the High Hills* is paralleled in Grainger's work by the two *Hill Songs* which, in the composer's own words, 'arose out of thoughts about and longings for the wildness of hill countries, hill peoples and hill musics (such as the Scottish Highlands, the Himalayas, the bagpipes, and the like)'. And Grainger was like Delius a nomad, a rootless wanderer, a cosmopolitan – was he Australian, British, Scandinavian, or American? He knew and loved all these countries and celebrated them all in his music. But did he really belong to any of them? Where did Delius really belong? They were both essentially folklorists; the main spiritual force which impelled them towards each other was undoubtedly their common response to folk-art. In this they were spiritual heirs of Grieg: their lives were spent in tireless quest for the roots of our culture in the native and characteristic. Grainger scoured the earth for folksong in an attempt to crystallise in his creative work the distinctive qualities of the Scandinavian, Celtic and English-speaking world. Delius as we know subscribed to no such creed of folk-worship nor did he participate in any systematic rediscovery or exploitation of folk music; nevertheless the saturated lyricism of his melodic writing is frequently a natural flowering from folksong, and in many ways of his works, especially those of the later Scandinavian period, there is an unmistakable aura of timelessness, an atmosphere of legend or myth. These two sharply contrasted personalities both lacked a stability of background, culture and environment; in their different ways they appealed to the folk to supply this deficit and, in so doing, found their way to a creatively fruitful mode of self-expression.

Grainger himself was more keenly alive than probably anyone else to this *natural* (in the widest sense of the term) impulse behind all Delius's characteristic work. Shortly after the latter's death Grainger wrote:

'He is the first great genius to have fully expressed in music the main stir of our period in music, i.e. the emotions underlying colonial expansion and all that goes with it – the "call of the wild", the passion for travel (Delius was a devourer of travel-literature) the hunger for adventure (he adored mountaineering) the yearning for the "wide open spaces" and much inquisitiveness about "native" races. The spirit behind a large part of Delius's music is at one with those same forces that drove Segantini to paint the Alps, steered the aesthetic courses of Robert Louis Stevenson, Pierre Loti and Paul Gauguin to the South Seas, and made sea-poets and outposts-of-empire-depicting bards of Kipling, Service and Masefield. For, although the amatory yearnings and philosophical introspections of civilised (and hyper-civilised) man find plenty of outlets in his music, yet it is obvious from the titles of many of his most arresting works that they grew out of rivers, mountains, the sea, sunsets, the "primitive" races and their basic emotions.

'Admittedly many other Nordic composers have based their compositions on similar themes, but the most successful among them (such as Schumann, Grieg and MacDowell) have expressed the urges in miniature rather than life-size. It seems as if Delius is the first composer to give us "nature music" on the grand scale of a Bach, a Wagner, a Richard Strauss; it is as if "nature music" –

dwarfed or childishly undeveloped before – has grown to man's estate for the first time in the music of Frederick Delius.

'He thus stands as the lone giant presiding over the musical expression of the major urge of the period which produced him – the "back to nature" urge that, in its various ramifications, has given us such very diverse manifestations as a world empire based on raw materials, nature cures, free love, touristism, jazz, athleticism and nudism. So if Delius is the first superlative genius among "nature-music" composers, as such he naturally excels in the musical depiction of those moods that invariably accompany the "nature" emotions : loneliness, wistfulness, dreaminess, turned-inwardness, vagueness, and a sense of distance.'

Scandinavia was not the only enthusiasm shared by Delius and Grainger, and it is astonishing the extent to which the older man's cosmopolitan personality is mirrored in the younger's. It argues an intuitive affinity of rare scope and profundity (and the wonder scarcely ceases when we come to examine the more severely technical relationship between them). *Scandinavia* we have dealt with. *America* now : Grainger eventually became an American citizen and settled in New York. He named *Leaves of Grass* (whence Delius drew the texts of *Sea-Drift* and *Songs of Farewell*) as a momentous contribution to his development, and dedicated his *Marching Song of Democracy* in gratitude to Whitman. Like Delius he was fascinated by the music of the American Negro. He was deeply moved as a child by hearing his mother sing him songs by Stephen Foster – that 'great American genius' as he described him, whose stylised imitations of Negro folksongs poignantly expressed the insecurity and uprootedness of modern man. In his *Colonial Song* Grainger attempted to express feelings aroused by thoughts of the scenery and people of his native Australia, particularly that 'patiently yearning, inactive sentimental wistfulness that we find so touchingly expressed in much American art, for instance in Mark Twain's *Huckleberry Finn*' (a favourite work of Delius's) 'and in Stephen C. Foster's adorable songs.' His *Tribute to Foster* (for five single voices, mixed chorus, musical glasses and bowls, solo piano and orchestra) is based on *Camptown Races* and grew out of his 'love and reverence for this exquisite American genius, one of the most tender, touching and subtle melodists and poets of all time; a mystic dreamer no less than a whimsical humorist.' It is Grainger's *Appalachia* or *Koanga*, if you will; the tune is treated first as a dance-song, then as a lullaby to some irresistible doggerel verses of Grainger's own :

> Foster's songs warn't 'darkie' quite *(Doodah! Doodah!)*
> Yet neider war dey jes 'plain' white *(Oh! Doodah day!)*
> But Foster's songs dey make you cry, *(Doodah! Doodah!)*

Bring de tear-drop to yo' eye. *(Oh! Doodah day!)*
    Gwine to still be sung
    'S long as de worl's heart's young.
Dese songs dey trabbel de worl' around *(Doodah! Doodah!)*
At las' dey come to Adelaide town *(Oh! Doodah Day!)*
When I was a tot on me mammy's knee *(Doodah! Doodah!)*
She sung dat race-track song to me. *(Oh! Doodah Day!)*
    Gwine to still be sung
    'S long as de worl's heart's young.

In the last section the original lively dance-movement is resumed, and then finally 'a tail-piece in which various tunes (sounded from various points on and behind the platform) gradually lapse into silence – like the quiet of night falling upon a countryside, from every farm and shanty of which jovial yet wistful song had been issuing in unrehearsed profusion. In my mind this tail-piece symbolises the fading-away of those untutored forms of Negro folkmusic from which we like to think that Foster drew inspiration for his art-songs' – from which we *know* that Delius drew inspiration for his art-music. There is no concrete evidence that Delius knew Foster's songs, but it is inconceivable that he did not and that he did not love them.

Grainger was also a great admirer of Gershwin; he made a pot-pourri for two pianos from *Porgy and Bess* and concert transcriptions for piano of the songs *Love Walked In* and *The Man I Love*. Referring to him as 'one of the most sensitive and many sided of recent composer-geniuses' he once drew attention to similarities of thematic procedure between the *Rhapsody in Blue* and the last movement of the Grieg Concerto, and *The Man I Love* and the slow movement of Grieg's C minor Violin Sonata. 'Gershwin knew his Grieg well; I do not call attention to these similarities in order to disparage Gershwin, whose music I worship. Quite on the contrary, I consider it a sign of genius in a composer to base his procedures upon an older, *original* composer, rather than on platitudes. . . .'

Scandinavia, America, and now Germany. The overwhelming literary influence on Delius's life was Nietzsche's, and there is a curious reference to the poet-philosopher in the simplified version of Grainger's *Country Gardens* for piano. Grainger's seemingly inexhaustible fund of mental and physical energy and his great personal beauty (his diminutive stature alone prevented his embodying an archetypal Siegfried blond hero) induced in him a slightly hysterical cult of bodily prowess – an athleticism prolonged into old age by rigid abstinence from tobacco and alcohol – which savours strongly not only of Whitman but also of Nietzschean precepts and those of the proto-Nazi Friedrich Ludwig Jahn (founder of the university fraternities of gymnasts known as the *Burschenschaft*, whose cause Wagner had espoused in a series of articles on German art and politics written for the Suddeutsche Presse in 1867). The egotism which made of Delius an embittered neurotic in his later years was also present in Grainger and manifested itself most strikingly in the extraordinary chaos of narcissism and necrophilia housed in the Grainger Museum in Melbourne.

Delius was educated at Leipzig, Grainger in Frankfurt. While they abominated the music of the Haydn-Mozart-Beethoven period they adored Wagner. The supremacy of late nineteenth-century Teutonic Romanticism in their musical thought rivals only that of Grieg. In Grainger's early music – notably the settings of love verses from *The Song of Songs* and the *Hill Songs* – Wagner is much in evidence, and the *English Dance*, employing a large orchestra with organ and piano, takes an unmistakable cue from *Die Meistersinger*, though Grainger named the slow section of Grieg's *Norwegian Dance*, Op. 35 no. 1, as a more immediate progenitor. Incidentally, if *Tribute to Foster* is Grainger's *Appalachia*, *English Dance* is surely his *Paris*, for this impressive piece is in no way an attempt on Grainger's part to write in the style of any particular English dance-form, nor is it based on folk or popular music, but instead 'is the result of an urge to express in large form that combination of athletic energy and rich warmth that is a characteristic of such English tunes as *Come Lasses and Lads* and of English music in general. I wished to tally in my music a certain bodily keenness and rollicking abandonment that I found typical and enthralling in English national life – as manifested in such things as furious football rushes, the love of sprinting, the high average speed of men and women walking in the streets, newspaper distributors swerving wildly yet cunningly through crowded London traffic on low bicycles, a profusion of express trains hurtling through the dark, factories clanging and blazing by night, and numberless kindred exhilarating things.' This is a fine big-boned piece with a Wagnerian massiveness, chromatic flux and melodic continuity ('endless melody') although the composer referred its formal technique and colour scheme back to Bach – 'particularly in the length of the sections, the uneventful "flow" of the form, in the eschewal of smaller contrasts and in the uniformity of almost unbroken peg-away even rhythms. And by laying the minimum of emphasis upon tonal "colour", by adopting an instrumentation of mainly "neutral" tints, I feel it is possible to concentrate the whole appeal upon what appears to me to be the strongest of all musical elements – purely intervallic expression. In nature at its sublimest (the desert, the ocean and the like) a certain monotony is generally present; the smaller elements of contrast do not intrude upon the all-pervading oneness of the overall impression. With Bach a somewhat analogous order of things still prevails in his colour scheme. A certain sameishness is wooed, consciously or unconsciously, in the interest of homogeneity.' So here we have an 'impersonal presentation of cosmic energy' which Grainger apparently felt to be of a peculiarly English cast, expressed through the medium of a thoroughly Germanic technique embracing Bach, Wagner (who evidently learnt much from Bach in the matter of long-lined form, music emancipated from the small sectionalness and constant thematic reiterations of sonata form) and ultimately Grainger himself. There is perhaps a reminiscence of Delius in the important upward-reaching, soaring, muscular theme introduced halfway through (Ex. 16).

Ex.16

More explicitly Wagnerian is *The Warriors* ('music for an imaginary ballet'). 'Often the scenes of a ballet have flitted before the eyes of my imagination in which the ghosts of male and female warrior-types of all times and places are spirited together for an orgy of war-like dances, processions and merry-makings broken, or accompanied, by amorous inter-ludes; their frolics tinged with just that faint suspicion of wistfulness all holiday gladness wears . . . I like to think of them all lining up together in brotherly fellowship and wholesale animal glee; a sort of Valhalla gathering of childishly overbearing and arrogant savage men and women of all the ages – the old Greek heroes with fluttering horse-haired helms; shining black Zulus, their perfect limbs lit with fire-red blossoms; flaxen-haired Vikings clad in scarlet and sky-blue; lithe bright Amazons in wind-swept garments side by side with squat Greenland women in ornately patterned furs; Red Indians resplendent in bead-heavy dresses and negrito-Fijians terrible with sharks' teeth ornaments, their woolly hair dyed pale ochre with lime; graceful cannibal Polynesians of both sexes, their golden skins wreathed with flowers and twining tendrils – these and all the rest arm in arm in a united show of gay and innocent pride and animal spirits, fierce and exultant.' This is pure hokum – magnificent, extravagant, riotous hokum – with all Grainger's deep-encrusted racialist fantasies and obsessions suddenly exploding in a burst of orgasmic Technicolor. If it sends shivers down our spine, as it undoubtedly sent shivers down Grainger's, its fanatical tone may also set our teeth on edge, for this brutal century has taught us all too plainly how the whole Wagnerian paraphernalia of racial purity, the glories of myth, the heroic achievements of legend, the cult of the body, virility, Nordic man-power, all can be turned inward to self-destruction, not outward (as in Grainger's and Delius's case) to creative self-fulfilment. In the case of *The Warriors* this pre-occupation with physique extends even to the parts for three pianos which are intended 'for exceptionally strong and vigorous players. If pianists of sufficient strength cannot be procured, do not hesitate to double or even treble on each piano part.' The orchestra is massive, for apart from the three pianos it calls for six horns, the rare bass oboe, and much percussion including wooden marimba, steel marimba, bell-piano and tubular bells. Yet if Grainger dreams in fire, he here works in clay. For all its experimentalism in the use of oriental percussion and aleatory rhythmic ensemble, the musical substance (which is consistently undistinguished) draws heavily on the harmonic and textural idiom of middle-period Strauss – a composer whom Delius loved in a limited number of contexts precisely for his manliness, as we shall see in the next chapter. *The Warriors* was dedicated to Delius. He and his wife were both ardent Nietzscheans, both imbued with the same kind of healthy animal sensuality as Grainger himself.

There was something of a reaction against Wagnerian inflation in the pre-Schoenbergian scoring of the *Hill Songs* for chamber wind ensemble (though these were written long before *The Warriors*) but Grainger was well aware that the basic temper and constitution of his chosen idiom were unassailably Teutonic and late-romantic-Teutonic at that. He was also aware that this 'sensuality' which he shared with Delius was, musically speaking, primarily a question of harmonic tissue. In a letter to Sir Thomas Armstrong – quoted here with all its eccentricities of syntax and spelling – he is speaking of those early works of Cyril Scott which were thoroughly representative in style and aesthetic of the 'Frankfurt Gang', to which Grainger belonged, notably *La Belle Dame sans merci*, the *Sänge eines fahrenden Spielmanns* to words by Stefan George, and the Rossetti setting *An Old Song Ended*:

'All these works are informed with some agony which I would be inclined to attribute to German influence. All we four composers (Grainger, Scott, Quilter, Balfour Gardiner) spoke German as fluently as English . . . I think it might be true that the exaggerated tenor of German emotionality had some influence on us all 4. The influence, if any, being in the willingness to take such an emotional view of things . . . And what musical medium could provide the agonized emotionality needed? I think the answer is the CHORD. The Chord has the heartrending power we musical prerafaelites needed. Based on Bach, Wagner, Skriabine, Grieg, and César Franck, Cyril, Balfour and I became chord-masters indeed.'

It was the originality of Cyril Scott, now forgotten, which first promoted the kind of luscious added-note harmony associated with Delius. Scott, however, lacked almost entirely the peculiar poetic sensibility of Delius; for all the superficial similarity of their harmonic idiom Scott rarely draws close to Delius on a more profound level, perhaps only in some of the Dowson settings and in a few isolated pieces such as *The Ballad of Fair Helen of Kirkconnel*, a particular favourite of Grainger's. Grainger on the other hand *did* possess a truly Delian sensibility; and if, as seems almost certain, his inborn harmonic sense was originally nurtured by Scott, a combination of the two led inevitably to a marked similarity in harmonic idiom between Grainger and Delius. I have here made a point of letting Grainger tell much of his own story in his own words, partly to give the reader some idea of his boyishly infectious enthusiasm, brimful of the awareness, assurance and vital enjoyment in his work which so endeared him to Delius and others; but also because his prose style is in many ways the equivalent of his harmonic style – rich, sonorous, often superbly wrought, prodigal of coinages, unfettered *à la* Whitman, sensuous *à la* Lawrence. 'My first contact with Delius's music almost overwhelmed me,' he wrote, 'when, in 1905 or 6, in Chelsea, I saw the full score of *Appalachia* and started to read the first *a cappella* outburst. I was amazed to find that anything so like my own chordal style existed. It struck my mother the same way. "What piece of yours is that?" she called from the same room, taking for granted it was mine, yet not able to recognise it.'

Grainger was always meticulous about noting the dates of his compositions, and many which sound as though they might well have been written in the wake of Delius turn out in fact to pre-date Grainger's discovery of *Appalachia* and Delius's music – *Walking Tune*, for instance, the two *Hill Songs* and certain of the Kipling *Jungle Book* settings. The setting he made in 1905 of *Brigg Fair*, a tune he had himself collected in Lincolnshire from that walking thesaurus of sterling folksongs, Joseph Taylor, is of particular interest, since Delius took that very tune for his orchestral rhapsody of the same name and gave it his own personal harmonic impress, as in the case of *In Ola Valley*. A comparison of the two settings emphasises the differences even more than the similarities between the composer's respective harmonic styles. Grainger's harmonic rhythms are here slower, dissonances diatonic rather than chromatic and resolved in a manner orthodox rather than iconoclastic; the harmony, in fact, respects the structural pattern and inflections of the melody. If we set this alongside, for example, the first orchestral *Brigg Fair* variation, we notice at once a greater fluidity of chromaticism, a more tenuous line of demarcation between consonance and dissonance; that the folktune is not distorted in the process is due to the composer's remarkable flair for reconciling a diatonically-oriented melodic line with an intensely chromatic harmonic substructure – we have seen how this technique sustains, for example, the entry of the multidivided un-accompanied wordless choir at the crucial point of *The Song of the High Hills*. Similarly, Grainger's harmonic writing flourished best under the stabilising influence of a pre-existent melody; where this discipline was absent, as in certain of the *Jungle Book* settings and the *Hill Songs*, his imagination was apt to run chromatically riot. But many of Grainger's folk and popular song arrangements are without peer in the delicate and subtle balance they maintain between the narrative mainspring of melody and the emotive complement of harmony. The character of the harmony is always determined by the character of the melody and by the emotional tenor of the text. *Willow Willow* is an excellent example. In the first verse the accompaniment consists basically of common chords; in the second (directed to be sung 'more tellingly than the first verse') a similar harmony is now decked out with discreetly placed added notes and extra suspensions, almost imperceptibly enhancing its expressive impact; only in the last verse ('impulsively and very feelingly') does the harmony give full voice to its pent-up intensity of chromatic longing with what Grainger termed 'moaning nature-voices' (imitation of the wailing sounds heard in nature) – harmony-changes on individual beats within the bar and poignant false-relations at 'In *love* I was true' and 'Aye *me* the green willow'. 'The cult of the chord, vitally furthered by Grieg,' wrote Grainger, 'was a marvellous device for engendering musical sensitivity and compassion' as here and in his setting of *The Sprig of Thyme*, when the 'moaning nature-voices' are invoked only at the pun on the word 'thyme' ('And time it'll bring all things to an end'). In the case of the splendidly boisterous *Seventeen come Sunday* for chorus and brass band, however, Grainger gives a couple of bars a quick taste of Delian chromatics simply to jolly along the proceedings (Ex. 17).

Ex.17

Grainger does on occasions eschew 'the cult of the chord' particularly in the setting of *Lord Maxwell's Goodnight* where the strong and simple melody is all of a piece with the strong and simple poetry. And it *is* poetry: oral tradition may perhaps perpetuate a verse like this, but it is the work of an individual poet:

> Adieu, madame, my mother dear, but and my sisters three, O!
> Adieu fair Robert of Orchardstane, my heart is wae for thee, O!
> Adieu the lily and the rose, the primrose fair to see, O!
> Adieu my lady and only Joy, for I may not stay with thee, O!

Grainger instinctively realises that the melody carried the poetry so superbly that a functional harmony is all that is needed; chromatic accretions would constitute superfluous 'expressiveness'. So his contribution is polyphonic rather than harmonic, strand added to strand. He also alters a crucial interval in the third line of the third and fourth stanzas ('His life is *but* a three day lease' and 'Now he's *o'er* the floods sae grey') and inserts a tiny 'tail-piece' for the accompanying string quartet between the two latter stanzas. We have only to listen to the result to understand why Grainger's settings of these folk and traditional tunes are still alive in the repertoire today, while most of Cyril Scott's are long sunk, encrusted with barnacles.

Mention of *Brigg Fair* raises the interesting question of Grainger's influence on Delius. According to Grainger, Delius was indebted to him on three counts:

1. 'After hearing my *Hill Songs* I and II he wrote his *Song of the High Hills*.
2. 'After hearing my Passacaglia *Green Bushes* he wrote his *Brigg Fair* and *First Dance Rhapsody* in similar passacaglia-like forms – as contrasted with the variation form he had used in *Appalachia*.
3. 'After hearing my "Wordless syllables" in such numbers as my choral *Irish Tune from County Derry* he adopted that method in *The Song of the High Hills* and elsewhere, abandoning the "la la" method employed by him in *Appalachia*.'

Grainger's two *Hill Songs* were composed in 1902 and 1907 respectively; they are rambling quasi-extempore impressions of mountain country, remarkably forward-looking both in their harmony and rhythmic patterns, but essentially the raw materials of musical composition, not the finished composition in themselves. They have all the appearance of a trial run at a transcendental hill music, an epic of the human spirit as reflected in the spirit of the hills, which ultimately materialised in Delius's *Song of the High Hills* wherein much of the 'feel', the potent atmosphere and melodic curves and shapes of Grainger's pieces are assimilated and recreated anew in the white heat of a superior musical intelligence. Some idea of Delius's indebtedness to Grainger may be gained if the ending of Grainger's first *Hill Song* (Ex. 18) is compared with the ending of *The Song of the High Hills*. In either case the harmony slowly comes to a standstill over an unresolved discord, and a lone voice (marked, in Ex. 18, 'as if from afar') is heard as an echo reverberating even more faintly until lost in the hills.

Ex.18

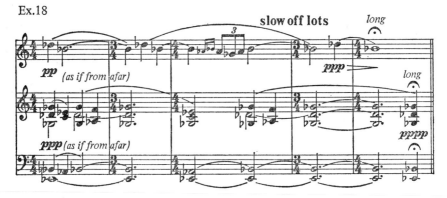

It seems almost certain that Grainger's splendid *Green Bushes* passacaglia *did* suggest to Delius a like procedure in *Brigg Fair*, particularly as it was Grainger who brought the tune to Delius's attention in his own rich, warm setting (just as he introduced Delius to Grieg's harmonisation of *In Ola Valley*). Grainger, however, saw sound practical justification for the treatment he accorded *Green Bushes*, reasons intimately bound up with the character of the folk tune itself, which struck him as being 'a typical dance-folksong – a type of song come down to us from the time when sung melodies, rather than instrumental music, held countryside dancers together. It seems to breathe that lovely passion for the dance that swept like a fire over Europe in the Middle Ages – seems brimful of all the youthful joy and tender romance that so naturally seek an outlet in dancing. My setting is a strict passacaglia unintentionally. In taking the view that *Green Bushes* is a dance-folksong I was naturally led to keep it running like an unbroken thread throughout, and in feeling prompted to graft upon it modern musical elements expressive of the swish and swirl of dance movements. The many-voiced treatment came of itself. My work should be listened to as dance-music – as an expression of those athletic and ecstatic intoxications that inspire, and are inspired by the dance – my new-time harmonies, voice-weavings and form-shapes being lovingly woven around the sterling old-time tune and in some parts replace the long-gone but still fondly mind-pictured, festive-mooded countryside dancers, their robust looks, body actions and heart-stirs.' The rather neutral harmonic colour of the

Mixolydian mode in which the tune was struck enabled Grainger to view it through a harmonic spectrum ranging over seven or more different keys, the tune itself remaining unchanged throughout and preserving that spirit of 'unbroken and monotonous keeping-on-ness'. Grainger adopts this procedure elsewhere in his folkmusic settings for various combinations – in *Seventeen come Sunday*, in *The Lost Lady Found* (another dance-song), in *Lisbon* (incorporating *Lord Melbourne* as a counter-melody), in *The Brisk Young Sailor*, in *Horkstow Grange* (the four last-named all form part of the brass-band suite *Lincolnshire Posy*). There can be no doubt that Delius was very taken with this demonstration of how a folksong can adapt itself *in toto* to constantly varying harmonic contexts and yet retain its own identity, and *Brigg Fair* is certainly closer to the passacaglia form than *Appalachia*. On the other hand, as Grainger himself must have recognised, both *Brigg Fair* and the *First Dance Rhapsody* also bear a number of the hallmarks of variation form – the key and speed and mood of the theme are altered and the theme is constantly transformed into new guises, both of which come under the classification of variation rather than the simple repetition which is of the essence of the passacaglia. It is probable that Delius would probably have treated *Brigg Fair* in the way he did even if Grainger's passacaglia had never been written, although it is possible that Grainger's prototype galvanised him into action. All he needed was the tune – and Grainger's harmonisation. Doubtless the melody would never have fired his imagination had he heard it in its pristine condition, naked and unashamed, any more than the *Appalachia* theme would have impressed him had he not heard it embellished with improvised harmonies by Negroes in a Danville tobacco factory; nor would *In Ola Valley* have caught his attention divorced from Grieg's harmonic context. It was always the *harmonic* implications or potentialities of a melody which attracted Delius. He was surely far more indebted to Grainger for his *Brigg Fair* harmony than for anything about *Green Bushes*.

Finally, the question of the use of the wordless chorus. Grainger's sensuous setting of the *Irish Tune from County Derry* for wordless voices (alternating between closed and open lips) was made in 1902, and elsewhere Grainger uses wordless voices always with poetic relevance – in *Brigg Fair* (1906) and in the *Scotch Strathspey and Reel* (there is a particularly lovely moment when the 'Reel of Tulloch' is first heard on a solo flute. The harmony is transformed as if by magic from an F minor triad to an F *major* added sixth, and all the harmonic support from here until the entry of the strings is given by the men's chorus, *pianissimo* and singing to 'mm'. Somehow there is here the joy of distances tenanted only by clouds and winds, of an early morning by Loch Lomond). In *The Lost Lady Found* voices singing to 'La' infuse the requisite sweet, tender, clinging, subdued quality into the fourth stanza; and in *I'm Seventeen come Sunday* and in the early part of the *Strathspey* some thrilling vocal effects are obtained through the chorus being given long, energetically rhythmic, thrusting passages to sing to 'ah' or 'la'. Now there is no doubt that the sound of the wordless chorus of the 1902 *Irish Tune from County Derry* is very much that of the 1911 *Song of the High Hills*, although in the former the actual harmony is much plainer; but it is also obvious from the sound of the *Appalachia* unaccompanied chorus (set to words) (1902) that Delius is gradually feeling his way towards a transcendental recreation of those Negro voices heard in close harmony over the water, and it is therefore only a matter of time before he eschews the use of words altogether in the natural order of things. Again, that is not to say that Grainger's work may not have helped to bring that far-shining summit of perfection some fraction closer; but Delius would assuredly have found his own way sooner or later to his hill of dreams. To say this is not in any way to disparage Grainger's own originality, nor to minimise the impact of his ferociously stimulating and anti-Establishment personality on Delius; from both points of view the relationship was a fruitful one. Grainger's exquisite 'room-music ramble' on the first phrase of the old English melody *My Robin is to the Greenwood Gone* (1912) is quintessentially Delian, yet there are intimations that Grainger was really a Janus-like figure, looking back in anguish and also in ecstasy on the glories of the Delian past whence he so gladly sprang, yet always keeping a weather-eye on the future. The strange way in which *My Robin is to the Greenwood Gone* seems at the end to lose all time sense, to dismember itself fragment by fragment and eventually to peter out on a sustained contrabass harmonic almost begins to look forward to the fusion of oriental and occidental philosophies and techniques in the work of Ronald Stevenson, John Mayer, Charles Camilleri and others. Grainger's many-sided relationship to Delius perhaps illustrates nothing so much in the old truism that musical composition is an art in flux, ever returning to its origins to replenish the energies expended in the pursuit of novelty.

CHAPTER THREE

Germany

1

Although Delius is traditionally bracketed with Elgar in the vanguard of the English Musical Renaissance, we do well to remember that both composers received their initial impetus from late Germanic romanticism, and both in the early stages of their career were more vociferously applauded in Germany than anywhere else. Delius was, of course, *echt* German; there was no single drop of English blood in his veins. His parents came of Prussian merchant stock and he himself, though reared in Bradford (where the father played the domestic Hitler almost as effectively as the son in his own declining years) terminated his residency there at the earliest opportunity. Travel soon took him to Germany and he acquired the language (doubtless Herr and Frau Delius would have spoken German between themselves) and snatches of German phraseology often tended to lodge themselves in his English vocabulary in later life. There are conflicting reports of the quality of his voice: Arthur Hutchings, Bax and Patrick Hadley all recall a 'Yorkshire harshness' but the first-named also admits that when Delius made his little speech at the end of the final concert in the 1929 Delius Festival, the intonation was decidedly German ('I mos tank you und Sair Thomas. . . .'). However this may be, Delius certainly had a strong pro-German bias which persisted throughout his life and manifested itself in a variety of ways, for instance in acidulous comparison between German and English attitudes or methods (political, economical, musical or whatever) to the distinct disadvantage of the latter. And there can be no doubt that for Delius, the music of Wagner was the parent stem on to which stylistic elements hailing from American, French and Norwegian sources were skilfully grafted.

Delius's formal musical training (though he claims to have derived scant benefit from it) took place in Germany, in Leipzig, and it was there, in 1888, that he first heard the sound of his music on the orchestra (the *Florida Suite*). It was not really until 1904, however, that his works began to make the profound impression in Germany denied them in England.

The enterprising Hans Haym of Elberfeld conducted *Over the Hills and Far Away* there in 1897, the first time (as far as we know) that any Delius work was publicly performed in Germany. Haym gave the premiere of *Paris – The Song of a Great City* in 1901 (the work was dedicated to him) and Busoni, no less, repeated it in Berlin a year later. Also in 1902 Haym gave the German premiere of *Das Nachtlied Zarathustras*, the *Urfassung* of what we now know as the finale of *A Mass of Life*. Thanks largely to his enthusiasm, other German conductors became interested in the *Nachtlied* – Julius Buths, Max Schillings, Hermann Suter (who gave it in Basel in 1903; he later gave there the world premiere of *Brigg Fair* in 1907). Germany began to wake up to Delius. He writes to Grieg in the autumn of 1903 :

'I'm writing exclusively orchestral music – every year I have three or four performances in Germany – Buths in Dusseldorf and Dr Haym in Elberfeld produce my latest scores every year – Buths has arranged *Paris – the Song of a Great City* a symphonic work of mine for two pianos and Dr Haym has done similarly for *Lebenstanz* . . .'

In March 1904 *Koanga* was staged for the first time at the Stadt-theater, Elberfeld (Haym's influence again) and in the same year Haym not only gave the world premiere of *Appalachia* but devoted an entire concert to Delius's works a bare nine days later (24 October 1907), the programme consisting of the Piano Concerto (played by Buths), *Lebenstanz* and *Paris*. The success of *Appalachia* led to its repetition in Düsseldorf in 1905 (at the Lower Rhine Festival, Buths conducting) and later in Berlin; but how strange it was, as Lionel Carley has pointed out, that this grimy industrial town of Elberfeld, south of the Ruhr – described by Jelka Delius as 'a dismal town, full of black smoke, modern industry, machines, rich and ugly people' – was the place where a performing tradition of Delius's spring blossom, orange afterglow music was first established.

After a highly successful first performance of *Sea-Drift* at Essen in 1906 – in the audience was the young Carl Schuricht who became one of the work's most enthusiastic exponents – Delius's music began to attain a popularity in Germany which seriously rivalled that of Richard Strauss, whose pre-eminence was becoming the subject of hot debate. 1907 saw the first production of *A Village Romeo and Juliet* in Berlin (conducted by Cassirer), and in 1908 the *Mass of Life* was given under Ludwig Hess in Munich, though not in its entirety; it was the indefatigable Haym who was responsible for the first complete performance in Germany which took place in Elberfeld in December 1909. In 1911 *Sea-Drift* was heard in Elberfeld and the *Mass* for the second time – and for the first time in Vienna. In 1914 *Songs of Sunset* came to Elberfeld; it was in fact dedicated to the Elberfeld Choral Society. Max Chop, a German music critic, published the first monograph on Delius in 1907.

It was those early German performances and their successes which really consolidated Delius's reputation. In the years immediately preceding the First World War, the names of Schuricht, Mottl, Mengelberg and other distinguished contemporary German musicians came to be associated with his work, German publishers vied with each other for the privilege of publishing it, and a number of major compositions were issued by Universal Edition, the publishers of Schoenberg and Berg. Yet in time the Germany which had discovered him gradually relinquished him; with the rise of the Second Viennese School he was branded as reactionary, and the war of course made everybody very nationality-conscious – and Delius, after all, was in theory an Englishman. As late as 1926, however, his works were still being produced in Germany with tolerable frequency. Mrs Delius writes to Norman O'Neill in January of that year: 'Did I tell you that the *Mass of Life* was given on December 18th with the greatest success at Coblenz, on February 4th it will be done at Hagen, later on at Duisberg and in May at Wiesbaden and Frankfurt. *The Song of the High Hills* is down for performance in Athens – *Sea-Drift* at Gotha – *Paris* was just done in Vienna. . . .'

Delius's music is now forgotten in Germany.

2

The xenophobic prejudice and naturalist arrogance of *fin-de-siècle* musical Germany would have repudiated any composer whose music did not show a recognisably Teutonic cast of feature, and Delius's early German audiences no doubt remarked in him an ostensible latter-day Wagnerian. Delius was indeed a perfervid Wagnerian. Much of the stylistic instability of his early period stems from a conflict between an eminently Wagnerian *grande envergure* and the deftly-chiselled, iridescent but definitely small-scale lyricism of Grieg – as we can see if we compare the latter's setting of Vinje's *The Homeward Way* with Delius's, for the compromise here reached is less successful than in the case of the rival setting of *Twilight Fancies* discussed on p. 62. Wagner's role in the formation of Delius's style is a curious one; it is perhaps true to say that if Grieg's influence was specific, Wagner's was general. *Autrement dit*, if the matter or substance of Delius's music is very often demonstrably Grieg-derived, its manner or spirit is generally Wagnerian. Grieg was a lyricist, a skilled practitioner of 'the art that carves on a cherry stone'; Delius built on an epic scale, although he could turn his hands to the beguiling intimacies of the *First Cuckoo*, *Song before Sunrise* and *Summer Night on the River*. But if these are sketches, *A Mass of Life*, *Sea-Drift* and *The Song of the High Hills* are enormous murals. In this quality – the ability to think in long paragraphs and construct over long time spans – lies Delius's outstanding debt to Wagner. One secret of this feeling for what Percy Grainger termed 'free form-flow' lies in the composer's grasp of chromatic harmonic technique, an endlessly proliferating sensuousness of sound. This also he acquired from Wagner, all of whose works he admired – with one exception. *Parsifal* was detested by Nietzsche; so *Parsifal* was detested by Delius.

No aspect of Delius's personality has been more discussed than the impact of Nietzsche thereupon. Through Nietzsche's *Also sprach Zarathustra* Delius experienced his true spiritual awakening, just as later Bax was to come to terms with his inner self for the first time through a reading of Yeats's *The Wanderings of Usheen*. Arthur Hutchings has examined almost every aspect of Delius's relationship to Nietzsche, but it may be useful here to recall briefly what Nietzsche taught Delius. He taught him that every man stands at an open door, that no man with an imaginative cast of mind need face a life twisted by drudgery; that man's pride as a man need not be measured by his capacity to shoulder work and responsibilities which he detests, which bore him, which are too small for what he could be; that such a man's strength should not be gauged by the values of the mystique of suffering. He instilled in him (or strengthened, for it was there already) an unutterable loathing of the society into which such a man is born : the stultifying mediocrity, the philistinism, the smug, directionless self-display of a bourgeoisie whose viciousness so often masquerades under the hypercritical leer of virtue. Delius had Olympian standards of refinement and discrimination, in music as in life, and those who proved themselves incapable of living up to them were ruthlessly cast aside. He was not cruel but he was hard; and we should remember that, in a way, his personality held a touch of the schizophrenic. What was the impulse which prompted the hard-headed, pragmatic, intolerant Teuton to a continuous outpouring of unfettered rhapsody on the evanescence of life and love, inextricably intertwined with profound obeisance before the mystery and beauty of nature? Few artists can have segregated the conflicting elements of their personalities into such mutually exclusive compartments. It is probably that, relatively early in life, Delius perceived his innate proclivity to introspection and almost pathological obsession with transience, and realised that unless effective measures were taken to counteract them, they would surely destroy him. Using *Also sprach Zarathustra* as a kind of moral crutch, he cultivated a facade of severity and imperviousness which enabled him to clear his early path of obstacles and maintain confidence in himself and his work, irrespective of a slow and erratic development and much unsympathetic and ill-informed criticism. For the other side of Delius, however, one has to look to his music, conditioned in every facet by those exquisite sensibilities which had to be so ruthlessly suppressed in everyday life. Add to this a capacity (later shared by Nazi intellectuals) for reading into *Zarathustra* exactly what he wished to find there, and the appeal of Nietzsche's work is crystal-clear. Had Nietzsche never crossed his path, it is no doubt feasible that Delius's development would ultimately have followed the same course; but the process would have been a protracted one and costlier in terms of fully mature creative achievement.

Ironically, Nietzsche and Delius just missed each other; it has been plausibly suggested by Hutchings that the former might have found in the latter the embodiment of the artist-superman whom he so tragically failed to see realised in Wagner. Like Wagner, Delius was self-centred and arrogant, almost impossible to live with (in his latter years, at any rate) bigoted, fanatical and intolerant. But unlike Wagner Delius was never sycophantic, dishonest in money matters, perfidious or insincere, he had a Northern (perhaps Yorkshire?) bluntness and directness and a lively Nietzschean contempt for those who would hold him subservient to them. Like all good Prussians, he enjoyed a discipline and routine of an almost military cast, and ordered his bouts of self-indulgence. Best of all – and this Nietzsche would have applauded above all else – he demonstrated uncomplaining fortitude in the face of prolonged bodily suffering. In nearly every way Delius was a better Nietzschean than Wagner, better even than Nietzsche himself. So it is predictable that Delius's most Germanic score is the one for which Nietzsche himself provided the inspiration; for the text of *A Mass of Life* was extracted from the book which Delius kept at his bedside much as others keep the Bible – *Also sprach Zarathustra.* It is from the viewpoint of the *Mass* that the Germanic orientation of Delius's style may be placed most realistically in perspective.*

A Mass of Life is built on an enormous scale, a pagan oratorio stemming in a direct line of descent from the 'An die Freude' of the Ninth, Bruckner's *Te Deum* and the choral finale of Mahler's *Resurrection* Symphony and anticipating the twofold structure of the mighty *Symphony of a Thousand* which had yet to be written. In the huge choral dithyrambs which open either part of the *Mass* and in the hymnic setting of Zarathustra's *Mitternachtslied* which forms the apex of the entire construction we find a

---

*The original German title was *Lebensmesse*, but the German poet Richard Dehmel pointed out that he had already given that title to a poem of his. So Delius changed his title to *Eine Messe des Lebens*.

sinewy architectural strength and a textural solidity and breadth of conception utterly Germanic in temper. These opening choruses are worth closer scrutiny. The first begins with an imperious attention-getting gesture, paralleled by Bruckner in the *Te Deum* and by Mahler in the 'Veni Creator' of his Symphony no. 8, for they all ring up the curtain on their apostrophes to a peremptory tonic chord giving way immediately to a tonic pedal. The wonderful 'Sunrise' of Strauss's own *Zarathustra* consists fundamentally in nothing other than a C major tonic chord; and Strauss is an influence we cannot afford to overlook in this context. In general terms, Strauss's contribution is contained in the virtuosity of his orchestral technique. *Paris* with all its ebullience, panache and self-conscious brilliance is directly indebted, and certain parts of *Appalachia* betray a familiarity with Straussian tricks-of-the-trade. In later years nothing whatever remained save a tendency (one which brands him as a true Germanic child of his time) to write for a larger-than-average orchestral complement. More specifically the impact made by the blazing unison horn theme in *Don Juan* was one whose repercussions would last almost to the end of Delius's life. Fenby recalls that he never missed an opportunity of hearing the piece and would listen for the high pedal G on the violins which precedes the entry of his favourite and, when it came, nearly wag his head off with pleasure. We need not look for any direct reminiscences of this horn theme in Delius; more striking in this respect is the way in which the fierily exuberant opening theme of *Paa Vidderne* of 1892 (Ex. 19) actually anticipates that of *Ein Heldenleben* written some seven years later. But the *Don Juan* theme came to symbolise for Delius manliness, robustness, health, youth, vigour, a healthy enjoyment of the good things in life; and I am confident that it is by reference to the spirit of this theme and others in

Ex.19

Don Juan, their energy, determination and fiery ecstasy, that we may explain the frequent presence in Delius of those angular leaping figures for the brass which on a first hearing may sound rather out of character. In the two great *Lobgesänge* in *A Mass of Life* these brazen brass figures are more to the fore than anywhere else – in 'O du mein Wille' at the first delivery of 'spare mich auf zu einem grossen Schicksale' where trombones echo the trumpets' clarion-call (which is none other than the omnipotent Ex. 6) and later pick up the sturdy thrust of pentatonic tune given out by the violins at 'eine Sonne selber und ein unerbittlicher Sonnenwille'. In 'Herauf du grosser Mittag' (part II) six horns, then four trumpets, spring to the defence of 'Dorthinaus, sturmischer als das Meer sturmt unsere grosse Sehnsucht' and later, just before the recapitulation, the entire brass section (with a motif deriving from the basic shape of Ex. 6), seems to throw all caution to the winds at 'Einem Sturme gleich kommt mein Gluck und meine Freiheit'. So too in other works burning at a similar emotional temperature – the approach to the first climax in *Song of Summer* is a notable example. These two choruses bring out the iron in the composer's temperament as does no other music of his. Their splendour of poetic imagery is no doubt responsible:

That I may be ready and ripe in the great moontide: ready and ripe like glowing ore, like cloud heavy with lightning and like swelling milk-udder – ready for myself and my most secret will: a bow eager for its arrow, an arrow eager for its star – a star, ready and ripe in its noontide, glowing, transpierced, blissful through annihilating sun-arrows – a sun itself and an inexorable sun-will, ready for annihilation in victory. O will, my essential, my necessity, dispeller of need! Spare me for one great victory.   (trs. A. K. Holland)

The flesh-and-blood of the music is Straussian, laced with a visionary heroism that Strauss could never rival. This is the music of the new Germany, of the race of Supermen, of the blond Teutonic god-hero who armed, brazen and beautiful, the fire of vision and victory in his eyes, stands flexing his muscles in a deluge of sunlight. How the Nazi culture-vultures (the colloquial term has a macabre appropriateness) could have overlooked this sterling musical prophet of their fondly-imagined thousand-year empire remains a mystery to me. We cannot fail to be thrilled by the music, though 'Herauf du grosser Mittag' is superior to 'O du mein Wille' largely because of the former's much greater strength of rhythmic impulse and the grainier, more muscular quality of its choral textures. 'Herauf du grosser Mittag' falls too into a neater ABA format with a tumultuously lyrical centrepiece for the three soloists, almost Skryabinesque in its welling, swelling ecstasy – the onrush of high summer to the mountain top. It seems that nobody has remarked on the recurrence here of two themes from the ten-year-old *Over the Hills and Far Away* – not reminiscence but literal quotation. The two themes are the very first heard in the earlier work (Ex. 11a and b) and they re-appear together here at 'mit kalten Quellen und seliger Stille'. Delius often repeats himself under stress of similar emotions, but this is deliberate self-quotation; it is astonishing that no comment was forthcoming from Haym (who gave the premiere of *Over the Hills*) in his published analysis of the *Mass*.

Delius considered Strauss's own *Also sprach Zarathustra* a complete failure, but the latter does relate to Delius in an intriguing if indirect manner through the intermediary of the Norwegian painter Edvard Munch. Munch and Delius were friends for over thirty-eight years, and two of their shared enthusiasms were Jacobsen and Nietzsche. A letter of Munch to Delius in 1899 mentions a scheme for bringing together etchings by Munch, writings by Jacobsen and music by Delius, though precisely what form this was to take is not clear – perhaps a recital of the Delius-Jacobsen songs to a decor by Munch. (John Boulton-Smith, who has investigated the Munch-Delius relationship very closely, suggests that the *Fennimore and Gerda* intermezzo offers a close musical parallel to some of Munch's paintings in which a lonely figure is seen sitting on the shore, as for example in *Melancholy: the Yellow Boat*.) Now Munch was also a Nietzsche disciple, and scholars have pointed out the affinities between the lithograph *Funeral March*, the painting *Golgotha* and *Also sprach Zarathustra*. Nietzsche dominates the Oslo University murals (upon which work was started in 1909), as in *Mountain of Man with Zarathustra's Sun*, and the centrepiece of the whole design, *The Sun*. Boulton-Smith suggests that the spirit of this mural is reflected in the burst of energy with which 'O du mein Wille' opens; but it can also hardly fail to suggest the resplendent opening of Strauss's own *Zarathustra*, one of the most elementally powerful moments in music. Strauss is in fact closer to Munch than Delius, since his sustained C major chord for the full orchestra reinforced by organ irradiates a cosmic all-enveloping but static energy, like Munch's; whereas Delius's chorus is energy in flux, dynamically constituted.

So we can see that the corner-stones of the *Mass* – 'O du mein Wille' 'Hereauf du grosser Mittag' and most of all the great hymn to eternal day 'O Mensch gib acht' – are weightily anchored in the great Austro-German symphonic past. There are parallels with Mahler, apart from the heaven-storming exordia – the process of thematic integration, for example. As in the Symphony no. 8 themes are introduced in embryonic form in Part 1 of the *Mass* to be subjected to a process of continuous evolutionary development throughout the remainder of the work, one which can be easily overlooked. The rising bell-like fifths (an echo of *Parsifal*) symbolising Zarathustra's midnight are generally recognisable enough whenever they occur, which is often; their effect is cumulative, so that the finale, in which they are scarcely absent from a single bar, seems the logical and inevitable outcome. Hence the use of the term 'symphonic'.

Other motifs are less all-pervasive. The long-limbed stalking theme for low cellos and basses which sets the finale in motion has already been heard in the Second Dance Song, both in the troubled, questioning orchestral introduction and in the long Zarathustra monologue which bisects the girl's choruses. The murky triplet theme for bassoon in

11. Munch, *Self-portrait at 2 a.m.*, after 1940. This bears a remarkable likeness to pictures of Delius in his bath chair.

12. Munch, *Delius at Wiesbaden.*

13. Munch, *Nietzsche*.

'Wehe mir! Wo ist die Zeit hin?' (the whole passage brings vividly to mind the spectre at the feast – the unclean spirits and their chill winds – in part 1 of Schoenberg's *Gurrelieder*) is heard again in the penultimate 'Gottes Wille ist tiefer du wunderliche Welt' but here is overpowered – magnificently – by another theme given earlier, a motif with a prominent falling sixth associated with the big climaxes both in 'Nacht ist es' and 'Gottes Wille'.

But in view of the text's special preoccupation with summer evening and night, it is interesting that the most subtle agent of motivic continuity is a shape whose only distinguishing mark is a falling fourth, yet whose

Ex.20(a)

(b)

(c)

(d)

presence is felt so tellingly in a variety of contexts that I am tempted to dub it a quasi-Mahlerian *Naturlaut* in general rather than an *Abendlaut* in particular – for one of these contexts is 'Heisser Mittag schläft nach auf der Fluren', where an atmosphere of 'silent noon' is in question, not the purple mists of even. Ex. 20 shows the various metamorphoses. There is no evidence that this represented a conscious effort; Delius was very much a composer who reverted time and again to the same vague outline of musical image in situations or scenes involving similar emotive forces, and so it is not at all surprising to find the germ of this motif in the earlier setting of the Jacobsen lyric *In the Seraglio Garden*, an *Abendstimmung* with Oriental overtones. There are *psychologically*-motivated similarities as well as those *musically*-motivated. Mahler's Day of Judgment in the finale of the *Resurrection* symphony – the lull before the storm – is heralded by a series of re-echoing, apocalyptic horn calls evoking a feeling of limitless vistas *à la* John Martin. The prelude to Part II of the *Mass* is stereophonically conceived in much the same way. Delius's great glorification of eternity ends on a chord of the added sixth to the word 'Ewigkeit', in B major (the Nirvana of *A Village Romeo*). *Das Lied von der Erde* ends with the contralto solo, drunk with beauty and longing, re-iterating the one word 'ewig' as if she was in a trance; the added sixth is never resolved. The romantic agony, which informs the music of both Delius and Mahler, here finds near identity of expression. There is a new quality of poetic awareness which may or may not reflect some Impressionist influence; a feeling for nature is built into the pattern and texture of, for instance, 'Der Einsame in Herbst' or 'Der Trunkene im Fruhling' and in the extraordinary night-music of 'Der Abschied' in a manner which makes Mahler's earlier pictures of dawn (Symphony No. 1) and night (his own setting of the *Mitternachtslied* as a solo song) seem by comparison laboured and contrived. *Das Lied* with its pagan delighting in the fruits of the earth, the good things in life, and its grieving at the inevitability of their departure, is a very Delian piece, spiritually and to some extent technically.

It is above all the influence which may conveniently be described as 'Impressionist' which so permeates certain sections of the *Mass* as to place them at some distance from the Teutonic sphere of reference, and to illuminate the true meaning of Donald Mitchell's classification of Delius as 'the only German Impressionist'. The two dance-songs are the most affected. The first ('In dein Auge schaute ich jungst, O Leben') is also the first nocturne of Delius's maturity, and one of his finest. Wordless voices sound over the water at night (the Delian Experience) and in the very first bars we recognise in Delius a quality not of Germany but of France – the beauty of sensuous sound *an und für sich*, to which the gentle soothing lull

of the much-favoured 6/8 rhythm is a significant contributor. The movement is neatly constructed : the chorus takes up a crisp, dapper little
folksong-like air which gradually gathers momentum in the wild glee of a
dance over hill and dale (in triple time, like the 'Tanzlied' in Strauss's
Zarathustra, even with the occasional waltz-like overtones). After the climax
the quasi-folktune returns and encloses a long meditation for the baritone
solo during which the music of the dance is slowly and nostalgically re-
moulded. Then a final reference to the folksong and the path is clear for the
real climax of the movement – the moving dialogue between Life and
Zarathustra and the first intimation of the *Mitternachtslied*, 'O Mensch,
gib Acht'.

In this movement the chorus sing throughout the dance-portion exclusively to 'la la la' as they have earlier done in Delius; but here more than
elsewhere are invoked the shades of the Flower Maidens in Klingsor's
magic garden. And in the *second* Dance Song, in Part 2, we are made more
than ever aware of how the world of musical Impressionism grew out of
the translucent singing textures of Wagner. The Second Dance Song is a
long and elaborate woodland idyll, a *Poème de la Forêt* inspired no doubt,
as was Roussel's, by the Forest of Fontainebleau. The music certainly seems
appropriately remembered in the context of the Fontainebleau forest at
dusk on a summer night. The opening of the orchestral prologue is particularly evocative, with its little swaying figure wafted through the muted
strings like a soft white mist arising from the earth and encircling the
trees. This is pure *Waldeinsamkeit*. Then a more agitated note creeps in
and the music becomes progressively more Wagnerian as it betrays the
tormented self-doubting presence of Zarathustra. Then his troubles are
forgotten as the spectacle of the wood-nymphs' dance unfolds before him;
and here, again, the sensuousness of texture, the economy of gesture – all
bespeak an Impressionist influence. The finest music is that of the epilogue,
'Die Sonne ist lange schon hinunter' – Zarathustra's moving soliloquy on
the going down of the sun and the feelings of melancholy it engenders in
him, a 'serene twilit brooding' *par excellence*. The forest glades are now
deserted, the bacchantes' voices no more than a distant echo; and the music
is an *Abenstimmung* the substance of which contains more than a hint of
the later *Summer Night on the River*. It is a miniature tone-poem, a quasi
Bartókian *musique nocturne* – rustling leaves, shimmering heat (violins
and violas, playing *tremolo*) the chirping of crickets (a syncopated
throbbing rhythm on clarinets and bassoons) even the distant calling of
night-birds in the forest (interlocking flute and oboe). This is nature-
Impressionism in a nutshell – nothing is really heard clearly, the instrumental sonorities are veiled, the listener is presented with a vague
impression in sound rather than a well-defined picture. And, if we stand

103

in the Forest of Fontainebleau at gloaming of an evening in high summer, Delius's music is what we hear.

The music of the *Mass* thus fluctuates constantly between the twin polarities represented by Teutonic romanticism on the one hand, and by Impressionist faery fantasy on the other. The common denominator is Wagner. Yet we are never allowed to forget that the massive cornerstones of the *Mass* – above all the great sacrament of the 'Mitternachtslied' which seems at its climax to fill the whole world with the clamour of bell-ringing and the paeans of a mighty concourse, roused to a frenzy of superhuman ecstasy with the light of the Everlasting shining in their eyes – are fairly, squarely and even slightly hysterically entrenched in an age-old, almost ritualistic tradition whose virility, gritty toughness of fibre and crackling extrovert brilliance effectively complement the recurrent refrain of *où sont les neiges d'antan*, Zarathustra's 'spirit of heaviness', the introspective melancholy of the dreamer and poet. *A Mass of Life* is *echt*-German, inspirationally, spiritually and technically oriented towards the *Vaterland*. Listening to it in this light we can well understand the enthusiasm of those young patriots in the Germany of the 1900s, those whom Bernard van Dieren termed the 'determined anti-Christians and New-silver Pagans' watching the rekindling of the flame of Imperial glory and asking of Delius 'Art thou he that cometh, or look we for another?'

Delius's response to German letters was not however limited solely to Nietzsche. If at first glance the range of poets he quarried for singable texts seems large, we quickly realise that their most distinctive feature as a group is uniformity of thought, however disparate their individual expressive techniques may be. The essence of Delius's art lies in its existence within a personally but rigidly prescribed set of formulas preserving identity of vision throughout, albeit in widely differing perspectives.

Broadly speaking Delius sought three principal themes in his literature: natural beauty, human love and the optimism born of self-reliance and earthly all-sufficiency. The authors he most admired – Nietzsche, Whitman and Jacobsen – offered him a concentrate of all three, and such verse as he (or his wife) selected from other poets revolved without exception round one or more of these seminal topics. Nevertheless it comes as something of a surprise to remember that the first score to bear an unmistakably Delian imprint – the opera *A Village Romeo and Juliet* – was not inspired by any one of the composer's great literary loves but by the comparatively obscure Swiss novelist and lyric poet Gottfried Keller, a prominent representative of that period in German literature known as 'Poetic Realism'. Delius's affinities with this literary school are worth commenting upon, and since *A Village Romeo* is not only Delius's finest opera but also anticipates in embryonic form most of the music that he was to produce thereafter, Keller's part in the sudden efflorescence of his genius may usefully be evaluated.

Poetic Realism in Germany was the name given to that period of the mid-nineteenth century when writers, under pressure from the steadily increasing turmoil and complexity of the contemporary scene, sought some measure of stability and coherence in what seemed to be the steadfast, enduring values of the trivial round and common task. 'Realism' implied the statistical norm, the social generality; subject-matter was drawn from the unexceptional rather than from the phenomenal, and settings tended to restrict themselves to the provincial and homespun. To avert the twin perils of triviality and tedium with which such an approach was fraught, writers concentrated on imbuing the *modi vivendi* on which they were focusing attention with meaning and purpose, finding in them positive values and intrinsic merit – this was the implication of the epithet 'poetic'. It was natural that these authors should be especially ready to exploit a trend which had become increasingly pervasive during the early years of the nineteenth century – a shift of emphasis from urban to rural communities as a fruitful source of thematic material. The prime incentives were undoubtedly the accelerating encroachments of industrialisation and the realisation that the advent of a technological age would engulf all traces of a folk and peasant culture, the full value of which had hitherto been imperfectly grasped. In England similar considerations prompted the writing of Hardy's Wessex novels, and the ubiquitous time-lag between music and literature is strikingly illustrated by the fact that the much later folkmusic revival came so perilously near to being still-born; had Sharp and Vaughan Williams been closer contemporaries of Hardy they would not have been obliged to extract much of their material from reluctant octogenarians in the remoter regions of East Anglia and the West Country.

Poetic Realism as a genre achieved considerable popularity among writers of the period. Today three of its most widely-read exponents are Adalbert Stifter, Theodor Storm and Gottfried Keller, and it was on a *Novelle* or short story of the last-named, *Romeo und Julia auf dem Dorfe*, that Delius based the libretto of his fifth opera. It is however a curious fact that he had less in common with Keller than with the other members of the triumvirate. Nature and the countryside form an integral part of their work – the Bavarian forest in Stifter, the marshes and heathland of the Schleswig-Holstein coast in Storm, Swiss pastureland in Keller; yet their relative importance as a structural constituent varies from author to author. In Stifter human activity is dwarfed by the magnitude and potency of nature; in one of his finest and most characteristic stories, *Der Hochwald* (which has become known as 'Das Hohelied des deutschen Waldes'), the huge Bavarian forest becomes a living, vibrant force with a life and personality of its own, although seemingly more benevolently inclined toward humanity than its Scandinavian counterpart as depicted in *Tapiola*. The plot and characters are little more than utilitarian devices to lend continuity and shape to the overall design, and to throw into suitable relief the indomitable grandeur of the forest. The true protagonist is nature, the human figures a mere background. Delius's *Song of the High Hills, North Country Sketches* and even works on a smaller scale, such as *In a Summer Garden*, similarly extol the majesty and all-pervasiveness of nature, compared with which puny man pales into insignificance. Delius, like Stifter, disdains to be caught up in the maelstrom of human activity and prefers to lose himself in pantheistic exploration of those phenomena which for Stifter constituted the truly significant facets of earthly existence: 'the stirring of the air, the rippling of water, the growth of corn, the movement of the sea, the growing green of the earth, the glowing of the sky, the shining of the stars'.

Although Delius, notably in *The Song of the High Hills*, is, like Stifter, irresistibly caught up in the intoxicating sweep and splendour of nature, a more typical attitude consists in the composer's seeing all things under the aspect of mutability, subject to the abiding laws of change and decay. In this he closely resembles Theodor Storm. Storm's preoccupation with transience gives his work that spirit of elegiac melancholy which is the quintessence of much of Delius's finest music; significantly he is remembered far more than Stifter or Keller as a lyric poet, although with the exception of isolated settings by Brahms and Reger his verse has been neglected by composers. In Storm's early period, of which the short story *Immensee* is the most celebrated example, frankly sentimental situations serve as a basis for discreetly aromatic and evocative writing in which the chief emphasis lies in atmosphere and colour; this corresponds roughly to Delius's early Macdowellesque phase, including the *Florida Suite, Summer Evening* and *Irmelin*. In later life Storm achieved a new intensity of vision in which the rather sentimental nostalgia of his early work is transformed into a hard-grained awareness of the tragedy of existence; the crowning achievement of his career is the story *Der Schimmelreiter*, a *Peter Grimes*-like drama of the individual against society in a maritime environment. There is a hard core of sturdy masculinity in this work which belies the author's age – Storm was over 70 when he wrote it. In Delius also, as we have seen, we can trace an increasing austerity of diction from 1910 onwards, at its most uncompromising in the *North Country Sketches* and *Arabesk*. In later works such as the Cello Concerto and *Songs of Farewell* he achieved a remarkable synthesis of sensuousness and asceticism, but the prevailing mood in many of his finest creations, as in those of Storm, distils the poignancy of time and chance and change; the most radical example is *Songs of Sunset*, which sustains the theme without respite from beginning to end.

A cursory review of Keller's life and works reveals at first glance a character considerably at variance with Delius's temperament and outlook. In early life he made abortive attempts to establish himself first as a painter (Stifter was also a painter while Storm was a musician), then, more half-heartedly, as a dramatist. Although in due course he obtained renown as a poet and novelist, he entered the Swiss Civil Service as 'erster Staats-schreiber' of the Canton of Zurich; the post was a responsible one and he performed his duties conscientiously for fifteen years. The change of attitude which turned an aspiring artist into a routine public administrator is highly significant in so far as his creative work is concerned, for Keller is particularly interested in the relationship between the individual and society and is critical of those who attempt to depart from the norm; in other words there is a strongly didactic element in his work. In these circum-stances we should expect him to strike a far steadier balance between subjective description and objective narration than Stifter; plot and dramatic interest are not subordinated to *Stimmung* and atmosphere as they are predominantly in Stifter, and to a lesser extent in Storm.

In Keller's *Romeo und Julia auf dem Dorfe* landscape and environment are not given small measure, indeed they are lovingly tended at every turn; but they are never allowed to usurp the function of positive action. From Delius's point of view this was a marked defect, for musical portrayal of much of the action specified by Keller lay well outside his potential. Conversely, the natural elements pre-eminent in Stifter and Storm and relegated by Keller, if not exactly to a subsidiary function, at least to a role which did not conflict with the main dramatic impulse of his narrative, were the very elements which commended themselves the most persuasively to the composer's refined sensibilities. In this respect Delius's additions to Keller's original story are as significant as his omissions, and certain re-interpretations of character together with the shifting of certain points of emphasis can be explained through the composer's personal involvement in the tragedy.

Keller's moral and social conscience generally asserts itself in his work in one form or another, and in *Romeo und Julia* the feud between the two farmers Manz and Marti over the strip of land separating their fields illustrates the unexpectedly far-reaching consequences of mild dishonesty, avarice and stubbornness. The decline of the two families is fully documented, and the tragic and poetic love of Sali and Vrenchen serves in the first instance merely to point the moral in an extreme and drastic manner – in fact the two themes seem to have occurred to Keller separately.

Now as we should expect, dramatically speaking Delius's main interest lies in the progress of the Sali-Vrenchen love-affair; consequently the parents and their increasingly ruinous strife are excised almost completely from the libretto. The composer pays lip-service to the exigencies of plot by illustrating the beginnings of the quarrel between the farmers and Sali's near-fatal clash with Vrenchen's father, but in each case characterisation falls limp and the musical argument grows threadbare; Delius falls back rather helplessly on stock melodramatic posturing with diminished seventh-ridden harmony and sequential two-bar repetition. One of the finest moments in the story is the dramatic encounter between the two hate-crazed men on a bridge in a thunderstorm, the climax of which brings to birth the nascent love of the two children :

Lightning struck and weirdly illuminated the dark melancholy of the waters all round : thunder re-echoed moodily in the grey-black clouds, and heavy raindrops began to fall as the two men, mindless with rage, leapt at one and the same time on to the narrow bridge. They grappled with each other and drove their fists into each other's faces, pale and trembling as they were with anger and the release of a pent-up deep distress . . . But by this time the children had come up and could see the pitiful spectacle. Sali sprang to his father's defence . . . Vrenchen too, with a scream, threw her arms round her father to protect him but succeeded only in hindering him. Tears were streaming down her face and she looked imploringly at Sali who was on the point of seizing hold of her father and overpowering him completely. In the process of forcing themselves between their parents in an endeavour to separate them, the children found themselves in close proximity one to another, and at that moment, through a break in the clouds, a flash of evening sunlight lit up the girl's face, so close to the boy's. Sali looked in this face, one he knew so well and which yet seemed now of a sudden so different and so strangely beautiful. Vrenchen noticed his amazement and amid all the tears and terror a smile flickered across her features . . . and as they turned to go their separate ways, unseen by their parents they quickly clasped each other's hands . . .' (trs. C. P.)

This is the *Wendepunkt*, the turning-point in the story, as far as the two children are concerned. Yet Delius jettisons it ruthlessly, and on the whole the love-scenes as such in the opera tend to lack conviction. Time is apt to weigh heavily on those occasions in the early scenes where the children are alone together, and Delius surely feels uncomfortable in his attempt to scale down the intensity of his conception to the level of two artless juveniles (Fenby tells us that Delius was always ill-at-ease with children). The final duet ('See the moonbeams kiss the woods') is soundly realised and generously written for the voices, its climax almost Puccinian in the magniloquence of its lyricism; yet the fact that it brings to mind so vividly certain passages in the *Idyll* (and anticipates 'Cease smiling dear' in *Songs of Sunset*) serves to emphasise its indebtedness to stock conventions of operatic expression, since the *Idyll* traces its origins back to the opera *Margot la Rouge*, written at much the same time as *A Village Romeo*. Magnificent rhetoric, no doubt, and rhetoric instinct with meaning and feeling, not empty posturing; but the music which expresses the very quintessence of the love-tragedy is devoid of rhetoric, of any acquired elements, dispenses with words, says little, implies a great deal. The peerless 'Walk to the Paradise Garden' is the tragedy of Sali and Vrenchen. It transcends the boundaries of time and space and verbal expression, and it is basic Delius in every bar.

The wonders of human love, then, and the wonders of non-human nature, and the infinity of their reverberations – these are Delius's preoccupations. *A Village Romeo* is unique among his works in its Swiss location. Delius was no folksy purveyor of pastoral-elegaic anonymity; his landscapes, whether Floridean, North English, French or Norwegian, are clearly differentiated one from another and sharply characterised; and here the lucidity and freshness peculiar to Alpine scenery, bracing yet benign, invokes in Delius a warm lyrical response never to be met with in quite the same guise again (the Norwegian mountain-country depicted in *The Song of the High Hills* touches a quite different nerve). This mountain panorama, not unduly insisted upon by Keller, is ever significant: for few composers have offered us so richly varied a range of mountain moods as Delius. A passion for high solitudes was rarely absent from his thought. In *A Village Romeo* this life-enhancing atmosphere (for Delius experienced it as such) is all-pervasive, and more often than not it is evoked in the traditional way by horns – six of them here. *Distant* horns, too, in two memorable cases – may I refer the reader back to Chapter 1 should he have forgotten the particular significance of distance in Delius's work. At the beginning of Scene 3 Delius (not Keller) describes in the stage directions the set he has in mind: 'The wild-land overgrown with poppies in full bloom . . . in the background fields and villages in the hills . . . in the distance the snow mountains.' In the brief prelude to this scene an orchestral wreath of no little complexity and miraculous beauty is worked by capricious, wayward woodwind figures as they offset a rhythmic polyphony of horns re-echoing multitudinously in the distance, piquantly flavoured by a Lydian-Dorian modality. Motivically, too, Delius knew what he was about, since the whole sound-picture grows out of the descending theme first heard in the very opening bars of the opera, here given simultaneously in augmentation (violins) and in diminution on the flutes where it breaks away into the tiny rivulets of Lydian triplets which set the bevy of offstage horns in motion. Structural subtleties of this nature are generally overlooked by those whose theory is that Delius's compositional technique was amateurishly defective.

The snow-mountains are again evoked by far-away horns at the beginning of Scene 6, where the Dark Fiddler, leader of the vagabonds, 'stands in the soft summer twilight with his back to the audience, looking at the high mountains with the last glow of the sunset upon them'. Horns in the far distance pick up the last three notes of the immediately preceding vagabonds' chorus ('Dance along') and repeat them, trance-like, over a soft timpani pedal through a kaleidoscope of harmony, reflecting the rapid shift of colour-combinations in a sunset's final stages – a strange and wonderful moment (Ex. 21). The very opening of the opera reveals the horns in an altogether different role – here they dance along merrily in block chords to suggest the exhilarating clarity of a fine September morning with the farmers happily at work in the fresh mountain air. This is one of those Delian passages almost visual in its suggestiveness; it has a fine realistic *alfresco* tang.

Ex.21

More often, however, horns in Delius are associated with moments of deep emotional import, and these, in their turn, are frequently associated with mountain scenery. In the fourth movement of the *Requiem* the soloist sings of the soul of man ascending to the mountain top which, like a throne, towers above the great plains that roll far away into the distance; and horns beneath a sustained added sixth chord (*the* Delius 'chord') sound a distant triadic fanfare, creating a sense of limitless vistas of space and time, air and light. Then the echo answers, as 'the sun goeth down and the evening spreads its hands in blessing o'er the world, bestowing peace'. In the spring awakening of the finale, off-stage horns again sound a fanfare, this time tellingly but discreetly bitonal, while horns in the orchestra peal out like bells, and a Lydian cuckoo calls on oboe and flute, until all the tangle and hum is lost in the distance. Delius was a legitimate heir of Weber and Wagner in that he succumbed time and again to the poetry and magic of the solo horn and the horn quartet. We may remember how in the first scene of Act 2 of *Meistersinger* Sachs is haunted in the cool of the summer evening by the music of Walther, including the 'spring' motif which fills the air about him with all the well-nigh unbearable sweetness of the elder's scent; it is the mellowness of the two horns in thirds singing the theme which so haunts and moves the old cobbler – and us. So too with Ex. 21 above; and it is appropriate that the little oft-heard oft-discussed ascending pentatonic triplet figure which in this work (as in no other to the same extent) is the mainspring of so much of the musical action – Ex. 6 – should be given on the occasion of its first appearance to the horns, i.e. bar 11 of the introduction to Scene 1. Its emotional significance is made nowhere more explicit than at that point in the Paradise Garden scene when Sali and Vrenchen are discussing the proposal of the Dark Fiddler and his colleagues that they should join their company and lead their free untrammelled existence in the mountains. 'What say you, Vrenchen?' asks Sali; 'shall we follow all those people to the mountains?' At the word 'mountains' there is a sudden irradiance of D major tonality with a solo horn intoning the ascending triplet phrase (Ex. 6) and flooding the distant snow-capped summits with light – a flawless synthesis of thought, word and musical image.

Throughout *A Village Romeo* Delius, unlike Keller, seeks to reduce to a minimum the impingement of the outside world on the quasi-fairy-tale romance of the children. It is not to be avoided entirely, however, for without some palpable indication of hostile or, at best, indifferent humanity, the lovers' suicide-pact could obviously not be rationally accounted for and would so lose greatly in meaning and poignancy. And so it came to pass that Delius decided to make as convincing a spectacle as possible out of the Berghald Fair scene. (A point of purely pedantic interest: Delius invests 'Berghald' with the significance of a proper name. In Keller the village where the fair takes place is not so specified, but the inn known as the 'Paradise Garden' is described as being situated some way from this village 'an einer einsamen Berghalde' i.e. on a lonely mountain slope.) Doubtless Delius would have dealt less successfully with such a scene in later life, but as noted in Chapter 1 in his early days he was perfectly at ease amid scenes of revelry and convivial gatherings; before *A Village Romeo* he had already produced his scintillating evocation of Parisian night-life in *Paris*, and very little later he was to write the brief but pungent brass-band variation in *Appalachia*. And, of course, at the back of his mind there must have been the opening of the fifth (final) scene in the last act of *Meistersinger*, which sets a festive scene in much the same way. Delius was surely mindful of Wagner already in the previous scene in which he prepares us for the fair: the children awake from their dream of being married in the old church to the sound of peasants yodelling in the distance, and the prospect of throwing caution to the winds for a day at the fair draws them out into the sunshine. The yodelling draws nearer, a jubilant paean of bell ringing begins (the bluey haze of these tolling bells has already enclosed the church-scene, and it will also take in the fair) and a pentatonic theme of rustic sturdiness (bringing to mind *Over the Hills and Far Away*) comes bounding up from the low brass of the orchestra, a variant of which will re-appear in the fair music. Then – and here a parallel to the end of Act 2 of *Meistersinger* occurs – everything quietens down suddenly, flecks and flickers of theme play casually about a long-held tonic triad *pianissimo*, until the curtain is run down on a snappy *sforzando* tonic chord which brings the audience to its feet. This is precisely the close of the fugal riot scene in *Meistersinger* – even the key is the same (E major).

The fair scene itself shows that Delius, no less than Humperdinck and Mahler, found the last scene in *Meistersinger* an invaluable object-lesson in the transmutation of pop into art. As far as we know there is no traditional melodic material here incorporated, and, of course, the representation is 'idealised' – there is no 'realism'; we are far (but not too far) even from the sophisticated realism of *Petrushka* which, incidentally, Delius admired. Yet how good his tunes are in this unlikeliest of contexts, and how fine his feeling, in terms of writing for orchestra, chorus and soloists, for the colour and tumult of the fairground scene! There is no sense of Delius's having wrested this music unwillingly out of himself, as he evidently did in respect of the Manz-Marti scenes; on the contrary it flows willingly and spontaneously with many an incidental beauty. Delius enjoyed this music, however untypical of his familiar manner it may have been, and he intended that we should enjoy it. In the other 'realistic' scene – Sali's and Vrenchen's dream of being married in the old church – he no doubt had a Nietzschean tongue thrust into a Nietzschean cheek as he penned the pious Gounod-like inanities of 'Lord before thy mighty will a loving couple humbly kneel' (the wedding march, a rather sombre one, and the peal of bells which conclude the ceremony are, however, perfectly 'straight'). The dream music is not particularly interesting, because Delius is 'dreaming' synthetically and therefore self-consciously. When we become conscious that we dream, the dream is on the point of breaking, and Delius's most delectable dreaming is that of which he is not aware and which therefore entails no loss of spontaneity in his poetry.

Virtually the entire fair-scene is in waltz-rhythm, and the main ritornello-like theme is an elegant little tune heard first on a solo trumpet to an *oom-pah-pah* accompaniment of the ice cream-cart variety. When the chorus takes it up to 'la' it reveals its kinship with the First Dance Song in *A Mass of Life*. The merry clamour of orchestral-choral-vocal polyphony – a real polyphony of unbound joy aided and abetted by an on-stage contingent of cornets, alto trombones and side drum – abates only when the children come upon the scene and when their presence is commented upon by the fair personnel; and even here there is one subtle sleight-of-hand. For at the end of the first 'la la la' chorus there is a lovely dreamy cadential progression, very Delian (p. 156 of the vocal score, p. 110 of the miniature). When this chorus and this progression recur later in the scene they are made to coincide with Vrenchen's words 'the "Paradise Garden" – how lovely that sounds', and to the sound of its loveliness is reflected, apparently fortuitously, in the music surrounding the lovers but independent of them (How fortuitous was it in fact? Did Delius know when he introduced this progression for the first time that he was later going to use it as a counterpoint to those words of Vreli's?). A final subtlety is that the melodic rhythm of the subsidiary waltz element (vocal score, p. 147, bar 3) is what later serves as a transition between the climax of the fair music and the start of the momentous 'walk'. And the sound of this transfigured music brings the lovers to their Nemesis; in the Paradise Garden they encounter for the last time the most enigmatic figure in the opera, the Dark Fiddler, and find the world well lost for love.

Who is this weird character and what does he signify in Delius's opera? There are crucial discrepancies between Delius's conception of Keller's 'schwarze Geiger' and the poet's own. In Delius he is incomparably more sympathetic, in every sense of the word – to us as a character, and toward the star-crossed lovers. The fact is that Keller wrote from within the narrow sphere of middle-class morality and was wont to cast a reproving eye on those who, like the Fiddler and his boon-companions, stood without the confines of that sphere and flouted its conventions. We can scarcely credit Delius with lending support to the type of bourgeois ideology promulgated by Keller, and in fact he would have identified himself personally more with the Dark Fiddler than with any other character. He, like the Fiddler, was in a sense an outcast, spiritually isolated, cosmopolitan in outlook and temperament but basically stateless; for routine morality and the standard ethical code of the society into which he was born he cared not a fig. The mode of life described at the beginning of Scene 6 by the chorus of vagabonds, who danced and fiddled their way over hill and dale, wild and free, 'ever journeying onwards, towards the setting sun' – this was Delius's own philosophy of life, and so autobiographical significance can be read into what we may almost term the Fiddler's 'theme-song', a miniature aria of haunting poignancy:

> O wandering minstrel, thou hurriest on
> Through the wrangle of trees and tangle of shrubs
> While I must limp after, thy fiddler forsaken,
> For are we not comrades, thou vagabond wind?

For Delius, the Fiddler symbolised not an evil or at best a sinister force (as in Keller) but absolute oneness with nature, unconditional freedom from

113

ties religious, parental or moral. When the two children first appear on stage they 'appear to be listening to something'. What they are listening to is a motif of consecutive ninths representing the wind to which the Fiddler's song is addressed. And when we first hear the song we do not see the singer: the voice comes, as so often and so meaningfully in Delius, from out the far distance. 'How strange the wind sounds sighing through the trees,' says Vrenchen before the song is heard. 'Listen, Sali! Perhaps 'tis fairy music.' And as the sound of the song comes closer, Marti exclaims 'How strange the wind sounds in the wild land' and Manz replies 'Is it really the wind? No, 'tis someone singing.' The Fiddler's ambiguity is immediately underlined – is he a real figure or merely an embodiment of the wild beauty of nature, the wind? And, very subtly, the composer characterises the disturbing, unnerving effect the Fiddler has produced on both children and parents by drawing the melody of his song into a silky web of tenuous fluctuating chromatic harmony – the first of many such passages in Delius. Delius, like the Impressionist painters, knew that Nature in all her tranquillities is never motionless.

This identification of the Fiddler with nature is further enhanced in that some of the happiest nature-music is enshrined in the extended lyrical passage in Scene 3 (based on his song) when he offers to show the children the wonders of the world:

And when you care to come into the world with me
The woods and dales we'll roam, and your merry guide I'll be,
My guide the sun and moon, towards the west across the sea,
The waving corn my daily bread to strange wild music from the stream
My bed's among red poppies.

This is matched in music of great lyrical expressiveness which anticipates the surging breakers and exhilarating elemental grandeur of *Sea-Drift*. Later, in the Paradise Garden, the Fiddler's description of his wild land through the changing seasons inspires beautiful music in the composer's most winning vein: here, as earlier, it is only when the subject of the feud between the peasants is broached that his muse fails him. There is a moment of infinite tenderness as the Fiddler preaches to Sali and Vrenchen the delights of free communion with nature and concludes 'And for your marriage bed there's soft and purple heather' – the thought, and the music, are evidently akin to the last line of the verse quoted above. Finally, the Fiddler's near-demented playing is superimposed on the ninths of the 'wind' motif to form a *moto perpetuo*-like accompaniment to Sali's ecstatic 'And I throw our lives away', a moment which foreshadows stylistically the paean to awakening nature and 'eternal renewal' in the *Requiem* of some fifteen years later. There is also, one feels, some intangible kinship or bond between the Fiddler and the unseen bargemen – 'travellers we a-passing by' were they not all? – whose distant song is one of the emotional pegs to which the finale is fastened. There are two bargemen to begin with, and then finally, as the boat drifts down the river and slowly fills with water, they are joined by a mysterious third to sing the epithalamium, tinted with the sombre richness of the Phrygian mode. Who is this third bargeman? A Charon-like figment of the poetic imagination? And what are we to make of the fact that the consecutive ninths of the Fiddler's nature-motif are absorbed into the tissue of 'Heigh ho, travellers we a-passing by?' This again marks a radical departure from Keller, since in the *Novelle* not only are the Fiddler and his set long out of sight and sound by the time of the *Liebestod*, but there is also no single trace of the bargemen. These bargemen – and the idea of a spiritual link between them and the Fiddler – are Delius's own invention, and a stroke of genius. Theirs is the song – like the Fiddler's, addressed to the wind – which transfigures the garden and turns it literally, in Sali's and Vrenchen's eyes, into a 'garden of Paradise' and prompts their last great lyrical duet in which they plight each other their troth in death; and theirs is the voice which, as the magic bark filled with hay drifts down the river and slowly sinks, beckons the deathbound lovers towards an immensity of richest expectation.

3

A Village Romeo was completed in 1901. It is an extraordinary coincidence that the same year also saw the completion of two other substantial scores both intimately related, as is *A Village Romeo*, to *Tristan und Isolde* and the apotheosis of the death wish in music. These were Debussy's *Pelléas et Mélisande* and Schoenberg's *Gurrelieder*. *Pelléas* will be discussed later; here we may profitably consider Delius's relationship to the Second Viennese School with which he is rarely to be bracketed. Yet a musical idiom so Germanically-oriented in temper and constitution needs to be seen within the contemporary matrix of post-Wagnerian chromaticism and its repercussions in Austria and Germany. Delius could not respond to Wagner's emancipated discords in a like manner to Schoenberg, because the clean, antiseptic, Nordic strain in his musical character was infiltrated by elements of a Latin sensuousness and hedonism. Yet there is one work in which their respective sound-worlds in some measure converge and meet, and that is the *Gurrelieder*. The chief common denominator – apart from a shared musical heritage – is the author of the *Songs of Gurre*, J. P. Jacobsen, the influence of whose work on Delius has already been examined. The reader may recall that the text of Delius's *Arabesk* issued from the collection of poems and short stories which had earlier given Schoenberg (in Robert Franz Arnold's admirable translation) the text of the work with which he bade farewell forever to post-Wagnerian romanticism.

To understand the nature of Jacobsen's appeal to Schoenberg, as to Delius, we have to review briefly the position of music *vis-à-vis* the other arts in the late nineteenth century. In these years music allowed itself to be influenced more than ever before by developments in the adjacent provinces of art and literature. Aesthetic concepts and their associated techniques which previously had remained the undisputed prerogatives of poetry or painting now began to be developed in musical terms, although there was the inevitable time-lag of approximately twenty-five years. Debussy is generally regarded as the key figure in this process of correlation, since his work is a complex synthesis of elements drawn from a variety of literary and pictorial sources – above all from the Impressionist movement in painting and the Symbolist movement in literature.

Now although these interrelated movements flourished exceedingly in France their repercussions were diffused over a wide area; and similarly the new ways of thinking and feeling musically to which they gave rise affected many composers in England, Germany, Russia – in fact no country could remain totally impervious to the winds of change. The case of Germany is particularly significant, for we should remember that the Symbolist movement in France took as its musical mascot not a contemporary French composer but Wagner, and that Thomas Mann in a famous Wagner lecture drew some interesting parallels between Wagner's appeal and Edgar Allan Poe's to Baudelaire, one of the unwitting founders of the Symbolist movement. We should also bear in mind that the evolution of musical Impressionism owed an incalculable amount to Wagner – to the vast, aery, Turneresque pictures of the elements (the *Flying Dutchman* overture, the *Rheingold* prelude, the Rainbow Bridge and the Magic Fire music, the destruction of Valhalla) and to the shimmering, translucent textures of the *Waldweben*, of the Johannistag music in *Meistersinger* (with its Debussian use of the dominant ninth) the music of the Flower Maidens and Klingsor's magic garden in *Parsifal*. Taking all this into account makes it easier to understand how Schoenberg could have been drawn to Maeterlinck's *Pelléas* (his symphonic poem was composed contemporaneously with Debussy's opera) and to the Impressionistic poetry of the *Gurre* cycle of poems.

Jacobsen had a wide following in Germany. In view of the affinities between Delius and the German literary school of Poetic Realism, it is interesting to remember that while he was a student at Heidelberg, Gottfried Keller had come under the influence of the atheistic philosopher

14. Delius (right), with Hans
Haym, c. 1907.

15. Sigfrid Karg-Elert.

16. Grez-sur-Loing; the river and the church seen from the bridge.

17. Grez-sur-Loing; Delius's house on left.

Feuerbach and become to all intents and purposes a free-thinker. The prevailing mood in his work is one of optimism: life is good and should be enjoyed for what it has to offer *per se*, not despised as merely a symbol of something superior. The very nature of the Poetic Realist movement postulated a degree of agnosticism if not of downright unbelief, and this together with certain other considerations justify us in classifying Jacobsen as a Poetic Realist, though in the terminology of Danish rather than German literary history he is known as a naturalist. He is particularly remembered for the impact he made upon the young Rainer Maria Rilke, who wrote of *Niels Lyhne*: 'It is a book of the glories and of the deeps. There is nothing that does not seem to have been understood, grasped, experienced and fully-known in the tremulous after-ring of memory.' A writer of the next generation, Stefan Zweig, recalls:

'*Niels Lyhne*! How ardently, how passionately we loved that book in the first wakeful years of youth! It was the *Werther* of our generation. A few of us even tried to learn Danish, just to be able to read *Niels Lyhne* and Jacobsen's poems in the original. They nurtured our emotions and our style, they helped articulate our dreams and gave us our first lyrical prescience of the world as it really is . . . and still they have that wonderful translucency right down to their porcelain base, so that you may discern each line, each arabesque so carefully composed in the most marvellous colours: and they still have their fragrance of soft melancholy. Jacobsen is one of the greatest water-colourists in words. He draws and paints *à la japonais*; he finds the most delicate colours for tremulous moods (*Stimmungen*) and their tiniest, most subtle fluctuations, *Stimmungen* of which the ordinary, healthy man is barely sensible. Jacobsen's feeling for the transparent stuff of reverie was perhaps the most perfect ever vouchsafed an artist in lyrical prose . . . The tenderly lyrical haze which suffuses all his scenes imbues the whole world with a fairy-tale-like feeling without ever depriving it of its reality . . . whoever in his inmost soul is a daydreamer recognises in him a master of dreams. Dreams do not age with men and the passing of years; and so this magical world of awareness and resignation will retain its wonder till the end of time.' (trs. C. P.)

We may easily relate these qualities to what we know of the creative sensibilities of Schoenberg and Delius. First, however, a word about the *Gurre* poems taken as a whole. They offer a highly personal recreation on Jacobsen's part of a very old Danish legend which first appears in the medieval ballads. It tells the story of one of the Kings of Denmark called Valdemar (it is not certain which – there were four between 1154 and 1375) and his illicit passion for the maiden Tove or Tovelil. The queen (generally known as Helvig) becomes jealous of the attentions Valdemar lavishes upon Tove, and during his absence she has murdered by burning

I   117

her to death in a *badstue*, a kind of primitive sauna in which steam was produced by pouring water on to stones which had been heated from the outside. Gurre in Northern Zealand, not far removed from the present Frederiksbourg Castle, is said to have been the dwelling-place of Valdemar IV and was apparently an area of lake and forest of such beauty that the king is purported to have exclaimed that God might keep his heaven if only he, Valdemar, could keep Gurre. It was here that the legend seems to have become involved with that of the 'wild hunt', different versions of which are found in Norway, Sweden, Germany, England and Northern France. There are overtones of the legend of the Flying Dutchman, for Volmer is condemned to hunt in the forests of Zealand until the Day of Judgment as a punishment for his blasphemy and his desire to have Tove rather than heaven. Jacobsen's treatment of the legend is an abstraction rather than a development, a personal interpretation heavily charged with an emotion which reflects the passionate, sensuous longings of a sensitive and highly-strung young man. It reflects, too, aspects of the prevailing temper of contemporary thought : the death-wish, in Tove's near-ecstatic surrender to death as a transfiguring, ennobling force ('Let us now empty our golden chalice to mighty Death, who restores us to beauty') the setting of God at nought and general disillusion with Christian doctrines (Valdemar : 'Lord! Do you know what you did when you took Tove from me? Do you not blush for your shame in having robbed the poor man of his one and only lamb? You, stern judge on high, you laugh at me in my wretchedness . . .'). Tove talks of a renewal of life after death, and in the finale, 'The wild hunt of the summer wind', Volmer is allowed to feel the quickening power of nature through love for Tove. The implication is that their spirits have been absorbed into nature; there is no renewal save in the summer wind.

The appeal of *Gurrelieder* to the Wagnerian mind is obvious. Nature in a variety of moods; a bedrock of myth and legend with a high proportion of violence and passion; and a love-affair of macrocosmic intensity of which the death-wish is the central core. Yet the score is less derivative than at first sight it appears, even those passages which appear to be re-living Wagner *con somma passione* – the ardent Volmer-Tove *Liebesnacht*, and Tove's glowing Novalis-like hymn to night and death. Nor has the nocturnal ride-past of Valdemar's spectral hordes (the 'wild hunt' of Nordic mythology) very much to do with Wotan's gleeful handmaidens in *Walküre*. Far better to invoke Delius's invocation of Scandinavian mythology and folklore in *Eventyr*. In Schoenberg the beginning of the ride is announced, spine-chillingly, by a big eruptive gesture on the ten horns, then by a sinister lumbering ostinato on contrabassi *divisi a 6*; but what sends the God-fearing peasant diving under the bedclothes in a paroxysm of terror is a wild 'Holla!' shouted *con tutta forza* by a men's chorus behind the scenes.

The climax of *Eventyr* is a 'wild shout' (two, in fact) hurled from behind the scenes by a group of men's voices.

Jacobsen follows the story in a series of self-contained impressions, monologues in free verse which denote an audacious break with the predominantly regular rhythms and verse forms of Romanticism. Hence the need for so many individual voices and combinations of voices in Schoenberg's score – Volmer and Tove themselves, the Wood-dove who describes Tove's funeral procession, the God-fearing peasant, Valdemar's men, the Court Jester who tells of his humdrum life at the court of the Most High, finally the summer wind which dances the legend to its close and goes out in a blaze of morning glory. While we can clearly follow the thread of the story through the sequence of monologues, the manner of its telling is deliberately vague, 'impressionistic', if you will; events are hinted at rather than stated explicitly. One of the most intriguing features of Schoenberg's realisation is the way in which his orchestra makes into solid fact events and emotions implied and even omitted in the poem. The orchestra prolongs Volmer's ecstasy at his first sighting of Tove (his climactic 'Volmer hat Tove gesehen'); and after the long Volmer-Tove love-scene an orchestral episode of extreme polyphonic complexity gathers up all the myriad thematic threads already woven into the love-music and culminates in a graphic portrayal of Helvig's murder of Tove. In the poem this is omitted altogether; we pass straight from Valdemar's rapt aria 'Du wunderliche Tove!' to the Wood-dove's account of Tove's funeral procession. Only at the climax are we told how she has met her death ('It was Helvig's falcon which so cruelly tore Gurre's dove in pieces'). At this point in the *music*, however, there recurs the vicious motif in bunched upward-shooting thirds which we remember marked the climax of the orchestral episode that preceded the Wood-dove's song; and so its subtle significance is made manifest. However much he may so depend upon his orchestra for elucidation of the text, Schoenberg never neglects his vocal lines; there is in fact great richness and variety of vocal characterisation, and the great strength of the *Gurrelieder* lies in this superbly calculated complementary blend of vocal and orchestral narrative technique.

The supreme example of this is one of the sections which on occasions approaches most nearly to Delius, namely the finale, 'The Wild Hunt of the Summer Wind'. Here we become conscious of a sudden stylistic gear-change, for this finale, a melodrama, was orchestrated a number of years after the rest of the score, by which time the composer had moved on to other worlds and new styles. Here the orchestral textures are scattered and pointillistic in the manner of Schoenberg's maturity, fantastic, evanescent, a kind of shadow-play illustration to the text which is declaimed by the narrator in *Sprechgesang*. Yet this change of stylistic stance is most happily

119

met: for it helps throw the events of the night before into a dream-like perspective and proclaims the reality of the new day (dawning, symbolically, for Schoenberg himself as well as for the protagonists of Jacobsen's poem).* Here Jacobsen in a quick succession of deftly-chosen, meticulously-annotated details suggests all the natural life of the woods and fields being roused to exuberant activity as the summer wind rampages on its way. The accompanying music consists of a myriad tiny flecks and dashes of instrumental colour – yet all subject to scrupulous motivic control. Now comes the sudden abatement in the wind's fury – quoted earlier as the spirits of the long-departed Volmer and Tove are borne in on the wind only to float away into the dim distance. Their names are not mentioned in the text; it is left to the musician to voice the poet's unspoken thoughts as he quotes their love-motif, scored with a searching tenderness and heard as if through a haze of memory. This is a passage of extraordinary beauty; the spirits of the lovers are enshrined in a phosphorescent texture of pentatonic harp figuration and flute arabesque markedly reminiscent of Delius, and the theme of human love and sorrow is set against a background of eternal nature in a manner very characteristic of the composer of *A Village Romeo and Juliet*. The music has a bittersweet, clinging Delian quality. Yet even more Delian is the orchestral *Abendstimmung* with which the work opens. Based on the chord of the added sixth, it is an exquisite sound-picture – an impressionist texture of multi-divided strings (violins in ten parts) four harps, glockenspiel, solo trumpet singing, dabs and dots of woodwind colour. This is the Delius of *In a Summer Garden* and *Summer Night on the River*. The music of Valdemar's opening aria grows out of this enchanted atmosphere, and Tove's response is a miracle of serenity and ecstasy. In an Impressionist painting, all the contours and colours of the earthly scene are dissolved in dream; and this is reflected especially in the miniature orchestral epilogue which in effect brings the first main section to a close – a tender, sweetly singing canon at the fifteenth between solo violin and solo 'cello, a polyphony of bird-song (two piccolos, two flutes, one clarinet) a wonderfully hushed horn fanfare dying further and further away into the distance, soft harp *glissandi* which help blur still more the already dim-focused polyharmonies (Ex. 22). In this music Schoenberg displays a rare feeling for poetic sonority and for beauty of timbre, one which in this context comes remarkably close to Delius. Schoenberg here is like Delius a true poet in sound.

The *Gurrelieder* finds Schoenberg at the junction-lines of *Im*pressionism and *Ex*pressionism and shifting the points as he wills. Both were sighted by Wagner; and if Delius, inevitably in the light of his admiration for Grieg and his exposure to French culture, chose the one direction,

*See also remarks on the ending of *Paris*, p. 134.

Ex.22

Schoenberg just as inevitably chose the other. For Thomas Mann, in an essay charting the influence of Dürer on German art and thought, made the point that in all spheres of creativeness the first loyalty of the German artist is pledged not to colour but to form. Blocks of pure colour – the *vertical* concept of a chord or sound-complex – have to be sacrificed or at least subordinated to fluidity of *horizontal* movement, to line, to polyphony. We can see that the *Gurrelieder* prelude and the reminiscence in the finale comes closest to certain of Delius's compositions because the harmony races backwards to Wagner, and the orchestral texture is affiliated both to Impressionism and Pointillism in painting. In a later work such as the Five Orchestral Pieces the *pointilliste* link remains and the titles of the individual movements even suggest some kinship of expressive intent, but by this time Schoenberg has so radically re-oriented his original concept of form and dialectic that no *rapprochement* is feasible.

So too with Webern whose orchestral textures may similarly be related to Pointillism: yet there is one early work with intriguingly Delian overtones, and that is the idyll for large orchestra *Im Sommerwind*. The title recalls the *Gurrelieder* finale;* coincidence, no doubt, just like the Delian flavour, for who writing a nature-poem for Delius's orchestra (six horns, two harps) in the immediate wake of Wagner could fail to sound like Delius? The answer is that Strauss very rarely does, nor Mahler; and the reason for our being able to categorise Delius along with Schoenberg and Webern rather than with Strauss and Mahler is, again, this fastidiousness in the latter's use of orchestral colour, the infinite sensitivity and subtlety of their brushstrokes. For the most part, Mahler and Strauss write musical prose, much of it magnificent; and as we have seen, Delius was far from insensible to the rich purple resonance of *Don Juan*. But Delius, Schoenberg and Webern, and the Berg of parts of *Wozzeck* and the Violin Concerto, are poets in sound. *Im Sommerwind*, written in 1905, finds Webern still stuck stylistically in limbo, although there are moments of straining towards a new idiom in his manipulation of individual points of instrumental sensation. But what is interesting from our point of view is the way he chances quite naturally independently and of his own accord on a recognisably Delian sonority or melodic curve. This gesture for stopped horns, for instance (Ex. 23a) is pure *Dance Rhapsody No. 2*, and 23b is a Delian *Naturlaut*. Broadly speaking we may relate Delius to the Second Viennese School in terms of texture and orchestral sonority rather than harmony, since their lines of harmonic thought, while stemming commonly from Wagner, diverged too rapidly to permit of any but coincidental points of contact such as these shown in Ex. 22 and 23.

* An odd coincidence is that Delius's song *Summer Landscape*, composed in 1902 to a text of Holger Drachmann, was originally entitled *Sommer in Gurre*.

This was not by any means the case with the German composer with whom Delius shares more common ground than any other. Donald Mitchell was not absolutely correct in referring to Delius as 'the only German Impressionist', for in fact he was one of two. His *frère en art* was Sigfrid Karg-Elert.

Although remembered today exclusively for his organ works, Karg-Elert was a prolific composer in a variety of genres. His output includes more than a hundred songs, piano music, chamber music, choral works, a symphony, concertos for flute and piano – not to mention theoretical treatises (on the logic of harmony and the relationship of harmony to acoustics), numerous technical tracts and manuals on harmonium playing, orchestrations of Bizet's *Jeux d'enfants* and, incredibly, piano solo arrangements of Elgar's two symphonies. Yet while the secular music is rarely heard today and is predictably difficult of access, the organ music is very much alive and nearly all in print. Although Karg-Elert's chosen instrument was the piano and he never became more than a moderately proficient organist, there is no doubt that he found in writing for the organ his true sense of direction as a composer. This has tended to hinder widespread appreciation of his talent which was by no means that of a mere hack purveyor of 'organists' music' – as those who might know him solely by the overplayed *Nun Danket* march might be led to assume.

Born into a poverty-stricken Bavarian family in 1877, Karg-Elert's musical training was erratic and he emerged in fact largely self-taught, seemingly destined for a career as a piano virtuoso. His originality as a composer might well have been stifled irremediably in the claustrophobically conservative atmosphere of the Leipzig Conservatory were it not for the timely intervention of Grieg, who helped him both artistically and financially. Already a parallel with Delius suggests itself (he said 'Were it not for the fact that I met Grieg . . . my studies at Leipzig were a complete waste of time'). It was no doubt from Grieg that Karg-Elert, like Delius, acquired his grasp of rich chromatic harmony, but the two brightest stars in his firmament were already set in position – Bach and the Lutheran chorale. There was thus rivalry between the Latin and Teutonic elements in his make-up, and a compromise proved difficult, at times almost impossible, to achieve. It is essential to grasp this point if we are to arrive at a true understanding of the nature of Karg-Elert's musical thought.

A digression is needed to place Karg-Elert's great mentor, Reger, in his proper position in our picture. Reger fed avidly off Bach and the Lutheran chorale, and fed his disciples on them; and he was one of the greatest contrapuntists of the century. He was also vitally interested in chromatic harmony, but tended to waver between the opposing polarities of Schoenberg and Delius inasmuch as he failed to acquire the intransigently linear orientation of the one or the feeling for physical beauty of sound, for timbre, of the other. Harmonically speaking, in Reger's work we are turned loose on a restlessly heaving sea of chromaticism and enharmonic modulation which exceeds even that of Schoenberg in *Pelleas und Melisande*; but Reger could never pause, like Delius, to revel in the loveliness of any one sound he had created. Now Karg-Elert could, and it is this above all which brings him within the Delian frame of reference. Like such diverse figures as Delius, Gershwin, Ellington and Stan Tracey, he was a natural and instinctive harmonist – no wonder he liked Grieg! – and a nature mystic to boot, as the titles of many of his works clearly indicate.

There is much of particular interest in the two sets of pieces for harmonium, *Intarsien* ('inlaid work') and *Idyllen*. The first piece in the latter collection, 'Sonnenuntergang', embraces some very Delian turns of melody and harmony which raise the question of whether or not Karg-Elert knew Delius's music. It is scarcely conceivable that he did not, bearing in mind his friendship with Grieg and Delius's popularity in Germany at the relevant time. On the other hand Karg-Elert's rich harmony – most strikingly exhibited in the fine 'Legend' (no. 1 of *Triptych* for organ) which has a slight flavour of one of Bax's Celtic inspirations, in the *Cathedral Windows* ('Saluto Angelico' and 'Lauda Sion') and in the *Seven Pastels from Lake Constance* – this harmony could have evolved logically and independently from Griegian and Wagnerian premises, just as Delius's own did. A resemblance is most marked, however, in a piece eminently *un*Delian in inspiration. This is the third of the *Three Symphonic Canzonas*, the 'Fugue, Canzona and Epilogue', one of Karg-Elert's finest works, which takes as its motto the plainsong motif *Credo in unum Deum*. The epilogue is a four-page conception of rare beauty. A choir of four single women's voices (from the heights like the boy's choir in *Parsifal*) sing an Amen in long finely-drawn polyphonic lines whose sensuousness and limpidity recall Fauré or even Duruflé. The final Amen hovers voluptuously between two notes with a sinuously ascending violin

Ex.24

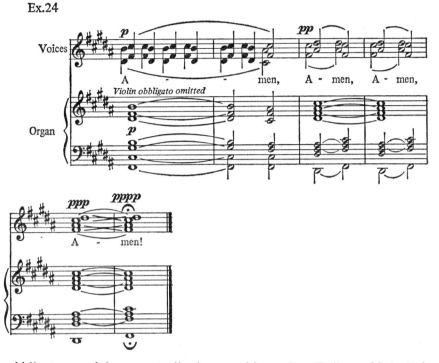

obbligato, resolving eventually into a shimmering Delian added sixth
(Ex. 24). The Delian radiance and serenity of these closing bars are rare
in twentieth-century German music. Karg-Elert once wrote: 'I love this
piece tenderly; it was written, frankly, in a vein of exaltation, and savours
of holy water and consecrated candles; that is the Catholic side of me,
which cannot be readily reconciled with my Lutheranism . . .' (Karg-
Elert's father was Catholic, his mother Protestant).

In these works this most industrious but unself-critical of composers
reveals himself not as an organist who regularly dabbled in composition
but as a composer who regularly wrote for the organ. And that, in the
organist's world, is in itself no small achievement.

CHAPTER FOUR

1

France

(*i*) *Ville*

'I want to be in the thick of people who are feeling and living. Whether I like them or their life does not matter so much, I want to find out what there is in human hearts . . . When I have had my fill of being this tumultuous being then I want one place for reflection and creation. Baudelaire used to call his descent to the city his *bain de multitude* and then he used to appreciate solitude. *Enfin seul!* he cried. I have the two cravings in my nature. . . .' (Enid Starkie to Alyse Gregory.)

Thus one of this century's greatest Francophiles, author of classic studies of two of her adoptive country's *mauvais garçons*, neatly but quite unconsciously summing up in terms of her own experience the place of France in the life and work of Frederick Delius, the *mauvais garçon* of English music. For the titles of the two sub-sections of this chapter I have appropriated those of two poems by Arthur Rimbaud (one of Enid Starkie's *mauvais garçons*) – *Ville* and *Départ*. For the first phase of Delius's association with France embraces his Paris years (1888–97) his *bain de multitude*; then *Départ*, he establishes himself in his rural retreat of Grez-sur-Loing near Fontainebleau, his home for the rest of his life and the physical, if not the spiritual birthplace of his most personal art – *enfin seul!*

No European city could have afforded greater stimulus to a young man hungry for culture and the good life than Second Empire Paris, then at the zenith of its aesthetic fame and power. Delius did not immediately move in on the city centre; he lived successively in Ville d'Avray (on the road to Versailles), in the village of Croissy (on the right bank of the Seine) and finally at 33 Rue Ducouëdic, near Montparnasse. He settled for some six years and participated to the full in the many and varied experiences offered him by life in the Latin Quarter. He was a habitué of an artists' restaurant known as 'Mère Charlotte's' in the Rue de la Grande Chaumière, where he met (among others) Alphonse Mucha, Strindberg, Gauguin and Edvard Munch; and often watching Gauguin clattering by in his sabots on the way to the *crémerie* in company with Delius was a young student of painting from Belgrade, Jelka Rosen. Later she was to become Mrs Frederick Delius. Jelka bought the property at Grez, and after his return from Florida in 1897, Delius's one and only permanent address became Grez-sur-Loing, Seine et Marne.

Delius consorted very little with French musicians during his ten-year-long sojourn in *la ville lumière*. Painters and men-of-letters were his preferred companions, and even these tended to be Scandinavian rather than French. We do find, however, that *Paris – the Song of a Great City* relates convincingly to certain manifestations in French poetry and painting of the period, for all that the compositional technique is basically that of Strauss. This gigantic Parisian night-piece represents the turning point in Delius's career in a number of ways. It reached its definitive form in 1899, after the composer had enjoyed the advantage, at the St James's Hall concert of the same year, of hearing how his most recent essays in orchestration sounded; but sketches go back to 1897 or thereabouts in the form of three fragments, 'Scènes Parisiennes', 'L'Heure d'Absinthe' and 'Heureuse rencontre'. These titles or subtitles were not retained in the final version, but they can be borne in mind, particularly the last one. Notice too that the dates coincide with Delius's transfer of allegiance from city to country; that this transfer coincides in its turn with the passing of his youth and the imminent onset of middle age (Delius was 37); that this onset of middle age coincides in its turn with the efflorescence of his genius; bear all these factors in mind and the very special place of *Paris* in Delius's spiritual development becomes clear. He had known the *bain de multitude*, and it had served its purpose; now he needed solitude.

It is appropriate that the work which marks both the end of a singularly long and gruelling apprenticeship and the first-fruits of a unique mastery should also assume the character of a valediction to the milieu which had fostered the slow growth of this mastery, and had given depth and strength to the final consummation. We shall see that some recognition of this symbolic import is even built into the musical character and structure of *Paris*, no doubt quite unconsciously. Perhaps Warlock had perceived something of the sort when he wrote that, for Delius, Paris was not so much the capital city of France as a corner of his own soul, a chapter of his memoirs. But neither this personal, autobiographical element in *Paris* nor its distinctly Straussian undertow satisfactorily explains the indifference it has always encountered in the city of its origin. *Paris* still awaits its Parisian première; but Parisians should appreciate *Paris* if for no other reason than that it is a landmark in the history of music. Delius is rarely given credit for his innovations. How many realise that *Paris* is the first score (or, at any rate, the first to have survived and to be regularly played) to see poetry in the city, to draw on the metropolis as a living source of inspiration? In this respect Delius's *Nocturne Parisien* closely parallels to the work of certain mid and late nineteenth-century French poets and painters.

We may seek the origins of a poetic consciousness of the city in the rise, in France, of the Realist and Naturalist movements in both literature and painting. In Baudelaire's first important work of art criticism, his *Salon* of 1846, he writes:

Now, today, a new beauty, a new spirit of the heroic has sprung up in our midst. Parisian life is rich in sources of poetic inspiration and wonder. Wonder surrounds us at every turn, we are steeped in it as in the atmosphere, yet we do not see it. In painting also, where there is no dearth of variety in motif or technique, a new element is clearly visible: the beauty of the modern age (*la beauté moderne*).

This 'modern beauty', considered by his predecessors and contemporaries as 'unaesthetic', Baudelaire saw in the spectacle of the teeming city. Théodore de Banville remembered how, even as a young man, Baudelaire would 'cherish with eagerness' the mysterious murmur and movement of the boulevards and streets at night, and in *Les Fleurs du mal* the opening of one of the *Tableaux Parisiens*, 'Les Sept Vieillards' is a cry of wonderment:

> Fourmillante cité, cité pleine de rêves,
> Où le spectre en plein jour raccroche le passant

– whose thrill of horror is surely echoed in Eliot's:

> Unreal City,
> Under the brown fog of a winter dawn
> A crowd flowed over London Bridge, so many
> I had not thought death had undone so many.

Awareness of the modern city lies behind a number of the finest of the prose-poems known as *Spléen de Paris*, and of at least two of the best of the *Fleurs du mal*: 'Le Crépuscule du Matin' and 'Paysage':

> Les deux mains au menton, du haut de ma mansarde,
> Je verrai l'atelier qui chante et qui bavarde;
> Les tuyaux, les clochers, ces mâts de la cité,
> Et les grands ciels qui font rêver d'éternité.

Il est doux, à travers les brumes, de voir naître
L'étoile dans l'azur, la lampe à la fenêtre,
Les fleuves de charbon monter au firmament
Et la lune verser son pâle enchantement.

'Paysage' here, of course, means cityscape, not landscape, and Baudelaire's city poems cultivated urban awareness in others. Several poems in Rimbaud's *Illuminations*, particularly those which took root in his mind when he and Verlaine were abandoning themselves to fascinated exploration of the London of the 1870s, are explosive indictments of the asphalt jungle – 'Métropolitain', for example, or 'Villes'.

Verlaine's vision is much less brutal, pastel-toned, imbued with romantic nostalgia. 'Il pleure dans mon coeur', based on a line of Rimbaud's from a poem no longer extant ('Il pleut doucement sur la ville') is too well-known to need quotation, and so are the two London poems entitled *Streets*. His rather Baudelarian *Nocturne Parisien* is less familiar; but there are lines which show a distinct affinity of mood with parts of Delius's:

. . . mais quand vient le soir, raréfiant enfin
Les passants alourdis de sommeil ou de faim,
Et que le couchant met au ciel des taches rouges
Qu'il fait bon aux rêveurs descendre de leurs bouges
Et, s'accoudant au pont de la Cité, devant
Notre Dame, songer, coeur et cheveux au vent.

Tout bruit s'apaise autour. A peine un vague son
Dit que la ville est là qui chante son chanson. . . .

Are these two last lines not precisely the opening of *Paris – The Song of a Great City*, with its 'vague son' – the distant rumbling pedal-point telling us that the city is there, singing its song? But, in Delius, this calm crepuscular Verlaine-like mood is not sustained for very long, and as the music erupts into a superb aural complement of the Parisian night-scene – lights, colour, glitter, glamour, crowds swarming feverishly in the pursuit of pleasure – we are reminded not so much of anything in French poetry of the period as of the cityscapes of the Impressionists and of Toulouse-Lautrec. The Impressionists' *plein-airisme* did not confine itself to rural locations, and in the concept of realism embraced a more open-minded and informal attitude to the modern city-scene – witness Monet's *Boulevard des Capucines* and *Rue Montorgueil Decked Out with Flags*, Renoir's *Les Grands Boulevards*, Manet's views of the Rue Mosnier where he had his studio, Pissarro's great series of pictures of Paris in the 1890s, the *Avenue de l'Opéra* and the *Boulevard Montmartre* by day and by night. Munch's 1891 neo-Impressionist *Rue Lafayette* is also relevant here. Yet if Delius's crowd-scenes in *Paris* are the work of a master painter in the colours of a Straussian orchestra, their ebullience and garishness are those of Toulouse-Lautrec rather than the Impressionists. Lautrec was certainly impressed by the Impressionists' use of colour and their free style of composition, but he was exclusively an artist of the city. Static landscape did not interest him: he was obsessed by movement and found the countryside tedious in the extreme. 'It is in the country,' he once wrote (and Delius would have agreed with him), 'that one becomes conscious of celibacy.' He would spend hours on café terraces watching the endless bustle in the streets, noting all manner of details in the nocturnal figures of the Montmartre – and, more generally, Parisian – underworld.* These are scenes portrayed on canvas for the first time in the history of art: the bar, the café concert, the circus, the brothel and its clientele. This is the night-world reflected in the stridency and glare of Delius's brass, the driving nervous energy of his rhythms, the rhapsodically impassioned development of a few germinal fragments of tune. Here, for the first time, the pulse and heartbeat of a vast metropolis is translated into musical terms. Ordinary city night-life is filled with a mystery and beauty which the paintings of the Impressionists surely helped him to find; it is probably true to say that the impetus came from Delius's experience of this painting since, like Debussy, he consorted not with musicians but with poets and painters and, like Debussy, he was driven to find expression in his own art for what had already found expression in his colleagues'. *Paris* was the result of this quest and also the stylistically cognate *Life's Dance*, the composer's least-known orchestral work. The first version was composed between September 1898 and February 1899, and *Paris* was completed later the same year; the title of this version was *La Ronde se déroule*, based as it was on a poem of the same name by Helge Rode (it was revised in 1901 and re-named *Lebenstanz*, and again, definitively, in 1912, when it assumed its present title. Delius informed an inquirer that by the time of the final revision it had completely disengaged itself from Rode's poem). In structure and substance the music is very much all of a piece with *Paris*, with these differences: first, the ending of *Paris* turns its face to the scorching sunlight, but *Life's Dance* collapses in disarray and disillusion, for Delius wanted apparently to depict 'the turbulence, joy, energy and striving of youth – all to end at last in the inevitable death' (hints here surely of Strauss's *Don Juan*). Secondly, the material quite lacks the strength and distinction of *Paris*, a work of infinitely greater scope and character. Perhaps we do best to regard *Life's Dance* as a testing-ground for *Paris*. Symptomatic of the new accession of emotional power is the fact

---

*The few paintings of Baudelaire to have survived show a marked affinity with those of Toulouse-Lautrec.

that the slow reflective episodes in *Life's Dance* are designed to complement the longer dynamic sequences with their dance-like gyrations. The corresponding episodes in *Paris* are much more than this. The *Adagio con espressione* which succeeds the first *Vivace* section and its recapitulation (*Molto lento*) just before the main climax give musical vent for the first time to the feeling of 'big city blues', urban desolation, a sudden realisation that, in the words of Verlaine's *Nocturne Parisien*:

> . . . L'on est seul avec Paris, l'Onde et la Nuit!

City of dreadful night. It is a mood recaptured again and again in twentieth-century music, particularly that of America, the American Negro: in the blues and nocturnes of Duke Ellington, and in the Nocturne (a blues) of Constant Lambert's Piano Sonata. It first finds concrete expression in Delius. Eric Fenby has commented on the stroke of genius whereby Delius gives the nostalgic melody of the *Adagio con espressione* to the violas, not to the violins – 'flighted with insight and artistry in performance it becomes a gesture – like opening a magic window to Innocence'. There are no blues elements in the music as such, but the mellow-toned eloquence of the violas approximates in terms of timbre to that of the saxophone, and Delius's use of the solo trumpet both to take the melody *in toto* for its second statement, and to inject a note of jazzy desperation high in its register at the climax of the passage, surely indicates that he was the first intuitively to recognise the emotional connotations of a sonority which jazz musicians were later to make peculiarly their own.

There are other instances where Delius creates an almost overwhelming sense of big-city loneliness – and also solitude, two very different things. There is loneliness – an infinite weariness – in the huge and darkling vista realised in the sound of high violins in octaves, low trombone and tuba in octaves with only a few winds in between to bridge the gap (6 bars before figure 17); but there is solitude, a welcomed solitude, in the passage which follows at figure 18 where a solo horn muses tenderly upon one of the salient themes over soft timpani beats. We may perhaps assume that this is the moment of the 'heureuse rencontre', the title of one of the early sketches – especially as this three-quaver theme recurs in the *Idyll*, which is the story of just such a 'heureuse rencontre' in the city by night. (And, what is more, one of the salient themes in *that* work, at the passage beginning 'This is thy hour O soul', reappears in its turn note for note in the third movement of the *Requiem*, addressed in French, 'A la grande amoureuse'.)

In a work afire with originality one of the most original parts of *Paris* is still its opening, which suggests to Eric Fenby some of Jongkind's calm vistas of the city – Jongkind, the Dutch landscape painter who was one of

131

the pioneers of Impressionism and whose work made a profound impact upon Monet. A long-held pedal-point (the droning murmur of the distant streets) and then a series of long-forgotten street cries. Everything suggests an approach to the metropolis as glimpsed from afar and gradually looming up before one, a frozen tableau slowly stirring to life. Delius wrote that he was here setting down his 'impressions of night and early dawn with its peculiar street cries and Pan's goatherd, etc. These cries are very characteristic of *Paris* and the piece begins and closes with them.' Now when Richard Strauss heard the Brussels performance of *Paris* in December 1904 he described it as 'a not quite successful imitation of Charpentier'. He was referring to the opera *Louise*, a protracted hymn to the splendours and miseries of Paris. Act 2 opens with a prelude, 'Paris s'éveille'; the scene is Montmartre, four o'clock on an April morning a light mist is hanging over the city. A deep pedal-point; a symphony of what we later recognise as the cries of the Bohemian street vendors and others – chair mender, rag-man, artichoke vendor, carrot vendor, old clothes man, and the piercing whistle of a goatherd's flute. At one point they are all enmeshed in a fantastic counterpoint and several enter the thematic weft of the score and recur without their proper context.* Act 3 begins with another cityscape over a low pedal, 'Vers la cité lointaine', a subtitle which would admirably have suited the opening of *Paris* (and also, as we shall see, of the *Idyll*).

The question is whether or not Delius knew *Louise* or parts thereof at the time of the composition of *Paris*. He himself claimed that he did not; he certainly cannot have heard it on the stage, since the first performance was given at the Opéra Comique in February 1900, and *Paris* was completed some time during the latter half of the previous year. Presumably, therefore, the two works were being written more or less simultaneously. We have no evidence that Delius knew Charpentier, but he did know André Messager (the first conductor of *Louise*) and he was certainly very familiar with the idiom of contemporary light opera – a fact to which many turns and twists of melody in *Paris* bear witness;** for Delius was no musical hermit or cave-dweller, however much it may have pleased him to give that impression. He was fully alive to what was going on around him, musically. So it is quite possible that rumours of Charpentier's innovatory realism in

---

*We may number Vaughan Williams's *London* Symphony, the street vendors' scene in *Porgy and Bess* and the Bloomsbury morning scene in Lionel Bart's *Oliver!* among the progeny of *Louise*.

**For instance the solo horn theme mentioned above, and the rollicking tune for brass (2 bars after figure 9). The *Idyll* is full of melodic phraseology deriving from the *lingua franca* of Parisian light opera, and so are some of the weaker parts of *A Village Romeo and Juliet*.

18. Mrs. Delius in the garden which slopes down to the river Loing.

19. Delius's study at Grez. Part of Gauguin's *Nevermore* is visible above the piano.

20. Sisley, *Misty Morning*, 1874.

Louise, being noised abroad in Parisian musical circles before work on the opera was finished, came to Delius's notice and registered with him, perhaps unconsciously. It would be interesting to be able to identify Delius's street cries, for with two exceptions they bear no resemblance to Charpentier's. The exceptions are the goatherd's flute which figures in both scores and presumably is related to the semi-rural character of contemporary Montmartre; and Charpentier's Old Clothes-man's cry which bears some resemblance to the bassoon motif in *Paris* (Ex. 25a and b). If Charpentier

Ex.25(a)

Mar - chand d'ha - bits___ A-vez-vous des ha-bits à vendr'?

(b)

Bsn.

mf

Ex.26

Ob.

p *espr.*

develops thematic material from street cries heard at one time or another *in statu quo*, several of the themes gathered by *Paris* as it proceeds may well be of street-cry origin even though they are not featured in the prologue or epilogue (e.g. Ex. 26). It is possible, too, that Delius may have remembered the gathering of Bohemians in preparation for the Crowning of the Muse of Montmartre when writing the Berghold Fair Scene in *A Village Romeo and Juliet*.

It may well be, then, that Delius when engaged on the composition of *Paris* was semi-conscious or even conscious of Charpentier's activities in a similar field; on the other hand it happens quite frequently in art that two artists, given a shared milieu and some affinity of technique, both started to work the same vein simultaneously but independently of each other. In any case, what is important in any artistic relationship is not the question of who influenced whom and when but that each artist should be appraised on his individual merits. What is beyond dispute is that Delius's technique of metropolitan evocation is incomparably superior to Charpentier's, not only in *Paris* but also in the work which emerged as a kind of pendant to *Paris*, namely the *Idyll* for soprano and baritone soloists and orchestra. This is a kind of extended *scena* assembled from the music for the one-act melo-drama *Margot la Rouge* written in 1902. By this time the Song of the Great City was ended, but its memories evidently lingered on; for the setting of *Margot la Rouge* was the Paris of Baudelaire and Toulouse-Lautrec and in the prelude the presence of a *cité lointaine* is again evoked over a persistent pedal-point. What is more, the text Delius finally compiled (with Robert Nichols's help) from Whitman exactly thirty years later begins with the line 'Once I passed through a populous city', and in due course the three-quaver horn motif referred to earlier appears, together with the theme associated with the *grande amoureuse* in the *Requiem*. *Idyll* is another metropolitan nocturne; the story is one of an *heureux rencontre* – a chance meeting, a liaison brief but deliriously happy, a tragic *finis* brought about by the departure or death of one or other of the lovers. The essential stuff of the music is vintage Delius, perhaps unexpectedly under the original circumstances : in the glorious passage which begins 'We two, how long we were fooled' and ends with the climactic 'Long, long have we been absent but now we return', the musical thought is shaped out of the upward-soaring triplet (Ex. 6) which Delius never uses unmeaningfully. What is again remarkable is Delius's feeling for the ambience of the mighty city by night, which he captures in terms of orchestral colour in a few deft brush-strokes – the suspicion of a distant street-cry or city noise on syncopated woodwind in the orchestral interlude which follows the baritone's 'All else has been forgotten by me'; an unfathomable depth of night-city solitude – 'Paris, l'Onde et la Nuit' – in response to the soprano's 'Double yourself and receive us, darkness' (again, solo horn and throbbing timpani). But by this time the Byronic, romantic, swashbuckling spirit of the more extrovert parts of *Paris* had departed for ever. The splendid main climax of *Paris* with its three gong-blows has something strangely fatalistic about it : midnight strikes, the magician waves his wand, but as he does so there flashes away something more than a night's revelry. If Delius is here symbolically bidding the glories of his youth farewell, his long trainee period is also left behind; and equally symbolic is the blinding sunrise which wells up out of the murmur of the empty streets (listen for the cock-a-doodle-doo of the 1918 *Song before Sunrise*, woodwind, 4 before 35) – we can almost see the quivering of heat and light in the physical movement of the string-players as they bow their *tremoli*. The new sun is herald of a Rimbaudian 'départ dans l'affection et le bruit neufs' and of a noontide of singular magnificence.

Départ

Frederick Delius, ever a painter's and poet's musician rather than a musician's, could have chosen no more suitable place than Grez-sur-Loing for the scene of his life's work; and it is not at all surprising that he should immediately have felt at home in the atmosphere there. For all of us, if we are lucky, there comes a sudden moment in the course of our search for a house, home, mate, *métier* or whatever it may be, when we feel instinctively that we need search no longer. Something of the sort happened to Delius in those very early Paris days when he had come down to Bourron, a village near Grez, to discuss *Koanga* with Keary, his librettist. Jelka Rosen, whom he knew from Paris, spent her summers painting in Grez, in the garden of a house owned by an eccentric, the Marquis de Carzeaux. Delius visited the place and was enchanted – 'Jelka, I could work here!' He could and did. Grez was his permanent base from 1897 to his death in 1934.

Grez possessed exactly the right kind of cultural-topographical ambience to appeal to Delius. It was a haunt beloved of Robert Louis Stevenson, who described it in detail in his *Essays of Travel*:

'It lies out of the forest, a cluster of houses with an old bridge and an old castle in ruins and a quaint old church. The inn garden descends in terraces to the river, stableyard, kailyard, orchard, and a space of lawn fringed with rushes and embellished with a green arbour. On the opposite bank is a real English-looking plain, set thickly with willows and poplars. And between the two lies the river, clear and deep, and full of leaves and floating lilies. Water plants cluster about the starlings of the low, long bridge, and stand halfway up upon the piers in green luxuriance. They catch the dipped oar with long antennae, and chequer the slimy bottom with the shadow of their leaves. And the river wanders hither and thither among the islets, and is smothered and broken up by reeds like an old building in the lithe, hardy arms of the climbing ivy.'

The ruined castle and the old church adjoined Delius's house, which had a long garden sloping down to the quiet river and beyond that the open country. Many artists were drawn to Grez and the region roundabout, both before the Deliuses' time there and during it. Lionel Carley has shown that in the last quarter of the century much artistic activity centred round the home of the American painter Francis Brooks Chadwick and his Swedish-born wife (née Lowstadt, herself a talented painter and engraver) later to become the Deliuses' house which, for some reason, never acquired a name. Two Swedish artist-friends of theirs were Carl Larsson and Karl Nordstrom, both of whom came to Grez and painted there; and the Deliuses themselves were to draw many artists, painters and sculptors to their rural retreat, among them Rodin, Munch, Matthew Smith, Edmond Kapp, James Gunn and Henry Clews. For those and other kindred spirits Grez was a favourite rallying-point. But most important of all, from the point of view of Delius's creative work, was the fact that the entire Fontainebleau area had been one of the happiest hunting-grounds of the Barbizon School of painters and the Impressionists.

Théodore Rousseau was the leader of the Barbizon group and it was he who 'discovered' the Forest of Fontainebleau which from 1833 onwards became his permanent theme. Diaz, Dupré, Millet, Daubigny, Corot, Courbet and a host of minor painters helped institute the *plein-air* methods which were later to bear fruit in the work of the Impressionists; and what more natural than that Delius, steeped as he was in Impressionist art and living as he did amid the very surroundings which had inspired some of the greatest of Impressionist landscapes, should have transmuted certain aspects of Impressionist pictorial techniques into musical terms? Was not also the most impressionist work of Albert Roussel his First Symphony, *Le Poème de la forêt* – a cycle of nature-impressions through the changing seasons – inspired by the Forest of Fontainebleau? It is arguable that the Impressionist movement in painting really began in the spring and early summer of 1864 when Monet and a group of his 'cubs' – Bazille, Sisley, Renoir – spent all their days in the forest making landscape studies in the open air, at the very spots where the Barbizon group had been painting for twenty years and more. Sisley's career committed itself to landscape from that time forth; and this is particularly interesting in that Delius stands closer to Sisley than to any other Impressionist. Sir Thomas Beecham pointed out the coincidence that they were both of English origin and both sons of well-to-do industrialists; both rejected the *vita activa* in favour of the *vita contemplativa*, and they both preferred the cosmopolitan isolation of the Ile de France to anything their country of origin might have offered for their delectation. In their early Fontainebleau days Sisley and Renoir would move in and around the village of Marlotte, staying at the popular painters' inn of Mère Anthony; the road between Grez and Marlotte was one of Delius's favourite walks, one on which any number of his works had been pondered. (Incidentally in Delius's day there lived in Marlotte an uncle of Philip Heseltine known as 'Joe' who was also a painter of sorts.) Renoir painted a scene from the inn showing Pissarro and Sisley together with the three-legged dog Toto. Sisley worked mainly in the Seine valley and retired in 1879 to the old walled town of Moret-sur-Loing, a little further down-river from Grez, where he spent the remaining twenty years of his life. Since both Sisley and Delius excelled in depicting the tenderness and melancholy of nature – Delius's preoccupation with transcience is reflected in Sisley's statement that 'there is a charm about things which are going away and I particularly like it' – we are surely justified in seeing in pictures of Sisley, such as *Misty Morning*, the 1870 *Landscape*, *June Morning*, *The Seine at Marly* and various other scenes of the banks of the Seine, the visual counterparts of the many aural landscapes of Grez and its surrounding country produced by Delius in the incredibly rich and fruitful decade which followed immediately on his settling there. The opening of *Brigg Fair*, *On Hearing the First Cuckoo in Spring* (whose subdued orchestral coloration is more akin to Sisley's than to any other Impressionist's), the river music of *In a Summer Garden*, the later *Song before Sunrise* (which could easily be contemporary with *Brigg Fair* but was written some ten years later), the nostalgic slow movement of the String Quartet, *Late Swallows* – these are all Sisleys.

On the other hand there are also a myriad echoes of other Impressionist and *pointilliste* painters. For after settling at Grez and fusing the atmosphere of his environment with that of the Impressionist and *pointilliste* art which he knew well – and we should remember that Jelka Delius was a painter of no mean ability affiliated to the Impressionist Pointillist school – Delius unconsciously began to recreate the flecked and dappled grain and texture of Impressionist art in terms of the modern orchestral palette. Thence his intoxicating sonorities. There is rich vibrancy of colour now, rather than harsh brilliance; a soft-grained translucency, an eggshell surface rather than a gloss. There is no sacrifice of compositional structure in favour of pure colour. *In a Summer Garden* is in fact quite masterly in its architecture: * its pulse firm, its control of tension such that it gives functional shape to what appears on paper to be an inchoate rhapsodic flow of glittering colour-charged particles. The colour-scheme in *Summer Garden* is that

---

*In a Summer Garden is one of Delius's supreme achievements. No other music so murmurs of sunlight and the bee, catches the sound of a little faint wind from the south rustling through the leaves of trees, conjures the scent of a thousand sweet summer flowers into the surge and fall and harmony of line. But *Summer Garden* as we know it is a 1914 revision, not the original version of 1908. In the revision Delius extensively cut and reshaped the quasi-recapitulation (or development: the music has such effortless continuity it is difficult to know how best to divide it into sections) to build the argument round one central climax instead of a number of subsidiary ones. The entire second part gains much in tautness and concentration, and it was a masterly move to bring the little chugging woodwind figure right up to the beginning of the piece instead of delaying its *entrée* for several pages. In the original version the tracery of woodwind over the river-song is much less finely-wrought, and the sleepy chromatic horn fanfare which introduces the latter is absent. On the other hand Delius jettisoned a number of rather attractive ideas in the revision – particularly the deep bell which sounds throughout the river-music and in the coda; and, in the latter, the dream-laden recollections both of the river-song (as in Moeran's *Stalham River*) and of the opening flute phrase given to a solo horn. Composers do not always know when to leave well alone.

of the Monet of *Woman with Umbrella* and *Red Poppies*, whereas *Summer Night on the River* recalls the Giverny water-garden. The quality of these great land-and-riverscapes justify us in numbering Delius among *les grands imprécistes du XXe siècle* in the company (as assembled by Léon Arnoult) of Turner, Wagner and Corot.

It is the vagueness and lack of precision in Delius's French canvases – their blurred, evocative effect, the subtle, indefinable and elusive appeal of their colour – which links him indissolubly with the world of the Impressionist painters. We do not perceive his imagined gardens, fields or water-surfaces with precision; indistinctness (as Turner said anent his *Fingal's Cave*) is his forte. The monotony of Delius's repeated ostinato-like figures which I discussed in connection with Grieg's nature-music may be related also to the divisionist technique of Pissarro or Seurat, the cumulative reiteration of sensation.

In this connection the relationship of Delius to Debussy naturally arises, for no musician was more aware of contemporary trends in the sister arts than Debussy. We can draw first of all a number of interesting parallels between their respective careers. They were both born in 1862, and survived a promiscuous youth to face prolonged suffering in middle age – Debussy was destroyed by cancer, Delius by syphilis. They both took long to reach maturity: the *Prélude à l'après-midi d'un faune* appeared in 1893, *Paris* and *A Village Romeo and Juliet* some six years later. It is possible that Debussy's advance over Delius here was the result of his more systematic and intensive training at the Paris Conservatoire during the years when Delius was still roaming around Scandinavia and North America. In about 1910 they both found themselves beset by a similar kind of creative crisis – a tendency towards self-repetition. They solved it in much the same way – by a paring away of harmonic flesh, a new directness and simplicity of melody and a gravitation toward abstract forms. Delius's thoughts veered away from the tropic luxuriance of the South to the austerity and bleakness of the North; and Debussy's orchestral *Images* and the ballet *Jeux* inhabit a very different world from *Pelléas et Mélisande*, *La Mer* or *L'Après-midi*. As for abstract forms, *En blanc et noir*, the *Études* and the three sonatas form a quasi-counterpart to Delius's sonatas and concertos, however they may differ in character and essence.

Debussy died in 1918, and Delius wrote progressively less thereafter in proportion as his health deteriorated. His *main* span of creative activity, then, approximated roughly to Debussy's. Finally, although both composers died of painful and wasting diseases, their creative powers were preserved intact to the end – witness Debussy's Violin Sonata and Delius's *Songs of Farewell*.

There are similarities in the moral and aesthetic attitudes of the two composers. Both were atheists – Delius a rabid anti-Christ fervently preaching the Gospel according to Friedrich Nietzsche, Debussy more naturally and instinctively. But they were both men of vision. Delius set a Whitman text with Christian implications as part of his last work, and Debussy provided music for D'Annunzio's mystery play *Le Martyre de Saint Sebastien*, his score for which Lockspeiser described as 'the work of a pagan musician who sees God in all things'.

Aristocratic, hedonistic, sensual – epithets we may apply as appropriately to Delius as to Debussy. They both loved the good things of life, and Delius never tired of urging people to free themselves from all ties, social, parental, or moral, and to enjoy the fruits of the earth. They both sought always to be *moved* – ideas were nothing to them until they had perceived their truth through the emotions, and no art was valid for them unless it provoked some form of sensual response. This was a prevailing aesthetic in the Paris of the '90s – we have only to cite such names as Pierre Louys, André Gide and even Oscar Wilde for corroboration. Their musical credos are practically identical. Music, said Debussy, should seek to please; extreme complication is contrary to art. Beauty must appeal to the senses, must provide us with immediate enjoyment, must impress or insinuate itself into us without any effort on our part. Eric Fenby tells us that for Delius, life was entirely a matter of feeling: he was contemptuous of learning and completely anti-metaphysical. Music, he said, is an outburst of the soul. It is addressed and should appeal instantly to the soul of the listener. Never believe the saying that one must hear music many times to appreciate it – utter nonsense. Music should be a thing of instinct rather than learning . . . it should never be complicated, for with complication it loses its power to move.

Closely connected with all this is the approach of both Delius and Debussy to harmony. It has long been realised that the originality of Debussy's harmony lay not so much in the chords he used as in the way he used them. He would seize on a chord he liked, lift it out of its usual context and enjoy it as a beautiful sound for itself alone, thus throwing overboard the classical concept of harmonic progression subservient to melody. Debussy was quick to appreciate the sensuous appeal of a chord like the dominant ninth: he might single it out and toy with it, trying it out on different degrees of the scale – or he might like the effect of the unresolved secondary ninth and *leave* it unresolved as at the end of Act I of *Pelléas*. So with Delius. The unusual *juxtapositions* of chords rather than the chords themselves is responsible for the distinction of his harmony. 'There's no theory. You merely have to listen. *Pleasure* is the law.' Thus Debussy, replying to an accusation that his harmonies were theoretically absurd. Delius would have said precisely the same. In Delius chains of chords usurp the function of chains of notes; yet only rarely does this descend to the level of wanton wallowing in sound. Examine the main climax of the *Walk to the Paradise Garden*. The harmony is rich, but there is a Gallic discretion and refinement in its application, moderation even in excess, taste in self-indulgence. This passage also highlights the principal quality which removes Delius's music from the technical orbit of Debussy – a Teutonic solidity, body, a weight of substance which has its roots above all else in a Wagnerian continuity of melodic impulse. Chords are always tethered by a melodic thread, even if the melodic thread is primarily chordal. There is none of the near-static quality of a Debussian mood-abstraction.

Delius was an aristocrat in music as in life, and shared Debussy's enthusiasm for Chopin, the composer-aristocrat *par excellence*. But they both realised that unalloyed harmonic opulence would merely cloy the palate, so they contrived to vary their textures by the subtle interpolation of common chords. These might be treated in the same way as discords – dislodged from their conventional contexts and relieved of their function of establishing tonality. The opening of 'The Court of Lilies' from *Le Martyre* and the strange sequence of consecutive common chords (with tubular bells) after the chief climax in *Eventyr* are both reminiscent of medieval organum, in which parts moved in successive octaves, fourths and fifths. The link here is possibly Grieg, one of the pioneers of Impressionist harmony. His influence appears in early Debussy – the *Petite suite*, the *Suite Bergamasque*, marginally in *Printemps*; but in Delius's case as we know he was the greatest single influence. Debussy reviewed some early Delius songs for *La Revue blanche* in 1901 – and he reproduced the same passage some two years later in reviewing some songs by Grieg.

Delius, like Grieg, was first and foremost a nature-mystic. Debussy spoke of the musician's claim to a unique interpretation of nature, and his pantheism and nature-mysticism – later to ignite *La Mer* and *L'isle joyeuse* – found eloquent expression even in a comparatively immature work as *Printemps* – 'the slow and arduous birth of things in nature, a gradual awakening and finally the joy and ecstasy of new life'. In *Pelléas* it is not so much the rather conventional love story that interests Debussy as the wide variety of natural phenomena serving either as a backdrop to the unfolding of the tragedy or – as so often happens – symbolically involved in the tragedy itself. Dark untenanted forests, the disembodied calm of a summer evening, a flock of sheep disappearing into the twilight – these were the aspects of the libretto that fascinated Debussy since they lent themselves so happily to his ability to evoke and suggest. In *A Village Romeo* too it is the setting more than the story which keeps Delius's muse alert. And in their respective personal interpretations of the *Tristan* myth,

Delius and Debussy tend to hit upon the same hints and dreams and note of haunting, the same aura of unreality. In *Pelléas* the characters are scarcely characters at all; they never emerge from the tenuousness of their surroundings, they do not develop, they make no attempt to force the hand of Destiny but meekly accept whatever it offers them. So, too, the two lovers wander through *A Village Romeo* as if in a dream, powerless to help themselves or to take any positive action to obviate their own destruction. Delius's opera, like Debussy's, has but the remotest connection with the world of everyday reality, and, similarly, there is no *real* fair in *Brigg Fair*: the strains and cries it evokes belong to some spectral fair of long ago, some long-vanished and forgotten past to which the woods and fields implicit in the idyll bear sole witness.

There are other links between Delius and Debussy – their power of sea-depiction in music, their use of the voice as a colouristic medium, their painter's approach to the orchestral palette (both enjoyed the company of painters and writers and avoided musicians with their technical prattle). They both set Verlaine; and inevitably the question of Debussy's possible influence on Delius arises. It is always difficult, when discussing similarities of expression in different composers, to distinguish between actual tangible influence and unconscious affinity of mind. There were certainly many affinities of mind between Delius and Debussy; and it is tempting to speculate as to whether or not Delius acquired any sense of direction from exposure to Debussy's music with all its complex network of associations with the other arts. My own belief now is that he did not. For one thing, we find Delius in 1908 writing to Granville Bantock: 'Do you know that I have never in my life heard *L'Après-midi d'un faune* or seen the score!' This after the opening of *Brigg Fair* written in the previous year, perhaps the most Debussian moment in Delius with flute arabesque *à la* 'Pan's goatherd', harp, muted strings, horn-harmony undermining tonal stability – the affinity with the opening of *L'Après-midi* is obvious. Delius told Fenby he admired Debussy's refinement and orchestration but that he considered his music deficient in melody; precisely the criticism we would expect from a man in whose own work melodic continuity is of paramount importance and who could conceive the great all-enveloping arc of melody which launches the final section of the Cello Concerto. It is true that Delius acquired a pianola roll of *L'Après-midi d'un faune* at the time of the composition of *Summer Night on the River* (1911). In the latter the *pointilliste* technique is once again applied to music, and the result is perfection. Yet every detail of orchestral procedure is implicit in the *Summer Garden* of 1908; no question of the later piece having been written in the glow of a first discovery of Debussy. No; Delius and Debussy shared a musical ancestry (Chopin, Grieg, Wagner) a physical environment (Paris, the French countryside); a cultural milieu (the world of French late-nineteenth-century painting and literature). But if Debussy was French, Delius was German; and what more natural therefore than that the latter should emerge as 'the only German Impressionist'?

CHAPTER FIVE

England

1

Lionel Carley, in his study of Delius's prophet and pioneer Hans Haym, remarks that none of the composer's works given in Elberfeld up to 1909 seems to owe very much, if anything, either to his English background or to the resurgent nationalist voices at the time discernible no less in English music than elsewhere in Europe. But 'what happened in about 1906 was that Delius, aware at last that his music showed signs of being ready and sufficiently well-established to cross the Channel . . . aware too that friends were tilling the ground on his behalf, was beginning to shed a part of his German self. He came to look more and more frequently to English themes – to the poems of Dowson and Symons, to English folksong, to English landscapes remembered from his youth. Pieces such as *In a Summer Garden* and *On Hearing the First Cuckoo in Spring* give us an instinctive feeling that, wherever the inspiration may be rooted, an essentially English setting is being evoked.' This is an interesting hypothesis, but I have no intention whatever of allowing myself to be caught in the peculiarly thorny thicket of Delius's Englishness; for in the last analysis it is all entirely a matter of subjective reaction. If Lionel Carley hears Delius in the mind's ear while walking the English country lanes, Eric Fenby hears Elgar, but Delius in France; for my part I find that he travels with all the ease and adaptability of a born cosmopolitan and is as much at home in the green fields of Surrey as in the woodland glades of Fontainebleau. He belongs to everywhere – and to nowhere.

Delius's relationship to the land of his birth was ambivalent. He grew up there, and the scenery of the Yorkshire moors made a big impression on him. Yet he was never really happy in England or among English people and regarded them to the end of his life with a species of niggling scepticism. His attitude is best summed up in a letter he wrote to Granville Bantock in 1911 on the subject of the, by that time, moribund 'Music League' which he and Bantock had instigated: 'I am afraid artistic undertakings are impossible in England – the country is not yet artistically civilised – There is something hopeless about English people in a musical and artistic way and, to be frank, I have entirely lost my interest and prefer to live abroad and make flying visits.' This attitude prevailed to the end, even after Delius discovered in England his ideal interpreter (Beecham) and one of his most devoted disciples (Heseltine/Warlock) and had ultimately seen England established as the country most likely to safeguard the future of his music after he was dead. And 'safeguarding the future' implied not only regular performances of his music, but a lively interest on the part of younger composers. Only in England, in fact, did Delius command any sort of a following among composers of the rising generation; and it is the relationship of this unique 'following' to the father-figure, the fountainhead, that I now propose to place in perspective.

And yet it is perhaps symptomatic of Delius's cosmopolitan breadth of vision that the first composer to call for some comment in this connection is not English at all, but American. For the American composer Bernard Herrmann (born 1911) undertook an opera on the only English novel which Delius ever contemplated submitting to operatic treatment and for which the *North Country Sketches* – the only work explicitly suggested by the English landscape – very probably served, originally, as draft pre-liminaries: *Wuthering Heights*. Delius as a Yorkshireman had always been a Brontë enthusiast and the wild moorland scenery of Haworth and the Brontë country impressed him tremendously. Yet the opera was never written; and it is as easy to see why as to predict that, had it been written, it could at best have been only partially successful. The range of characteris-ation over which Delius had musical control was small, as *A Village Romeo and Juliet* shows only too clearly. Manz and Marti in their aggressive moods are woefully feeble; what then would Delius have made of Heath-cliff? As far as the natural element is concerned, Delius would have been happy enough creating the seasonal moods of the *North Country Sketches* – the autumn winds in the 'bare ruin'd choirs' where no birds sing, a silent snowbound winter landscape, the resurrection miracle of spring. But the role of nature in *Wuthering Heights* demands a composer who can find a musical equivalent not only for her tranquillities and lyrical outbursts, but also – and it is a very important 'but also' – for her uncompromisingly elemental manifestations. This is a cardinal factor in *Wuthering Heights*, for here rural passions and the elements are not merely joined in symbolic harness (as in Hardy's *Return of the Native*, for instance) but they are actually one and the same. Every effect of natural phenomena – cold, heat, storm, sunshine – is felt both as a physical sensation and as a spiritual force emanating from the tensions between the protagonists. Bernard Herrmann explores this facet in a depth and subtlety comparable to Britten's in *Peter Grimes*; and many of the best moments in his *Wuthering Heights* spring from this enmeshment of inner and outer conflict. As in the vivid, almost Turneresque sea-and-storm music in the cantata *Moby Dick*; as in the music for Jane's encounter with Rochester on the fogbound moors in the 1944 film version of *Jane Eyre*; here, at the end of Act 2 of *Wuthering Heights*, as a distracted Cathy vanishes over the rainswept moors with Joseph and Nelly in hot pursuit, a miscellany of motifs from various contexts erupt into some of the most harrowing storm-music ever penned. Herrmann so reveals himself, like Bax, a true heir in music to the vast elemental frescoes painted by Wagner, the storms and hurricanes in *The Flying Dutchman* and *Die Walküre*, the flooding waters of the ultimate Götterdämmerung, the fire-music of Loge. This lay without the scope of Delius's pictorial sense.

Herrmann has long been a devotee of Delius (as conductor-in-chief of CBS Radio for seventeen years he introduced a number of his works together with those of numerous other English composers) and is a devout Anglophile; his music does not bear any recognisably American signature, and the lyricism of a piece such as the *Fantasticks* (six settings of the seventeenth-century poet Nicholas Breton) is as English as anything in the work of Quilter, Armstrong Gibbs or Warlock. Something of a debt to Delius here becomes apparent – in 'April', for example, a fragrant piece with liquid harp ostinato and solo violin obbligato. Cecil Gray would surely have acclaimed its sensuous sweetness as exclusively English, exclusively Delian! The cream of the set is undoubtedly the last poem, 'May', with its enchanting barcarolle-like lilt and a freshness which comes from an ear for vocal colour and the subtle balancing of vocal and instrumental timbres (very Delian). The first entry of the voices is a moment of exquisite beauty; until now each poem has been allocated to one individual singer, but in this case all four soloists enter one after the other and then together, eventually dispensing with words in the sweetness of their ecstasy, a lovely paean to the prime of the year.

It is of this music that the fine lyrical scene in Act 1 of *Wuthering Heights* is born. This is where Delius would have excelled – and he would surely have been appreciative of Herrmann's realisation. Cathy's aria 'I have been wandering in the green woods' and the love-duet 'On the moors' both seem to catch in their impressionistic, birdsong-studded orchestral textures the feeling of the wind, the expanse of moorland and the wide open sky; the sudden rush and sweep of string figuration at Heathcliff's 'Yes, and with a west wind blowing, and bright white clouds flitting rapidly above' make for an almost physically-experienced sensation. The sunset is played out to music of a familiar Delian cast – a broad singing melody sustained in the tenor of the orchestra over *ostinato*-like figuration, basically pentatonic, in woodwind and harps. The orchestral nocturne which closes this first scene, after Heathcliff has dismissed the sordidness of the day-world to harmonic progressions of melting beauty ('Grim world, go hide thee till the day'), is knit to a similar pattern, but in reverse: the song is carried on high by the violins, the ostinato by winds and harps in the tenor. Antique cymbals let fall their tiny needle-points of moonlight, and in the final bars the high sustained string chords are lost to stardust in a manner not unlike the ending of *Cynara*. The whole of this long first scene of Act 1 pays homage to Delius, yet there is no direct reminiscence; the musical personality is Herrmann's own. As André Gide once put it: 'L'influence ne crée pas: elle éveille.'

2

In 1910 the young Peter Warlock (then known by his rightful name as Philip Heseltine), an unhappy 16-year-old schoolboy at Eton, chanced on the music of Delius in the form of a hearing of the unaccompanied part-song *On Craig Dhu*. This came as a revelation to him, a fact which is faintly puzzling since this is by no means one of Delius's best works or even one of his most characteristic, the harmony being for the most part comparatively conservative in idiom. (Had it been the *Appalachia* unaccompanied chorus which so electrified Percy Grainger, one might have understood.) But however this may be, *On Craig Dhu* was evidently sufficiently novel and exciting to spur the 16-year-old on to familiarising himself with every note of Delius then obtainable; and, what is more, the decision to devote himself to music took firm root in his mind as a result of this experience. In a now famous letter, he wrote to his old music master, Colin Taylor: 'I spend most of my time saturating myself with Delius's music. I am sure there is no music more beautiful in all the world; it haunts me day and night – it is always with me and seems, by its continual presence, to intensify the beauty of everything else for me!' Heseltine lost no time in establishing personal contact with Delius and in furthering his cause in a variety of ways – making piano transcriptions, vocal scores and English translations of his works, publishing articles and eventually a book on him, making the composer's name and his music known among his contemporaries. One of these was the poet Robert Nichols, later to make himself useful to Delius in the matter of resuscitating *Margot la rouge* and re-furbishing it in the form of the *Idyll*. It was Nichols who noted how Warlock's enthusiasm for Delius came in time to join hands with an interest in English folkmusic and the man to whose creativity it was central – Ralph Vaughan Williams.

And here we must consider the question of Delius's relationship with Vaughan Williams and his position *vis à vis* the other homegrown composers of the English Revival. Delius (b. 1862) is generally linked with Elgar (b. 1857) in the vanguard; yet their music has nothing in common apart from a basic grounding in German romanticism; even a superficial hearing suggests a much greater affinity between Delius and Vaughan Williams (b. 1872). But if such an affinity exists it was evidently far from apparent to the composers themselves. In fact their attitude towards each other's music was one of inveterate hostility. Vaughan Williams once said that for him Delius's music always savoured too strongly of the 'restaurant' and that it had a tendency to sound 'like the curate improvising'. He once described an occasion in London when he forced himself in on Delius's privacy and insisted on playing him the *Sea Symphony* in its entirety – 'Poor fellow. How he must have hated it!' – although apparently his gracious comment was 'Vraiment ce n'est pas mesquin' (why he should have chosen to address an English compatriot in French remains, as Michael Kennedy has said, one of life's mysteries).

This incident, trivial in itself though it may be, nevertheless serves to highlight an important facet in the Delius-Vaughan Williams relationship: namely, their mutual response to Whitman, a poet greatly admired and set to music by other composers of the Revival, notably Holst (*Ode to Death*) and Harty (*The Mystic Trumpeter*, also set by Holst). Now on three occasions* Delius and Vaughan Williams set identical texts: 'Away, O Soul! Hoist instantly the anchor' (from *A Passage to India*) appears in No. 3 of Delius's *Songs of Farewell* and also in the finale of the *Sea Symphony*; 'Joy, Shipmate, Joy' (from *Songs of Parting*) is set both in *Songs of Farewell* and in Vaughan Williams's *Three Poems by Walt Whitman* for voice and piano; and 'A Clear Midnight' ('This is thy hour, O Soul') is set as No. 2 of the *Three Poems* and is also included in the Whitman miscellany compiled by Robert Nichols for Delius's use in the *Idyll*. From the point of view of direct comparison, the first of these shared texts ('Hoist instantly the anchor') is the most revealing. What strikes us immediately is that, stylistic disparity notwithstanding, Delius's approach to Whitman is essentially similar to Vaughan Williams's. They are both great visionaries and mystics, happy like Whitman to view the sea as the symbol of man's spiritual odyssey into the unknown – 'Away, O Soul!'. The only difference is that the *Sea Symphony* inaugurated Vaughan Williams's career as a composer, and, as in *Toward the Unknown Region*, he cuts himself adrift on the seas of life; whereas the *Songs of Farewell* are the last proud unflinching choral legacy of the composer of *A Mass of Life*, cleaving the breakers on his way to a Baudelairean rendezvous with death.

*Four, if one includes Vaughan Williams's unpublished *Two Vocal Duets*, for No. 2 sets a passage from *Out of the Cradle Endlessly Rocking*, used by Delius in *Sea-Drift*.

The sea-nocturne 'On the beach at night alone' in the *Sea Symphony* is inferior to Delius's night-sea-music in *Sea-Drift*, but the symphony is an early work and there are many authentic sea sounds elsewhere in the piece, notably in the scherzo and in the orchestral swell and surge which precedes the rapt ecstatic duet 'O we can wait no longer' in the finale. Nor must we forget the mysterious dove-grey twilight epilogue ('O my brave soul, O farther sail') looking backward to the close of Part 1 of *The Dream of Gerontius* and forward to the interstellar infinities of Holst's 'Neptune'. There is too an arresting similarity in temper between the B flat minor/ D major exordium of the *Sea Symphony* and the no less rhetorical tempest of F major sonority which launches the *Mass of Life*. There is the same utterly romantic note of heroic endeavour, hard-grained masculine aspiration, expressing itself in a markedly similar cast of pentatonic theme (Ex. 27a/b).

We do not have to look far for further parallels. The Second Symphony, the *London*, is city-music like *Paris*, and the Third, the *Pastoral*, is music of the open country like *Brigg Fair* or whatever. The first movement of the *London* is almost a kind of *précis* of *Paris*, with the city gradually stirring to life *dans une brume doucement sonore* (to borrow an evocative expression from *La Cathédrale engloutie*), and there is a like enclave of stillness, a moment of pause for reflection at mid-point; and in either case all is to end in the bright light of day.

The *Pastoral Symphony* is a landscape, not so much the Cotswolds as the wastes of wartime Flanders. Here human figures recede from the scene; we are closer to the pantheistic spirit of *The Song of the High Hills*, in that landscape is viewed divorced from its function as a background to human activity, yet further away in that there is no element of 'man in nature'. There is a world of difference between music depicting human figures in a landscape (as for instance in d'Indy's *Summer Day on the Mountain* or Britten's *Peter Grimes*) and music depicting the *reactions* of humans in the face of natural beauty – Delius's *Song of the High Hills* or Carl Nielsen's

Ex.27(a)

(b)

21. Munch, *Rue Lafayette*, 1891 – Delius's 'Paris'.

22. 'Lonely Waters'; an East Norfolk scene at the turn of the century.

Sinfonia Espansiva. Yet Nielsen, Vaughan Williams and Delius, no less than Debussy and Holst, have this in common : they are nature mystics, and they invoke the power of the wordless human voice to sound paradoxically *un*-human in the musical representation of un-human nature. In 'Neptune' the sexless female chorus is both agent and symbol of the Infinite; the 'Andante pastorale' of Nielsen's *Espansiva* carries the ear to the 'soothing, gentle roll of Danish fields in high summer' (as Robert Simpson puts it), the whole orchestra is bathed in a *pianissimo* sunset glow of E major (the key of Delius's and Gershwin's Eden) and the two wordless voices, projecting their beautiful wordless melismata from the far distance to soft fanfare-like clarinet and horn figures, drone-basses and birdsong, hint at some eternal bond of blessedness between man and nature. So they do too in *The Song of the High Hills*, written at much the same time as the *Espansiva*, in a glorious evocation of the immensities of time and space as experienced in high solitudes. In Debussy's 'Sirènes' the voices have all the coldness of white Carrara marble, and in the *Pastoral* the soprano solo bears a remoteness bordering on indifference – Housman's 'heartless, witless nature'; the wordless chorus in *Riders to the Sea* and the *Sinfonia Antartica* is quite definitely a spokesman for hostile, elemental force – the sea in the one case, a polar wilderness of ice and snows in the other. Much closer to *The Song of the High Hills* is the use of voices to articulate the naked, earthy passion of *Flos Campi*, the most sensuous of all Vaughan Williams's works; in the melancholy pastoral lyricism of the opening pages, in the great flood of choral-instrumental sound at 'return, return O Shulamite', in the impression of overwhelming sadness always left by the closing bars, we recognise a Delian affinity. Delius would surely have appreciated moments in certain other of Vaughan Williams's nature-pieces – *In the Fen Country*, the coolly atmospheric opening bars of the *Norfolk Rhapsody No. 1*, the enchanted bird-song of *The Lark Ascending*, in *Job* the distant cornfields stretching away in to the sunset far as the eye can see, and Elihu's dance of youth and beauty with its violin arabesques of an almost unbearable sweetness. Delius wrote for the violin in similar vein in the Violin Concerto.

The basic fact here is that both Delius and Vaughan Williams were nature-mystics and folklorists (in the widest sense of the term). As such they were both spiritual descendants of Grieg. Were they nature-mystics because they were folklorists, or *vice versa*? Nature-mystics could not have existed in music before the rise of nationalism and consequent re-appraisal of folksong, because the far-reaching changes in melodic, harmonic and formal syntax which the repatriation of folksong brought in its wake were endemic in musical representation of the folksong milieu, i.e. nature, the countryside. Nature was simply not realistically 'available' in musical terms before. With the enhanced awareness of the purely sensuous qualities of harmony and timbre fostered by Impressionism (of which Grieg was an established progenitor) came the means of exploiting the evocative properties of orchestral and piano sound, and so it came to pass that a wave of nature-mysticism* swept like a rushing mighty wind through all those countries whose composers had directly or indirectly been bitten by the folksong bug. Delius was bitten, indirectly, through Grieg and also through the American Negro; Vaughan Williams was too, very directly, through exposure to English folksong. Elgar never was. Holst was; Bax was; John Ireland and Frank Bridge and William Baines were, largely through their attraction to varying facets of Impressionism. We cannot carry the Delius/Vaughan Williams parallel too far, but it is important to remember that both were first generation atheists (although Delius was certainly not, like Vaughan Williams, a disappointed theist) and that the rise of Darwinism, the speedy erosion of faiths and beliefs to which men had clung steadfastly for centuries, the general re-orientation of the European mind in which Nietzsche played no insignificant role – all were contributory factors in the insurrectionist 'back to nature' movement in music. That this should have coincided, musically speaking, with the new nationalist awareness which carried on its wave's crest the emancipation of Impressionism and all its wide new range of expressive dimension *may* be simply coincidence; more likely is it evidence of a deep underlying *rapport* between a spiritual need and the technique which provides for its fulfilment.

With no composer of the Revival, even counting those who were directly influenced by him, does Delius have more in common than with the strange faun-like figure of Arnold Bax – Bax whose early work bears broad signs of many an enthusiasm but never, overtly, of Delius. Yet his affinity with Delius is no doubt all the closer therefore, since it is first and foremost an affinity of *matter*, spiritual matter, thence of technical *manner*. And the secret of this affinity lies in one word: ecstasy. They both had known the splendour and the glory, their eyes had seen the enchanted light. Bax wrote:

'I am absolutely certain that the only music that can last is that which is the outcome of one's emotional reactions to the ultimate realities of Life, Love and Death . . . I believe in conditions of ecstasy – physical or spiritual – and I get nothing from anyone else. I think all the composers who appeal to me – Beethoven, Wagner, Delius, Sibelius – were primitive in that they believed that the secret of the universe could be solved by ecstatic intuition rather than by thought. All our unrest and melancholy is caused by conscience and remorse

*See Percy Grainger's theory given on p. 8.

inhibiting nature. I do believe that all original ideas derive from some condition of untrammelled passion and ecstasy . . .'

This might easily be a statement of Delius's artistic credo, except that he would not have included Beethoven and Sibelius in the list of composers that 'appealed' to him; but neither would he have composed Bax's seven Beethovenian, Sibelian symphonies. Delius, it seems, had no time for Bax the symphonist; but he adored Bax the tone-poet. We can see why, for there are many moments in the tone-poems – *Tintagel, The Garden of Fand, November Woods, Summer Music, Moy Mell, Red Autumn* – which Delius might easily have written himself. In Bax there was a wild, hungry sensuality, a strong streak of pagan mysticism, a throbbing pantheistic response to nature, an *ecstasy* of a kind which visited his English contemporaries but fitfully (John Ireland in 'Song of the Springtides' in *Sarnia*, Frank Bridge in *Enter Spring*). Bax is really best considered in the company of Delius's Nordic inspirations and their sources. His response to nature was Nordic-Celtic; Russia, Bavaria and later Finland were the countries to which he was most drawn, but a more central experience than any of these was his discovery of Ireland. Stumbling across Yeats's *The Wanderings of Usheen* at the age of 19 induced in Bax a state of considerable spiritual excitement, and when he first visited Ireland he was overwhelmed by the wild extravagant loveliness of the landscapes, the lakes and windy heights – and the sea.

'The endless grey sea sorrow and the murmuring miles' – a line from one of the poems of Bax's *alter ego*, Dermot O'Byrne. Like Delius, Bax wrote a deal of sea-music. Apart from *Tintagel* – 'in which enormous breakers may be imagined crashing against the coast of Cornwall' and *The Garden of Fand* in which is envisioned the land of eternal youth, of Celtic mythology, the opening bars and the coda of the first movement of the Fourth Symphony are said to represent a choppy sea at floodtide on a sunny day. There are distinct *Fand*-like echoes of an enchanted Atlantic in the slow movement of the Piano Quintet, and in the slow movement of the Sonata for Two Pianos; and if *The Garden of Fand* was the last music Bax heard, one of his last sights on this earth was that of the Atlantic as viewed from the old Head of Leinsale in County Cork, burnished to beaten gold in the rays of the setting sun. A matter of hours later, Bax was ready to follow Usheen and Niamh from Ireland into that sunset.

Colin Scott-Sutherland has pointed out that the languid, chromatically drooping 'sick Tristan' motif which comes increasingly to dominate the *Tintagel* development section also occurs in Debussy's *La Mer*; he might also have mentioned that it is to be found alike in Delius's *Sea-Drift*. Wagner, Debussy, Delius, Bax . . . is it mere coincidence that all four composers should have been drawn to the same sea image in the music? We should remember that the chromatic language of *Tristan* was first forged to articulate feelings of sexual desire and passion, and that a shared characteristic of these four great sea-poets in music was the strength of their sexuality. None could be fettered in the usual way to conjugal and family fidelity or responsibility, and it is surely true that any denial of this constant and restless need for gratification of the senses would have impaired the force of their creativity. The sea has always had a Freudian symbolic import – did not Grillparzer once treat the Hero/Leander myth in the form of a play entitled *The Waves of Love and the Sea* – and the *Fand* legend is very explicit. It is perhaps permissible to describe the chromatic textures of Wagner, Debussy, Delius and Bax (who were all at one time or another fulfilled in love both physically and spiritually) as 'wet' music, those of Ravel and Ireland (who were repressed) as 'dry' (Ireland was more indebted to Ravel than to anyone else). There is here a promising line in post-Freudian research for some disciple of Edward Lockspeiser or Gaston Bachelard.

Delius is constantly referred to in connection with Bax's gentler nature-music – *In the Faery Hills, Moy Mell* (a tone-poem for two pianos which, like *Red Autumn* for the same medium, cries aloud for orchestration), the fine *Romantic Overture* for piano and small orchestra (dedicated to Delius), the slow movements of the Third, Fourth and Sixth Symphonies, piano lyrics such as *The Princess's Rose-Garden, The Maiden with the Daffodil, Apple-Blossom Time, A Hill Tune, A Mountain Mood*. Most Delian of all is *Summer Music* (dedicated, appropriately enough, to Beecham) which is intended to depict some hot, windless June mid-day in some wooded place in the South of England. Here is a Delian scene set so many times before by Bax, notably in the nature poem *Nympholept* (which takes as its motto Meredith's 'Enter those enchanted woods you who dare') and the setting of Shelley's *Enchanted Summer* for two sopranos, chorus and orchestra. In all this music, and in *Summer Music* and the central interlude in *The Happy Forest*, the atmosphere evoked is the same: a burning heat dimming the outlines of all things and all distances with a faint mist, the scent of flowers mingled, the odour of the woods, of cool shaded places and, with all the myriad hum and murmur of the summer, an infinite silence. In the magic of the spell woven by the music, in the deep folds of dream, there is a mystic presence. In *The Happy Forest* the enchantment lies in the triadic fanfares sounded on muted trumpets as from a great distance (not unlike those in *Moy Mell*) in which, as we feel the heated air beating in gusts about our face and see the shimmer rising from the turf, we are made dimly aware of the mystery which lies beyond. In *Summer Music* we are brought straight *in medias res* with a long lovely melody sung by the cor anglais to a hushed backdrop of muted strings – the span and stretch of which Delius would have admired, no less than its folksong-like curves and undulations (Ex. 28). A later return sprouts capricious flute and clarinet arabesques and a light flickering orchestral texture bearing witness to the Impressionist tendency to dissolve links of form and colour with subject – thence leading to the more fugitive manner of thematic development exemplified by the flanking sections of *Summer Garden*. The same applies to *November Woods* whose form corresponds to the ABA tripartite scheme of *Summer Garden*. The only part in the latter in which melody is

Ex.28

is allowed freely to grow, flow and exult is the central section, the 'Song of a Great River'; and in *November Woods* all the tossing battle-scarred turmoil (the music is full of blood and pain and the First World War) is forced into temporary oblivion by a broad-flowing, singing melody first heard on the violas speckled with cool flute, harps and celesta figuration. Here is music sunk, like Delius's, in nature-worship and nature-mysticism, imbued with an earthy spirituality, intoxicating in the depth and redness of its sunset hues. Above all it is the work of a poet. Bax and Delius were the two supreme poets of the English Revival.

So much for Delius's relationship with, as opposed to influence upon, the other English romantics. Now Warlock's natural predilection for modal melody was nurtured and strengthened by his knowledge of Vaughan Williams's work and by that of other folksong enthusiasts, especially E. J. Moeran of whom we shall hear more later. Warlock made occasional use of actual folksongs but more often stamped his own melodic invention with the impress of folksong, especially in *Lillygay*, a set of five songs which could be mistaken for arrangements of authentic folksongs. Ironically, the words and tunes stand a better chance of surviving than the arrangements, which have dated badly. There is an element of preciousness even in the best of the set, 'The Distracted Maid', though there is beauty in the chiming harmonies to which the demented girl spins her skein of fantasies around her lover and herself. By contrast the *Folk Song Preludes* for piano seem hardly to have dated at all; written in 1918, they are the first *echt*-English music (excluding that of Delius himself and Percy Grainger) to show that Delian harmony can adapt itself to a folksong context.

Apart from Delius, the other great musical and spiritual influence on Warlock was that of the Elizabethan period, not only its music but also its literature; and we must try to establish how it is that these two apparently disparate spheres of influence do not conflict with each other in the music of their recipient, but rather complement each other creatively. To the transcribing and editing of Elizabethan and Jacobean music – that of Dowland, Whythorne, Campion, Ravenscroft *et al.* – Warlock brought the scrupulousness of a scholar and the sensibility of an artist, and his re-searches into the byways of Elizabethan literature led to his discovery, editing and publishing of a collection of early seventeenth-century lyrics, *Giles Earle, His Book*. He introduced Delius to the Elizabethan poets, several of whom he later set; an early letter from Warlock encloses a vol-ume to him of plays by Tourneur and Webster. And herein we have perhaps the first intimation of a shared attitude of mind, a kinship of sensibility be-tween the two composers – their patrician taste, their exquisite feeling for *poetry* in the widest sense of the term. To paraphrase Percy Grainger, theirs was 'bed-rock aristocraticness of mind and sensibility, not top-layer aristo-craticness of birth or upbringing or acquired culture'. And the kind of poetic sensibility Warlock found manifest in the lyrics of Shakespeare, Peele, Marlowe, Robert Wever, Fletcher and others, he also found manifest in Delius's music. This, for instance:

> In a garden so green in a May morning
> Heard I my lady pleen of paramours;
> Said she: 'My love so sweet, come you not yet, nor yet,
> Heght you not me to meet amongst the flowers?'

or this:

> Rest, sweet nymphs, let golden sleep
> Charm your star-brighter eyes,
> While my lute her watch doth keep
> With pleasing sympathies.
>   Lullaby, lullaby,
> Sleep sweetly, sleep sweetly,
> Let nothing affright ye,
> In calm contentments lie.

In these two stanzas is all the sweet spring and summer sadness of *On*

Hearing the First Cuckoo in Spring and *In a Summer Garden*; and hand in hand with the Elizabethans' instinct for felicities of *verbal* utterance, there goes a special talent for felicities of *vocal* colour, an instinctive grasp of the sensuous qualities of the human voice – just as in Delius. The madrigalists' fa-la-las and la-la-las and other conventions of syllabic vocalise find their counterparts in the *Mass of Life* and other choral works, even though the immediate prototype in these cases was no doubt the Flower Maiden's music in *Parsifal*. Then, reading through the above-quoted *Rest Sweet Nymphs*, without any knowledge of Warlock's delectable setting one senses straightway the drowsy Delian lilt of the 6/8 metre. The Elizabethans seem to have been particularly fond of the trochee which translates itself into music precisely in the form of this barcarolle-like 6/8 or as a 3/4 with the first two beats tied together, which comes to the same thing. How frequently do we find this in the music of this period – and how frequently in Delius! So that when we discover it in Warlock, as we do at almost every turn, we know not to which of his two great loves he is swearing allegiance.

The same applies to other characteristics shared by Delius and the Elizabethans. The modality of sixteenth-century music, particularly the ambiguity of the seventh, attracted Warlock, Vaughan Williams and Moeran precisely because they had discerned similar characteristics in folksong; Delius being an unwitting folklorist with a predilection for non-major and minor diatonic formations, it follows that a degree of stylistic compatibility between his idiom and that of the Elizabethans may be taken for granted. We have noted how useful a folk-tune can be to a composer like Delius with a penchant for harmonic variation; its modality offers him scope and flexibility for the elaborate harmony he delights in, and to move a single tune through a harmonic kaleidoscope as Delius does in *Brigg Fair*, the *First Dance Rhapsody* and the central section of the Second (with the solo oboe) not only gives shape and purpose to a composition but sustains a specific identity throughout. This is essentially the technique of the old Elizabethan variation form, and Eric Fenby has mentioned Byrd's *The Woodes so Wild* in connection with *Brigg Fair* – though doubtless Delius had never heard it, or of it. Incidentally, Delius never evinced the slightest interest in any 'old' music of any kind, notwithstanding his relationships with Grainger and Warlock. His own settings of Elizabethan poets make no attempt to assimilate any archaic elements. A figure of special relevance in this context is that of Herbert Howells, since he, like Warlock, left ample evidence of his ability flawlessly to recreate the dance-forms and vocal idioms of yesteryear, in no spirit of pious or condescending antiquarianism nor as a gesture of derisory modernism, but in true creative deference to the demands of his musical personality (*Howells's Clavichord*,

155

Lambert's Clavichord, Sarabande for the Morning of Easter, Master Tallis's Testament). Howells drew much nourishment from the English Cathedral tradition and from English folksong (Vaughan Williams was one of his closest friends), yet his sensuous and passionate nature led him also to the poignancy of Delian chromatic harmony – though in his case it is always a polyphonically-orientated harmony, compounded of what Frank Howes has aptly described as 'impressionist' counterpoint. Transience, the Delian sense of loss, is always keenly voiced in Howells, and, as in Delius, expressed in terms of a kaleidoscopic, dissolving harmonic texture. The great climaxes of his choral works are cases in point – 'Holy is the true light and passing wonderful' in *Hymnus Paradisi*, 'Et exspecto resurrectionem mortuorum' and 'Et vitam venturi saeculi' in the Credo of *Missa Sabrinensis*, 'Per te, Virgo, sim defensus' in the 'Fac ut Portem' of the *Stabat Mater*; not to mention shorter choral pieces such as the wonderful *A Maid Peerless*, *The Summer is Coming, Like as the Hart* and *A Sequence for St Michael*, songs such as *King David* and *The Lady Caroline*: mention of all of which merely scratches the surface of this fine composer's contribution to English music of our century. As Hugh Ottaway has put it, Delius's vision is never-more, Howells's evermore; but there is no mistaking a sunset, whichever way you happen to be facing.

Now Warlock never wrote anything on the extended scale of *Brigg Fair* or Grainger's *Green Bushes*, but on the principle of melodic stability *versus* harmonic changeability are conceived a large number of his songs and choral pieces. One of his finest songs, *The Frostbound Wood*, is a supreme example. The poem by Bruce Blunt (who often inspired the composer to his best efforts) is declaimed by the singer very slowly and quietly to the timelessness and impassiveness of a phrase of quasi-plainchant which remains unchanged (apart from a few minute variations in rhythm to accommodate the words) throughout. By contrast the harmony is ever changing, reflecting in masterly manner the shifting undercurrents of tension and emotion implied, suggested, sensed as from a great distance. Notice in Ex. 29 the numb, icy bleakness of the first three bars where almost nothing is happening; and then under 'lovely' a simple added-note chord, barely articulated, but one which seems to point tacitly to beyond the horizon to a mystic dimension of space and time existing without our powers of perception. It is a movement of pure vision, just like Debussy's ordinary F sharp major triad when Sebastian sees the face of the Crucified in the garden (*Le Martyre de Saint Sébastien*).

Warlock employs the same device in 'The Distracted Maid' from *Lillygay* already discussed and in many others, including *The Passionate Shepherd, The Sweet o' the Year, Sweet and Twenty, Sigh no More Ladies*. A song such as *Roister Doister* is particularly striking for the way it applies added-note chords and a species of whole-tone chord peculiar to Delius to an utterly un-Delian context – and it works, just as it does in *Yarmouth Fair, Twelve Oxen, Away to Twiver* and a number of the other more boisterous songs. Some of Warlock's most subtle effects of 'harmonic variation' are however reserved for the choral works, since Delius taught

Ex. 29

him that human voices are a far more malleable and expressive medium for the articulation of chromatic harmony than the piano. *Carillon Carilla* is a conspicuously lovely example; the verses ring the changes on the harmony in accordance with the text, but there are two landmarks which come constantly into view – the E major flavour of the refrain ('Carillon, Carilla') somehow suggesting bells heard faintly in the distance, and the warm glow at the end of each verse as the E minor melts into G major for 'And the small child Jesus smile on you'; the music literally smiles. But all the points are made harmonically: e.g. a moment of infinite tenderness for a boy soprano at 'it was very, very cold when our Lord was born' with a magical chromatic progression on 'born' out of G major into a dominant seventh on A flat. *The Five Lesser Joys of Mary* is another gem. Here the first four stanzas are basically diatonic in their harmony, although chromatic elements are guardedly admitted. But for the fifth, telling of the Mother's vigil on Calvary and her regret for the passing of the happy days she had experienced with her son, the harmony is chromatic *à la* Delius throughout. Perhaps the most arresting example in this context is the sequence of carols for choir with orchestra – *Tyrley Tyrlow, Balulalow* and *The Sycamore*

157

Trees, in each of which the harmonic texture becomes increasingly complex as the stanzas progress, although the tunes themselves never alter.

It is not surprising that Warlock should have written so many carols, given his predilection for the pastoral 6/8 so beloved of the Elizabethans. Most of them also have a strong modal flavour, especially *The First Mercy* (Bruce Blunt), with its delicately modulated harmony and a haunting refrain of a falling fourth in the accompaniment, which ultimately dissolves in the blissful consummation of the *tierce de Picardie*. There is the magnificently rough-hewn *Cornish Christmas Carol*, the Marot *Noël*, the extraordinary *Corpus Christi Carol* to be discussed presently, *Adam Lay Ybounden* with its unexpected and thrilling peroration, *I Saw a Fair Maiden*, almost Howells-like in its blandness but liberally spiced with false relations . . . but more directly relevant to this context is the splendid *Benedicamus Domino* which sports a favourite device of Warlock's, no less than of Grainger's – that of throwing in a short pregnant phrase of Delian chromatic harmony to enliven a consistently diatonic norm. Grainger does it in *Seventeen Come Sunday* in the verse which begins 'O it's now I'm with my soldier lad' at the words 'the drum and fife is my delight' (Ex. 17); and Warlock does it tellingly in *Benedicamus Domino* in the first two lines of the last stanza ('In hoc festo determino/Eya nobis annus est') (Ex. 30). In the New Year Carol *What Cheer? Good Cheer!* Delius would have liked the 'squelch' of the clotted chord at 'birth', the sole 'pimple' in an otherwise blamelessly diatonic harmony. And in his anthem *Thee, Lord Before the Close of Day* Balfour Gardiner introduces Delian chromatic inflexions only in the nocturnal unaccompanied choral part, at 'Keep us from Satan's tyranny'.

Ex.30

It would be misleading to suggest that Warlock learned his harmonic trade solely from Delius, since in his case the luxury of Delian chromatics was braced and tempered by the modal diatony of Vaughan Williams's harmony and by the more linear polychordal tendencies of van Dieren. These formed the basic ingredients of his harmonic personality, and it is when this distinctive personality allies itself to a tripping, lilting Delian

6/8 that the spirit of Delius is invoked – far more surely than were he merely to imitate various Delian harmonic tricks-of-the-trade, which any skilled hack could have done. As so often it is a question of the spirit rather than the letter. *Rest Sweet Nymphs* is, one feels on a first hearing, unashamedly Delian in mood; yet when one comes to examine the score there are few progressions or chord-formations which could legitimately be described as basic Delius. The final cadence for example – Delius never used fourths-chords or polychordal blocks (the exquisite final upbeat is an amalgam of a dominant seventh on C and a triad of D flat major). The same can be said of *Cradle Song, After Two Years, Ha'nacker Mill, Thou Gav'st Me Leave to Kiss, Sorrow's Lullaby, Spring the Sweet Spring*, and others. In some of these, as in *Robin Good-Fellow* and *The Sick Heart*, the proportion of recognisably Delian elements is higher than in others; yet we turn to *The Birds* and find harmony which could not possibly have been conceived without the example of Delius, but which in itself is quite *un*-Delian. So too in the case of the tenderly modal and only very cautiously chromatic *Bethlehem Down* and the closely-related 'Pieds en l'air' in the *Capriol Suite*.

Warlock's first experience of Delius was, as we know, the unacc-companied chorus *On Craig Dhu*, an 'impression of nature'. It was inevi-table that he should try to recapture something of this experience in his own work. He comes closest to it perhaps in *The Full Heart*, dedicated 'to the immortal memory of the Prince of Venosa' i.e. Gesualdo, another of Warlock's lifelong enthusiasms. A few lines from Robert Nichols's rather Whitman-like poem give some idea of the nocturnal atmosphere the music tries to convey:

> Alone on the shore in the pause of the night time
> I stand and I hear the long wind blow light;
> I view the constellations quietly burning
> I hear the wave full in the hush of the night

And the poem ends:

> O my companions – Wind, Waters, Stars and Night.

An 'impression of nature', in fact; and like Delius in the admired *On Craig Dhu*, Warlock resists the temptation to find musical equivalents for individual words or phrases; his response is solely to the mood of the poem taken as a whole. The harmony is, however, very much more *recherché* than Delius's, though the sensitivity to vocal colour is ever on the watch for undue density or muddiness of texture. The dirge *All the Flowers of the Spring* is in a similar league, and this is one of a number of choral pieces which take Delius's experiments in the expressive use of wordless voices a stage further. The last word, 'wind', is prolonged over a total of twenty-one slow-moving bars, the 'd' being enunciated only on the twenty-first. The singers are directed gradually to close their lips and sustain the 'n' sound, as chromatic step-wise movements are etched against long internal pedal points. The effect is almost mesmeric, almost as if the chorus had picked up the sound of the low-singing wind and had identified themselves with it. In the *Corpus Christi Carol* the chorus are wordless for almost the entire length of its duration, singing to 'ah' and 'mm' throughout; they provide a gently but insistently rhythmic *susurrando* background, a kind of subdued ritual keening, a frieze of monochrome sound out of which contralto and tenor soloists rise at intervals to declaim the text of the Old English carol to long melismas of a modal/pentatonic cast. At only one point does the chorus itself advance the story: when the presence of the Crucified is first mentioned ('And in that bed there lieth a knight'). The soloists are silent, the chorus assumes control: but all the modal/pentatonic stability of what has preceded is lost, instead a plaintive liquescent chromatic harmony of unutterable desolation. Then at the end of the couplet a reversal to the *status quo* – until the final couplet, when the soloists are no more and contraltos and basses spell out the text on a monotone, *senza espressione*.

Apart from the oft-performed *Capriol Suite*, Warlock wrote two short orchestral pieces. The later of these, *Serenade for Frederick Delius*, was composed in 1922 as a 60th birthday present for his great idol, and is clearly modelled on *A Song Before Sunrise*. In several ways the earlier, *An Old Song*, is the more interesting. It dates from 1917–18, the year Warlock spent in Ireland in which he found himself as a composer. He wrote of *An Old Song* 'The tune is Gaelic but the piece, for me, is very much the Cornish moor where I have been living. The tune should emerge, as from afar, chiming in with one's thoughts while walking. The curious way in which it seems to end on the supertonic gives the impression that it fades away into the distance, unfinished. One stands still, attentive to catch another strain, but there is only the gentle murmur of the wind – and only fragments remain in the memory, and a mood half-contented and half-sad.' *An Old Song* catches odd echoes of another fine paean to the wide far distance, *The Song of the High Hills*; there is in it too something of the bleakness of Moeran's Norfolk landscapes, and it even looks forward to the moody, desolate atmosphere of Bridge's *There is a Willow Grows Aslant a Brook* (the critic who dubbed the piece 'On hearing the second cuckoo in spring' may have heard it, but he certainly did not *listen* to it). The opening triplet on the clarinet (a very Delian figure) is immediately wafted back in particles, echo-like, as if from the distance; and at regular intervals strings come to a standstill on a sustained chord as the lone singer is heard again, now on clarinet, now on flute, now on solo horn. The composer's reference to the supertonic is puzzling, for the music ends fairly and squarely on a tonic chord of G major; but the music does convey that poetic feeling for nature which informs those songs of Warlock where nature is a background and signally affects the musical imagery. *An Old Song* represents the type of natural beauty to which Warlock was particularly susceptible. Robert Nichols recalls that when they were fellow-students at Oxford they would take walks together, and '. . . was any fragment or ghost of beauty, whether in cloud-crag's edge or in stretch of vapour hovering between us and the willows, to be discerned, Philip would discover it . . . indeed I have never known anyone more sensitive to the more retired moods and fainter beauties of nature than he. This loving observation of nature was entirely poetical, non-scientific . . .'

Again, the shadow of Delius looms large, Delius who in the depiction of nature's tranquillities – her 'more retired moods' and 'fainter beauties' – excelled all others. Many of Warlock's songs with a natural setting are in fact exquisite tone poems in miniature – for instance the setting of Arthur Symons's *Autumn Twilight*, in which a *Songs of Sunset*-like landscape is evoked in musical terms which scarcely bring to mind for one second the composer of *Songs of Sunset* (quite a feat for someone as drunk with Delius and Dowson as Warlock – in a letter to Delius he described himself as one of those, who, in Dowson's words, 'deem no harvest joy is worth a dream'). *Autumn Twilight* is one of Warlock's loveliest songs, and so is *Late Summer* in which some turns of Delian harmony are requisitioned to portray the drowsy warmth of an August afternoon and the ripe passionate contentment of the old couple who in youth 'loved with strength and loved with truth' and who now 'in heavy age are beautiful'. Most poignant of all is the part-song *The Spring of the Year* which begins quite winsomely with consecutive modal sevenths in the manner of Vaughan Williams.

Ex.31

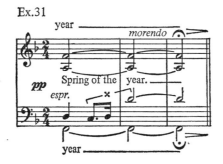

Very soon, however, the harmonic temper changes, and Delius tells us at 'I could sleep in the wild woods where primroses blow' that the poet is one of those for whom, as for Dowson, 'the Spring of the soul cometh never again'. In the final cadence one of the most hackneyed of all Delian clichés, the added or unresolved sixth, is used to inexpressibly moving effect as the tenor leaps upon the octave (Ex. 31) – the words being 'Let none tell my father, or my mother dear/I'll meet them both in heaven at the Spring of the Year'.

3

We must now consider something of Warlock's effect on his contemporaries. We tend to forget that Warlock acted almost as a kind of liaison man for Delius in England, not only between the great composer and those who felt drawn whole-heartedly to embrace his aesthetic (Moeran and C. W. Orr), but also for those whose musical outlook tended in quite different directions – Constant Lambert and William Walton. It is safe to say that those reminiscences of Delius which crop up from time to time in the music of Lambert and Walton are more probably Delius filtered through Warlock. Richard Shead has shown convincingly how Lambert was affected by the atmosphere of the Warlock circle. He was on intimate terms with van Dieren and Cecil Gray as well as with Warlock with whom he had much in common: cats, limericks, an interest in early music and a romantic pessimism which found expression in Warlock in *The Curlew*, *The Shrouding of the Duchess of Malfi* and other works voicing a black despair, in Bax in *This Worldes Joie,* and in Lambert in the Piano Concerto, Piano Sonata, in the very Warlockian *Dirge* from Cymbeline, and most of all in his great choral work *Summer's Last Will and Testament*. Shead has interestingly suggested that because of the musical time-lag between England and the continent not only nationalism but also the grim and grisly romantic movement of the mid-nineteenth century reached Britain fifty years late and expired in these doomed and deathstruck compositions of Warlock, van Dieren, Lambert and others. Delius, of course, plays no part in this; yet Lambert, as we know from *The Rio Grande*, was ever a Delius enthusiast, and there can be little doubt that his love and knowledge of Delius's music was enhanced through his familiarity with Warlock's.

The factor which unites Delius and Warlock with Lambert and Walton above all others is the almost uncanny fascination the 6/8 rhythm appears to have held for all of them. In Lambert this took the form of the siciliana.

Angus Morrison, dedicatee of *The Rio Grande*, writes: 'The strange sadness of its characteristic 6/8 rhythm, as well as the poetic overtones and associations of the name itself, always had a fascination for him, and in both ballets (*Romeo and Juliet* and *Pomona*) he used this form for the emotional core of the work.' In *Music Ho!* Lambert described the siciliana which forms the finale of the Mozart D minor quartet as a 'dance tune into which and its variations Mozart seems to have compressed the emotional experience of a lifetime'. The siciliana in *Pomona* is certainly the most personal music in the score, infinitely more so than its counterpart in the earlier *Romeo and Juliet*; but for a siciliana in which Lambert diverts Delian harmony to his own purposes we need only turn to the 'Allegretto piacevole' of the woman's variation (Section 5) in the lusty and lyrical ballet-score *Horoscope*. Lambert's finest work is *Summer's Last Will and Testament*, a masque for orchestra, chorus and baritone solo, 'words taken from the Pleasant Comedy of that name written in 1593 by Thomas Nashe' – which Comedy includes the famous lyric set by both Delius and Warlock, *Spring the Sweet Spring*. In the 'Intrata', wherein are presented themes structural to the entire work, Lambert very quickly slips into his favourite siciliana-type rhythm, whether in 12/8, 9/8 or even 15/8, and at the climax (vocal score, p. 5, bar 6) the upward-thrusting pentatonic triplet of Negro-Delian origin makes a significant appearance, returning again briefly shortly before the dissolve into the 'Madrigal con ritornelli'. For Lambert this phrase, and the Delian poignancy of the 6/8 rhythm, seemed to lie at the nerve-centre of his deepest emotions.

The siciliana-like 6/8 also seems to have possessed a particular emotional significance for Lambert's great friend and contemporary William Walton, who acknowledges Lambert as the greatest influence on his development. Walton and Lambert used to visit Warlock for convivial evenings, and while Walton fortunately managed to steer clear of the dipsomaniac and pathologically depressive tendencies of the van Dieren/Warlock/Gray circle (as Lambert alas did not) Warlock's *musical* personality impressed itself upon Walton in a number of ways which seem to call for comment in this context. There are echoes of Warlockian chromatic harmony in the early *Litany* to words by Phineas Fletcher, and, more perfectly assimilated into a personal style, in the Jews' song of lament in the first part of *Belshazzar's Feast*. A lazy lotus-eating 6/8 underpins the Mediterranean elegance of *Siesta*, but it is in the scores for Louis MacNeice's radio play *Christopher Columbus* and Olivier's film of *Henry V* that the rhythm seems to have picked up its Delian overtones, *via* Lambert, *via* Warlock. In *Christopher Columbus* there is a lovely song in this rhythm for Beatrice, 'When will he return' (and if anyone wishes to be reminded of how well the age-old modes seem to adapt themselves to this age-old rhythmic framework, let him delight in the dexterity which builds a plainsong 'Kyrie' into the song to effect the transition between Columbus's last meeting with his lady and his farewell to the Prior of La Rabida). And in *Henry V* everybody knows the moving siciliana for muted strings (perhaps 'quasi-siciliana' would be more accurate, since no title is specified) for Pistol before the embarkation – 'Touch her soft lips and part'. As in Warlock, the matrix is stylised, acquired; but the emotional stuff, the personal involvement, lies in the harmonic tissue which makes no attempt to conform to the style of the period. Genius reconciles and unites two potentially conflicting entities; and a point which emerges with some force from these portions of *Columbus* and *Henry V* is that the 6/8 rhythm seems to be associated in Walton's mind, as in Delius's, with love and the sorrow of parting. Many have remarked on the 'bitter-sweet' quality of Walton's lyricism, an epithet so frequently applied to Delius's that it has now become a cliché; but as far as I know no one has commented on the most explicitly Delian moment in Walton, which again is to be found in the *Henry V* music. In Act 5 scene 2 the Duke of Burgundy speaks at some length on the devastation being wrought alike on the French countryside and on the minds and spirits of the French people; he entreats movingly for peace. Now Walton's obvious course of action would have been to underscore this in a sombre-hued music, perhaps using low registers of wind or brass and muffled drums. Instead he sees as the emotional crux of the passage the ideal of peace, contentment and quiet prosperity to which Burgundy refers in his opening lines, and evokes this vision constantly throughout the speech in music of a gently pellucid beauty. Based melodically on one of Jean Canteloube's lovely folksongs from the Auvergne, it is

Ex.32

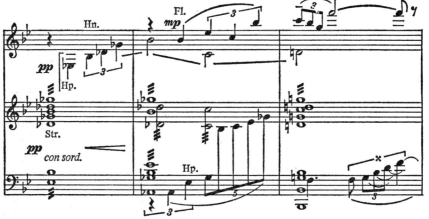

23. C. W. Orr.

24. Arnold Bax as a young man in Norway.

25. Bernard Herrmann.   26. Patrick Hadley.

27. Christmas card from Peter
Warlock to C. W. Orr.

To C.W.O.
with all good wishes
from P.

Christmas 1927.

pure Delian poetry, no water added – shimmering *tremolo* strings, a rustling background to exquisitely-turned woodwind triplets, harmony focusing upon the chord of the added sixth (Ex. 32). This is unique in Walton, although something approaching a precedent comes to mind – the sudden lull just before the heaven-storming peroration in the finale of the Symphony No. 1, with solo trumpet sounding a last post which is also a reveille (Oxford score, pp. 188–9) – a memorable moment in which a solo oboe and then a flute muse over a very Delian woodwind figure, the basic harmony that of the added sixth. A similar moment – a nostalgic backward glance, a last lingering look at the sunset – occurs at the corresponding juncture in Delius's *Second Dance Rhapsody*, and in John Ireland's symphonic rhapsody *Mai Dun*.

If Lambert and Walton thus hovered on the periphery of Delius's English discipleship, E. J. Moeran and C. W. Orr are located precisely in the centre. Moeran is another in the small band of English romantics who are gradually coming back into favour after a long period of eclipse. He is difficult to evaluate fairly. He seems ever confused by a multiplicity of influences; echoes of virtually everybody working within a romantically-oriented frame of reference in the England of the twenties and thirties can be discerned at one time or another – Vaughan Williams, Delius, Bax, Ireland, Warlock, van Dieren, even Lambert and Walton, and (most prominently in the case of the G minor Symphony, written at much the same time as the Walton Symphony) Sibelius, the sole continental cult-figure of the period in England. The question is whether Moeran succeeded in evolving a classifiably 'personal' style out of this welter of potential catalysts. My own view is that he did not. In fact I wish to suggest without impertinence – and I speak as an admirer of Moeran – that his distinction lies not so much in any recognisable or striking individuality of idiom as in a recognisable and striking ability so to order this assembly of often disparate currents and cross-currents of musical thought to produce thereof a musical substance fine-textured, subtle-mannered, eloquent and expressive – but in the last analysis deficient in personal presence. Proportions are balanced with an infallible sureness; there is no grinding of gears, no sudden braking out of one style and equally abrupt acceleration into another; the music flows with a smoothness and inevitability, it *sings* ever radiantly, and before long we find ourselves accepting this skilful and painless concatenation of acquired stylistic elements as something original and personal. Perhaps it is. Is this tantamount to saying that Moeran *did* possess a language of his own? Surely, however, a composer's 'language' should be more than the sum of its component parts, however faultlessly these parts are integrated and aligned.

If Warlock drew his 'component parts' chiefly from Delius on the one hand and the Elizabethans on the other (with English folksong as a sub-ordinate contributor) Moeran's loyalties were divided primarily between Delius and folksong, with the Elizabethans gesticulating in the background. It was undoubtedly through Warlock, with whom he was on intimate terms (they shared a riotous cottage at Eynesford in Kent), that Moeran learnt to love Delius and the Elizabethan madrigalists. Awareness of England's folkmusic heritage, however, came to him suddenly, and he described once how he had arrived in London as a raw student just before the First World War 'my own conception more or less defined by the dreary platitudes of Parry and Macfarren. It was on a wet evening in early spring that I attended St Paul's Cathedral to hear a Bach "Passion" and, finding the building packed out, rather than spend a blank evening and with decidedly lukewarm enthusiasm, I made for Queen's Hall and paid a somewhat grudging shilling to sit through one of those concerts of modern British music. There was a rhapsody of Vaughan Williams based on folksongs recently collected in Norfolk by the composer. This, and other works which I heard that night, though not all directly inspired by actual folkmusic, seemed to me to breathe the very spirit of the English countryside as it then was.' The next day, filled with enthusiasm, he acquired the Cecil Sharp collection of folksongs from Somerset.

'The following Sunday I was home at Bacton and, after church, I tackled the senior member of the choir on the subject of old songs. He immediately mentioned *The Dark-Eyed Sailor*, but the day being Sunday, I had to curb my impatience to hear a real folksong, sung by a traditional singer, until the next day. I soon discovered that in Bacton and the immediate district there seemed to be a very few songs left, and these I succeeded in noting down. The war soon came to put a stop to my activities for the time being. The only songs I had heard had been sung to me by elderly people who assured me that the old songs were fast dying out, and the singers with them. By the time the war was over, I assumed that there was no longer anything to be had, and I did not resume my attempts at collecting. However, in the late summer of 1921, I received an urgent message from the folksong enthusiast, Mr Arthur Batchelor, to come over to Sutton, near Stalham. It appeared that he had accidentally overheard an old roadman singing softly to himself over his work. This turned out to be none other than the late Bob Miller, known for miles around, I have never discovered why, as "Jolt". Bob admitted that he knew some "old 'uns" but he was at pains to point out that he had not really been singing, but "just a-tuning over to himself". I soon fixed an appointment to spend the ensuing evening in his company at a local inn, and he gave me a splendid batch of songs, some of which were hitherto unpublished. Moreover, by his enthusiasm and personality, he opened the way to a series of convivial evenings at which I found that the art of folk-singing, given a little encouragement, had by no means died out.'

166

Bacton, Sutton and Stalham are all villages in East Norfolk. Moeran's grandfather was rector of Bacton (his mother was East Anglian but his father Irish) and this accounts for the large amount of time he spent in this area in his most impressionable years, drinking in the landscape which was to determine the character of much of his best music. The whole of this part of Norfolk is incredibly isolated, although Stalham is a busy little market town; but the junction of the River Ant with the channel leading to Stalham (which is what Moeran must have had in mind when he entitled one of his early piano pieces *Stalham River*, there being no 'Stalham River' as such) is the centre of a circle two miles in radius with no village and scarcely a house – water, reeds, marsh, sedge and scrub. In winter it is completely lifeless and in summer sports wild-flowers, birds, insects and reeds. This is the desolate scene evoked in one of the finest of Moeran's nature-impressions, *Lonely Waters*. It is based on a folksong collected by the composer from the village of Sutton (he refers to it in the quotation above) which lies on the perimeter of this wilderness; and the singer was obviously susceptible to the barren bleakness of the scene:

> So I'll go down to some lonely waters
> Go down where no-one they shall me find,
> Where the pretty little small birds do change their voices
> And every moment blow blustering wild.

Moeran writes at the head of the score that the song 'is still frequently to be heard on Saturday nights at certain inns in the Broads district of East Norfolk' (this was in the thirties before the Broads became commercialised). 'Whenever possible it is preferable to perform the piece in the version with a voice part' (just before the end both words and music of the original song are written in); 'but it should be understood that the singer need not be a professional one, in fact anyone with a clear and natural manner of singing may perform the verse. And in any case, the singer must be in an unobtrusive position, sitting at the back of the orchestra or out of sight altogether.'

We are immediately reminded of the solo voice in *Appalachia*, its mystery and remoteness, Delius's concern to safeguard its anonymity and naturalness. *Lonely Waters* is a work in which Delius and the Vaughan Williams of *A Pastoral Symphony* meet and are one; the music ebbs and flows on chordal strings flecked by woodwind arabesque which occasionally takes flight and soars like a bird over the marshes, and with what sensitive forethought does Moeran make provision for the deliciously nutty, reedy timbre of the oboe and the dark-hued melancholy of the cor anglais! The tune itself is heard integrally twice, elsewhere in half-remembered snatches, its shape and outline serving elsewhere as starting points for new trains of thought, ever mindful of their theme whether akin to it or not. Some may associate this music with the Norfolk landscapes of Crome and Cotman, of the Norwich School; others may find in it an exact, if unconscious, musical equivalent of one of Helen Waddell's lyrics from the Chinese:

> The rushes on the marsh are green,
> And in the wind they bend.
> I saw a woman walking there
> Near daylight's end.
>
> On the black water of the marsh,
> The lotus buds swim white.
> I saw her standing by the verge
> At fall of night.

In Moeran's other nature-piece with specifically East Anglian associations, *Stalham River* for piano (the topographical implications of whose title were discussed above) the harmony of his teacher John Ireland is tempered by awareness of Delius. It was written at Bacton in September 1921 and so is one of Moeran's earliest published compositions; it is also one of his finest. The bleakness, the salt air, the wide East Anglian sky – we can see and sense them all in the opening section, almost diffidently rhapsodic, chromatically side-slipping an expected progression or resolving it elliptically, limning the silver thread of the water as it dissolves and is lost to view in the misty blue of the horizon (Ireland's bi-tonally-flavoured harmony serves its purpose here). Then however a signal change of stance: the river begins to sing of itself, gradually the onlooker becomes more and more wound up in the swelling, surging song, the current of the water deepens and a full-hearted climax is reached. Here is the architectural sharpness of *In a Summer Garden* – a tracery of pentatonic figuration (quasi *moto perpetuo*), the tenor inscribing a wide-spanned arc of modal melody (the main theme of the opening section, transformed as if by magic) a growing exultation; the difference in atmosphere is perceptibly realised in the music. And in Moeran's music there is a paradisial wonder – the paradise of childhood when all is drenched in a golden sunlight and day seems never-ending. This is surely the enchantment he works here. Soon the dream breaks, the bleakness of the opening returns; yet as the music is gradually lost in an exquisitely Delian fade-out, echoes of the river-song linger on in the atmosphere.

Most of Moeran's music can be related to a compromise, generally happy and successful, between the rival harmonic claims of Vaughan Williams and Delius, facilitated by their melodic grounding in modality and pentatonic phraseology. This is apparent in Moeran's folksong settings, whether of Norfolk or Irish melodies or those of his own devising – for instance in 'Donnycarney', No. 5 of the *Seven Poems by James Joyce* for voice and piano, in which the folksong-like melody attracts a modal harmonisation to begin with, but one which becomes increasingly rapt and chromatic as it not only reflects the summer bliss of the moment but anticipates the autumnal, Delian quality of the next song in the cycle, 'Rain has fallen'. Surprisingly, perhaps (in view of the dedication) a subtle admixture of Vaughan Williams and Delius also characterises the lovely *Nocturne* for baritone, chorus and orchestra, composed in 1935 for the Norwich Philharmonic Society in memory of Delius. Perhaps Moeran was anxious to avoid appearing over-sycophantic, even posthumously; more likely is that he simply wound the fine gold skein of his imagination around the Robert Nichols poem, and the result was the result. The poem is the 'Address to the Sunset' from Nichols's play *Don Juan Tenorio, the Great*; it is another of those 'impressions of nature' to which Delius and his aerial perspective of a white crane, and the spirit is enjoined to find out disciples were so addicted. The glories of the sunset are viewed from the wings and mount with him, wheel and soar with him,

> Hang where now he hangs in the planisphere –
> Evening's first star and golden as a bee
> In the sun's hair – for happiness is here!

For the first half – the setting of the evening scene – the chorus is used wordlessly, both harmonically and polyphonically; the writing for the voices is more linear than in Delius, less a matter of massed blocks of chordal sound. As in so many of Delius's scores, the solo baritone is the protagonist, and the centre-piece is a long narrative surveying the sunset world through the crane's eyes (in the E major of *Sea-Drift*) with an easy flowing undulating movement; the chorus now enters with words ('Now spirit! find out wings and mount to him') and in an out-pouring of visionary lyricism in the manner of Vaughan Williams (e.g. in the *Sea Symphony, Towards the Unknown Region* and *Dona Nobis Pacem*) a fine climax is reached. The emotional crux is only laid bare in the epilogue, voiced by soloist and chorus together; for at the first 'happiness is here' muted horns sound an explicit reference to the sunset horns in Ex. 21 from *A Village Romeo* – E flat over a timpani dominant pedal. We have already heard these horns once before – at the very beginning, just after the first entry of the wordless chorus. There they were unmuted; now they are veiled, buried even deeper at the rainbow's end, and reveal to us their true significance. As in *A Village Romeo* – as so often in Delius – they are

169

symbols of the Transcendent. This is a perfect little piece.

The two best of Moeran's piano pieces are *Stalham River* and *Summer Valley*, the latter of which also bears a dedication to Delius; it is more self-evidently Delian than the *Nocturne*, easefully trochaic and fluidly chromatic, an evocation of wet-warm afternoons in late summer overhung in appointed places by a cool shadowy stillness. The 6/8 metre often haunts Moeran, generally to Delian effect – in 'Where the bee sucks' (*Four Shakespeare Songs*) and particularly in the *Seven Poems by James Joyce* – 'Strings in the earth and air', 'Now, O now, in this brown land' and the beautiful 'O Cool is the valley now' which quotes the opening phrase of *Summer Valley* rhythmically translated from 6/8 into 5/8. Through all these Joyce settings – and to a degree in *Summer Valley, Stalham River* and *Lonely Waters* – there is always in the harmony a faintly astringent coloration, the suspicion of a bitonal bleakness, which it is always tempting to relate to the East Anglian landscape and climate.

In the Joyce album are also two skilful imitations (on the poet's part) of Elizabethan lyrics – 'Who goes amid the greenwood' and 'Bright cap and streamers'. Moeran negotiates them enchantingly – pretty, fresh, engaging melodies with the characteristically Elizabethan ambivalence of the seventh and a harmonic framework incorporating modal pleasantry, Delian dissonance and the false relation, all three the happiest of bedfellows. Moeran is at his best when he does not consciously affect the Elizabethan idiom, as he does in his choral suites *Songs of Springtime* and *Phyllida and Corydon*. These are tainted by too obvious and literal a pastiche of the Elizabethan

madrigal (which Warlock's Elizabethan choral pieces and songs never are), and wherever the harmony breaks loose from its self-imposed straitjacket it veers none too dexterously into the chromatic 'expressiveness' of Warlock. Here is one instance in Moeran where a conflict of styles is not so successfully resolved. Far more worthy a tribute to Warlock is the dirge for unaccompanied chorus *Robin Hood Borne on his Bier*, a setting of a poem from Munday and Chettle's *Death of Robin Hood* (1601). The grain and texture of this short piece is extraordinarily cogent and vital; emotionally it is one of Moeran's most concentrated and powerful utterances. It contains at least one of those rare phrases so perfectly realised that words and music linger on in the mind as an indivisible entity (Ex. 33). Another telling simplicity is the last chord, an added sixth, but with this difference: that the bass is not the tonic, but the dominant, enhancing the impression at the *niente* close that the music does not really end at all. The humming voices, like those at the end of 'Neptune', are merely lost in the vastnesses of space and are still humming to this day.

There is however one work in which Moeran does achieve an original and striking synthesis between idioms ancient and modern, and that is in the orchestral sketch *Whythorne's Shadow*. This is based on a part-song by Thomas Whythorne published in 1571, and according to Moeran the poem of Whythorne's song tells us all that we need to know about his 'shadow':

> As thy shadow itself apply'th
> To follow thee where so thou go,
> And when thou bend, itself it wry'th,
> Turning as thou both to and fro:
> The flatterer doth even so,
> And shapes himself the same to gloze,
> With many a fawning and gay show,
> Whom he would frame for his purpose.

If Moeran is hereby giving us to understand that he regards himself as a 'fawning flatterer' by way of his treatment of Whythorne's part-song, he is showing himself in an unnecessarily discreditable light. What he does here, in fact, is to gather together in a single brief movement the whole complex chain of technical and spiritual affinities relating Delius, the folklorists and the Elizabethans. Here is the English Delius movement in a nutshell. How easy it is for Moeran, *vis à vis* Delius, Vaughan Williams, and Whythorne, to 'shape himself the same', to 'frame' them all together for his purpose, simply because of the common technical currency they share – the trochaic pulse, the modality, melodic constancy versus harmonic changeability. They all draw in their different ways on the same stylistic bank. The first section of *Whythorne's Shadow* is, harmonically speaking, unimpeachably Elizabethan; but gradually, although Whythorne's melodic base retains its pre-eminence, the *personae* of twentieth-century harmony begin to take shape – first Vaughan Williams, then Delius, so that by the end of the piece the Delian era of chromatic romanticism is fully upon us. It is as though Whythorne, from the comfortable vantage-point of his own period in history, were suddenly vouchsafed a vision of how his colleagues three and a half centuries hence would be recreating and regenerating his work. And the chief catalyst in this remarkable metamorphosis is Frederick Delius.

Unlike Moeran, who oddly failed to make much personal contact with his idol, C. W. Orr enjoyed a period of some twelve years during which (with the exception of two years spent in the army) he corresponded regularly with Delius and met him quite frequently, either in London or at Grez. Delius played an important part in the development of a composer who has produced a handful of songs which rank among the finest written in Britain – perhaps anywhere in the world – this century.

Charles Wilfred Orr was born in Cheltenham in 1893 and has spent the greater part of his life in the Cotswolds. Plans for a military career were thwarted through persistent ill health, and although he joined the Coldstream Guards at Windsor in 1915, he had to be discharged the following year. He had earlier shown musical promise and, late as it was, he went to the Guildhall in 1917 to study under Orlando Morgan. By this time the Delian magic had him utterly in its spell, following a first hearing of the *First Cuckoo* in the early years of the war. 'Then and there I determined to go to every concert at which a work of Delius was announced' he recalls.

'Fortunately, there were frequent performances of his works at that time; and in fairly quick succession I heard *Brigg Fair*, *Life's Dance*, *In a Summer Garden*, the *First Dance Rhapsody* and the *North Country Sketches* (these last at their first performance). My enthusiasm grew with what it fed on, and even Elgar had to give place for a time to the worship of this new divinity revealed to me. It was an admiration quite uncritical, which is in some respects the happiest way of enjoying music; but it was none the less sincere, like so many of the idolatries of youth. Meanwhile, I had got to know the composer by sight, as he frequently came on to the platform to acknowledge the applause – a thin slightly stooping figure, with the face of some ascetic Catholic priest. To such lengths was I carried by my hero-worship that I would hang about the concert halls after a performance in order to see him come out; and it was due to the boldness of inexperience that I achieved a semi-introduction to the great man. It occurred after a concert at which May Harrison and Hamilton Harty had played the First Violin Sonata in its revised version, and I found myself immediately behind Delius and his wife as they left the Aeolian Hall together. Without any very clear idea in my mind as to what I proposed doing I followed them up Bond

Street, into Oxford Street and finally into a restaurant, where I chose a table as near to them as possible. I waited a few moments, and then, walking boldly over to where he sat, I heard myself say: "Excuse me, but are you Mr Delius?" (Fatuous question!) On his replying "Yes I am," I stammered: "Oh, then, I wanted to tell you how much I love your music." Banal and stupid as the words must have sounded I think he must have felt they were the expression of genuine feeling, for he greeted me warmly, introduced me to his wife and invited me to sit down with them.

'Of our conversation then I remember little, save that I was impressed by his easy, unaffected manner, with nothing in it of the condescension of a great man towards a nonentity. I remember the quiet charm of his wife, and her smiling encouragement. Which helped to put me somewhat at my ease and enabled me conceal an inward elation under what I hoped was a fairly calm exterior. Some weeks later he invited me to spend an afternoon with him at Hampstead, which concluded with a visit to the Proms, where we heard the *Dance Rhapsody*. Thereafter I kept up an intermittent correspondence with him while he was abroad.'

'Of the man, as distinct from the composer, I can only write as I knew him. An enemy of pose or insincerity in others, he was himself absolutely free from affectation or eccentricity. Indeed, I think his chief characteristic was his hatred of anything that suggested these twin vices. I remember two amusing examples of this. The first was a description he gave me of a charity matinee to which he had been invited, and which was organised in aid of the Russian aristocrats who had been exiled through the revolution. These poor down-and-outs, who did not know where to turn for the next thousand pound note, were present in force – the ladies garlanded with expensive jewels, and every emigré looking remarkably well-fed and prosperous. Delius's comment was very typical: "I went in hating Bolshevism as much as anyone, but I came out feeling like a Communist. Why, do you know, my dear chap, Jelka (his wife) and I were the only two who went home by bus!" The second example was when a young musician was trying to interest him in a quartet by one of the "advanced" school. Delius listened to the rhapsodic praise of the work, and then said, "Well, play me some of it, dear boy." The young man (whom I will call X) demurred on the grounds that it was impossible to play for two hands. "Then let's do it as a duet," said Delius promptly: "you take the first and second fiddles, and I'll do the viola and cello." But X, who was either unable or unwilling to submit his idol to this stringent test, made some excuse and left Delius master of the field. "Don't try to take me in with that sort of talk, dear X," he said, "I am too old to be bluffed in that way!"

'It was just this ingrained commonsense and balanced judgment that made it impossible to imagine Delius as a beer-drinking Bloomsbury aesthete or an absinthe-sipping cafe-crawler of Montparnasse. A propos of that curious tribe, he said to me once: "I'm no Bohemian, nor ever was. I like my meals at regular hours." He responded modestly to genuine appreciation of his work, and suffered patiently (but not gladly) the gush of certain feminine leaders of London "Musical" society – those vaporous females who could hardly distinguish B flat from a cowslip. But I believe he was happiest in his country home at Grez-sur-Loing, with a few intimates for company.'

The Orr-Delius correspondence includes on the older man's part a deal of amusingly caustic dismissal of his contemporaries and their music:

'I find Elgar's musical invention weak: whenever he gets a promising theme or good harmonies they remind me of *Parsifal* or Brahms. His manner of composition is also that of Brahms, and so is his orchestration which is thick and clumsy. And then the A flat symphony is very long, and the musical matter in the last three movements is very meagre . . . They play a lot of Mahler in Germany at present, and we have already heard three of the symphonies. I find them dull, pretentious and unoriginal . . . Only Ernest Newman had the acumen to discern what *Elektra* really was – long, tedious and dull, and Wagnerian at that. It is now entirely forgotten, even in Germany.

It was through Delius that Orr came to know Warlock* (or Philip Heseltine, as he was then and always signed himself to Orr in their correspondence) to whom he had good cause to be grateful:

'I think it was some time during 1918 that I first met him. I had gone to see Delius at his Hampstead flat and on my arrival I was introduced by him to a tall, fair youth of about my own age, whose name meant very little to me, except that I knew him to be a great admirer of the composer. He had risen from the piano as I came in, and then, after a few words together, Delius asked him to continue playing from a score which was on the piano. This was a work of van Dieren, a setting, if I remember rightly, of some Shakespeare sonnets, and it soon became evident to me that Delius was taking very little interest in the music as it went on. Instead, he kept up a running commentary of adverse criticism such as: "Not very original, this," or "Rather a banal passage, don't you think?" and so on, and eventually poor Philip gave up his attempts to persuade Delius that a new musical star had arisen in the shape of this unknown Dutch composer. Subsequently he and I walked to the tube together, and as we parted he invited me to come and see him some time. From then until the autumn of 1919 I went quite a number of times to the flat where he was then living, and got to know him fairly well.
'Knowing that I shared his admiration for Delius's music, he would produce piano solo or duet arrangements of some of the scores, which latter we would play through together, ignoring any wrong notes or mishaps on the way, and accompanied at times by Philip's whistling, which was of a peculiarly musical

---

*Warlock's song *Consider* is dedicated to C. W. Orr.

kind that I have never heard equalled – it was quite flute-like in quality and purity. I well remember our performing the *First Dance Rhapsody* and Philip saying to me as we came to the penultimate variation: "This is one of the loveliest passages he ever wrote," and then as we began the last one: "And this is one of the worst."

'In the autumn of 1919 I went abroad for reasons of health and was away from England for about 18 months. During that time I was surprised to get a letter from Philip expressing great interest in the MSS of three songs which I had had the temerity to send to Delius for his opinion, and which Philip had come across while staying at Grez. I am glad to say that I destroyed these jejune efforts, but his letter encouraged me to continue writing, and later on I sent him the MSS of some more songs early in 1922. While recommending me to scrap two of them (advice which I was wise enough to follow) he not only copied the others out in his own exquisite hand, but went to the trouble of arranging for them to be printed in Austria at a ridiculously low price, owing to the current rate of exchange at the time, and induced a London firm of publishers to take them over. From then on he always showed interest in anything I wrote, and I now bitterly regret having destroyed all but two of his letters I received over the years, including a wonderful postcard written in concentric circles, with his own signature neatly inserted in the centre! I write this, not with a view to advertising my own wares, but as an example of Philip's never-failing generosity and kindness where other men's work was concerned.

'Our last meetings were during the Delius Festival of 1929, during which I saw him frequently at the rehearsals and preparations for that event, and at his request shared the writing of the programme notes for the *Mass of Life*, each of us taking alternate sections. By this time Philip had come to take a more critical and detached attitude toward Delius's music, while still retaining a whole-hearted admiration for the greater works, especially *Appalachia*, of which Beecham was to give a superb performance during the Festival.

'Shortly afterwards I married and left London for good, to live in the Cotswolds, and it was there that I read in the paper of his tragic death. It was something for which I was quite unprepared and had never anticipated. But in retrospect I think there may have been some truth in Cecil Gray's idea that Philip had come to believe that his creative powers were exhausted, and that he would not face up to living as a mere shell of what he once had been. It has been well said that whereas genius is always renewing itself, talent can only end by becoming self-repetitive, and this, I have come to believe, was what Philip feared for himself. If it really was so I cannot think of a better epitaph for him than lines which Housman wrote in another context:

> Now you will not swell the rout
> Of lads that wore their honours out,
> Runners whom renown outran
> And the name died before the man.'

Apart from a few miscellaneous instrumental pieces, Orr's output has consisted solely of songs. The first he published was *Silent Noon* which dates from 1921; the last, a characteristically eloquent and full-blooded setting of Bridge's *Since Thou, O Fondest and Truest*, was written in 1957. Discernible influences are three: German lieder, particularly those of Wolf (here Elena Gerhardt's singing acted as a valuable incentive); Delius's music; and the poetry of A. E. Housman, to which Orr was introduced by a chance hearing of Graham Peel's setting of *In Summertime on Bredon*. In fact, of his 35 songs 24 are Housman settings, a total equalled by none of Orr's many contemporaries who were attracted to the poetry of the Shropshire Lad and whose persistence caused Lambert once to exclaim with a weary despondency: 'It is now some ten years since the Shropshire Lad published his last poems, and it may without impertinence be suggested that it is high time his musical followers published their last settings.'

The Cotswolds look north to Housman's actual Worcestershire, just as the latter looks north to his mythical Shropshire (he was a Shropshire Lad only by projection of spirit, by westward yearning from the extreme eastern bounds of Shakespeare's homeland). Orr was impressed from earliest childhood by towering vistas and 'high-hilled plains' of the type which succeeded also in *de*pressing Housman, and it is significant that in the work of those who also set Housman and set him well – Bax, Moeran, Howells, Gurney, Ireland, Butterworth, Vaughan Williams – nature was ever a potent inspirational force. Yet very few of these settings are wholly satisfying in every respect, for despite his enormous popularity Housman is in fact one of the most difficult poets for a composer to negotiate. As is now universally acknowledged, Housman was a repressed homosexual who deliberately charted for himself a pilgrimage of the deepest loneliness; of the passionate attachments he conceived for others, and the desperate agony of mind he suffered as a result, he allowed only the Shropshire Lad and his successors to speak – and that obliquely. For in the poems the stress of an overwhelming emotion is contained with a finely-turned precision of outline and a deceptive nonchalance of metre, and it is in his own resolution of this deliberate conflict between inner turbulence and outer equanimity that Housman offers his most taxing challenge to the composer. For if the latter observes the form of a poem he runs the risk of merely scratching the emotional surface (e.g. several of Somervell's settings); if on the other hand he penetrates the rose to find the worm, the chances are that the rose will suffer grievously in the process (e.g. 'Is my team plough-ing' in Vaughan Williams's setting). It is in the delicate balance he so often achieves between these two extremities that the unique distinction of Orr's Housman settings lies, and the secret is to be found in the harmonic texture.

Orr's harmonic language is not derived solely from Delius or from Delius through Warlock; in fact in a number of his best songs – *When I Watch the Living Meet, The Earl of Bristol's Farewell, Whenas I Wake* – the influence of Wolf is paramount. The familiar Delian insignia – a weft of lush chromatic discords woven to the hypnotically seductive barcarolle-like 6/8 – are most apparent in the *Cotswold Hill-tune* for strings, a fresh, strong piece instinct with all the tangy exhilaration of the open air and inexplicably neglected by modern orchestras. The *Midsummer Dance* for cello and piano is influenced, and also *Tryste Noel*, a gem-like carol-setting discreetly tinctured with melancholy, more consistently Delian than any of Warlock's carols. An early Housman setting, *'Tis Time I Think by Wenlock Town*, flows well but it is rich and heavy Delius, overripe, too full-flavoured. Eric Sams once described *Silent Noon* as an 'overripe plum of a sonnet . . . but Orr makes delicious jam' and here in fact Delian excesses are rendered almost mandatory by the very nature and texture of the poem, stagnant and almost cloying. Here it works; and in one of Orr's most dramatic and powerful songs, *Farewell to Barn and Stack and Tree*, he achieves that oddly moving synthesis of simple, unsophisticated modal-pentatonic melody and sensuous Delian harmony which we have already witnessed in Moeran and Warlock (implicit in Delius himself, made explicit in the work of his disciples). Housman's models here were the Scottish Border Ballads, and Orr contrives a melody which bears the impress of a Scottish folktune yet which is amazingly all of a piece with its close-worked, almost Baxian harmonic undertow. Bax actually heard this song when it was sung by John Goss at the Central Hall in Westminster in 1928, and was moved to introduce himself to the composer. Later he wrote to him: 'I heard that song at the place in Westminster, and have never forgotten it; it is a most lovely tune.'

Orr never professed any allegiance to the folksong movement as such, yet the modal ring of English folksong is not infrequently detectable; for example, *When Smoke Stood up from Ludlow* and Ex. 34 from *Is My Team Ploughing*. Ex. 34 also illustrates a peculiar strength and distinction of many of Orr's Housman settings, which is that Delian chromatic harmony is not used consistently throughout, but instead elements are encompassed within a basically diatonic or modal framework in order to make a particular point or to convey specific shades of meaning implied rather than stated directly by the poet. In *Loveliest of Trees* the harmonic temper is consistently diatonic, the key-centre hovers consistently between F minor and A flat save for the two occasions on which the text refers to the bloom on the cherry trees. At this point the harmony poises on a radiantly un-expected added sixth in A major. Time stops, and we catch a momentary glimpse of an enchanted world. In *When I Was One-and-Twenty* the chromatic inflections at the climax – 'and I am two-and-twenty, and O, 'tis true, 'tis true' – arrest the lightly skipping motion and strike a note at once wryly rueful and tragic; similarly too in *The Lads in Their Hundreds*, where the bitter-sweet quality of the whole-tone chords at the punch-line – 'The lads that will die in their hundreds and never be old' – gives the lie to the easy lilt and swing of the 6/8 plus 9/8 metre, which both Somervell and Butterworth perforce employ without applying this crucial cutting edge. The most subtle example of this skilful interpenetration of diatonic and chromatic elements occurs in *Is My Team Ploughing*, surely the most successful setting of a poem which has attracted and baffled a number of composers. Orr's realisation avoids both the over-studied simplicity and directness of Butterworth's and the hysteria of Vaughan Williams's. Notice how in Ex. 34 the modal seventh chord in bar 1 and the drooping fifth in

Ex.34

bar 2 both suggest the living man's terrible heaviness of heart as he approaches the climax of his revelations, and the darkening of the whole scene by means of the chromatically altered chords in bars 6 and 7 as he reaches it. The setting ends on an unresolved dominant seventh exquisitely echoing the question implied – and shunned – in the last line ('Never ask me whose').

Another fine song whose climax is achieved solely by means of harmonic intensification is the last and perhaps the loveliest of all Orr's Housman settings, *In Valleys Green and Still*. This is one of those poems in which the pastoral and the military are starkly juxtaposed:

> In valleys green and still
> Where lovers wander maying
> They hear from over hill
> A music playing.
>
> Behind the drum and fife,
> Past hawthorn wood and hollow,
> Through earth and out of life
> The soldiers follow.

In the second pair of stanzas the maying lovers are now lying beneath the hawthorn, sighing at the *memento mori*. The music follows the guidelines of the first two stanzas but with subtly significant changes: edges are blurred and softened as melodic contours are flattened, harmony veers to a magnetic Delian north and becomes more emotionally 'loaded'; the atmosphere grows pregnant with bitterness and the beauty of bitterness. The crisis is yet to come:

> And down the distance they
> With dying note and swelling
> Walk the resounding way
> To the still dwelling.

The 'dying note and swelling' is for Housman a mere incidental detail; but Orr makes 'swelling' the climax of the entire song by fixing thereon the full weight of a Debussian or Delian chord which has been subject to almost as much abuse as the added sixth – the dominant eleventh, or augmented eleventh, as it is sometimes referred to (i.e. B flat – D – F – A flat C – E natural). Orr very cannily *hints* at the chord at the corresponding place in the earlier second stanza ('past hawthorn wood and hollow'), but now its disposition is such as to make the maximum impact. There must be few instances of this shockingly hackneyed chord being used so meaningfully or to voice such deep intensity of emotion.

In Valleys Green and Still brings to our notice the importance of Orr's piano parts (they are often elaborate and quite difficult – another legacy from Warlock? – although they never challenge the supremacy of the vocal line). These piano parts frequently transcend the merely functional. Like Warlock, Orr will often take some hints from the text and fashion therefrom a Delian nature-poem in miniature. For instance *Along the Field* marries a fine-sprung, long-breathed lyric line of vocal melody ('Along the field as we came by a year ago, my love and I') to a quivering *Waldweben*-like piano figure which persists throughout and shades in the sound of the whispering aspen (its 'rainy-sounding silver leaves') – an inspiration of rare beauty. So too in *The Isle of Portland* where a rising-and-falling left-hand figure with interpolated triplet suggests the gentle murmur of waves in the gloaming. In this way does Orr impart a consistent flavour and unity of natural background to his settings. A much-favoured musical image is the cascading, rippling *moto perpetuo* of arpeggios which first appears in the Arthur Waley setting *Plucking the Rushes* (taking in its stride a splash of *pointilliste* colour from the Summer Garden after 'We rested under the elms till noon'). In *The Lent Lily* it evokes the breathy freshness of spring among the 'hilly brakes' with primrose, windflower and daffodil; and again in *The Time of Roses* (Thomas Hood) and *While Summer on is Stealing* (Helen Waddell) it seems to be associated with flowers in springtime – the world newly crowned with flowers, Phoebus high in heaven, and fled the rime. The last-named songs also share a similar cadential formula, sensuous and sweetly Delian. In Joyce's *Bahnhofstrasse*, a particularly moving and deeply-felt song, the ebb and flow of Delian harmony is overpinned constantly by a syncopated inverted pedal G – the 'trysting and twining star', the 'signs that mock me as I go'. Small wonder that in Orr, as in Wolf, the piano epilogue is a crucial feature of many a song – nowhere more so than in *In Valleys Green and Still*. For in response to the final stanza quoted above there arises in the piano a clamour of spectral bugles bringing to mind Owen's 'Bugles calling for them from sad shires' (Ex. 35). Why does that repeated C flat evoke the sound of distant bugles with such uncanny realism? Whatever the reason, it certainly sets a most haunting seal on over thirty years' devotion to a favourite poet.

Ex.35

Eyebrows may be raised at the slenderness of Orr's output over a period of some thirty-five years, but it must be remembered that he never acquired facility in composition ('I just worried and worried at the things until they came right'); and he also had the good sense to recognise and respect

28. Peter Warlock (left) and E. J. Moeran (right), with members of the Shoreham (Kent) Dramatic Society, c. 1928.

29. At Eynsford, Kent, outside the 'Five Bells'. Left to right: Hal Collins, Warlock's manservant; E. J. Moeran; Constant Lambert; Peter Warlock.

30. Peter Warlock (left), Jelka
Delius and Delius, in London
(Regent Street), for the Delius
Festival of 1929.

31. Patrick Hadley and R. Vaughan
Williams, King's Lynn, 1952.

the limits of his talent. And in the last analysis many composers have written much more and achieved much less.

We pass finally to a composer profoundly influenced by Delius's musical outlook but in a class by himself, namely Patrick Hadley (1899–1973). An individualist, one who moved in the Warlock-Lambert-Walton circle, his work is hardly ever played today, not through any lack of intrinsic merit but because, one's impression is, it failed to receive the right kind of promotion at the time when the musical climate was most favourable (much the same sort of fate has befallen Orr's songs). Hadley is however a composer worth reviving. Born in Cambridge, he was brought up in North Norfolk (his father was Master of Pembroke College and also owned a large house by the sea at Heacham, near King's Lynn) and inherited Irish blood from his mother. So a parallel with Moeran immediately suggests itself, the more in that Hadley became as much attracted to the music of Delius as to the folksong revival (unlike Moeran he was never a collector). In company with Balfour Gardiner he was a visitor at Grez in the early thirties (their exploits are entertainingly recounted in Fenby's *Delius as I Knew Him*) and was responsible for disinterring the long-lost score of *Koanga* from a London publisher's warehouse – upon his triumphant arrival at Grez, replete with score and victory, 'champagne was served'. Hadley was a fine conductor; during the war, while deputising for Boris Ord as conductor of the Cambridge University Musical Society, he introduced *Appalachia* and *Song of the High Hills* to Cambridge, using reduced orchestrations by Edward Dent, and memories of those performances still linger on in the minds of those who heard them.

For all their affinities of topographical sympathy, it is misleading to bracket Hadley too closely with Moeran, for whereas in Moeran the respective contributions of Vaughan Williams, Delius, John Ireland and others are comparatively easy to identify, Hadley has so thoroughly absorbed his influences that the extent of any direct stylistic debt to Delius or Vaughan Williams is difficult to gauge. He is not what is often slightingly referred to as a 'folksong composer'; flattened sevenths, clod-hopping six-eights, amiable pentatonic doodlings and all the other trappings of synthetic folkery play no part in his work. It is not, in fact, difficult to see why his works never became popular; for he lacks the warm-hearted, expansive gestures of Vaughan Williams on the one hand, and the luxuriant subjectivity of Delius on the other (except in such juvenilia as the *Ephemera* of Yeats for voice and chamber ensemble, an elegy of long-lost love, sunset embers and decaying leaves with many lovely and evocative moments). In his mature manner Hadley eschews the familiar appurtenances of 'juicy' harmony; he inclines to austerity of texture rather than lushness, understatement and a species of tough-fibred introspection rather than passionate self-revelation or assertiveness. In his settings (for voice and chamber ensemble) from Tennyson's *Mariana*, Shelley's *Cenci* and Hardy's *Woodlanders* (Marty South's lament) the stress of an overwhelming emotion is suggested with exemplary reticence and economy of expression, and there also falls into a similar category an enchanting lyric for small orchestra entitled *One Morning in Spring* (written, as was Lambert's *Aubade Heroïque*, in honour of Vaughan Williams's 60th birthday). In his later choral works *Fen and Flood* and *Connemara* (less in the moving *Cantata for Lent*) Hadley leans toward a degree of conservative Englishry very much less apparent in the period bounded roughly by 1930 at the one extreme and 1945 in the other. During these years Hadley produced a number of fine choral pieces all of which have been allowed to fall into oblivion. Two of them fit with special relevance into this context – the Symphonic Ballad *The Trees so High* (1931) and the cantata *The Hills* (1944). Hadley's personality is a strong and distinctive one; the free-ranging folksong-oriented lyricism of Vaughan Williams is fused with a spirit of a more Delian nature-mysticism, and the result is original Patrick Hadley. Folksong colours the melodic countenance of both works (conceptually in the case of *The Trees*) yet the guiding force that of Delius the moving *spirit* rather than the letter. For although in either case a programme governs the sequence of musical events, the real protagonist is nature – the shadows of high trees and high hills loom large over the entire proceedings, and the wonder of Hadley's music is that it is able to convey constant visual suggestiveness of these phenomena, these all-embracing backdrops, even when no specific allusion is being made to them. The generative force of *The Trees so High* and *The Hills* is profoundly Delian.

The Trees so High is a landmark in the English Revival; why it is so consistently ignored is a mystery. Those who seek evidence for the possibility of happy co-existence between the rival forms of symphony and a folksong sufficient unto itself need look no further than here; not even Vaughan Williams attempted to build a four-movement choral symphony around a solitary Somerset folk-tune. This was the challenge Hadley set himself. For being moved by the tale of the 'pretty lad' who was married at 16, a father at 17 and laid in earth at 18, he determined to dramatise it in the form of a 'symphonic ballad' (the very title epitomises the all-besetting dichotomy). He takes the utmost breadth of ground: the actual telling of the story, using words and music of the original song *in statu quo*, is reserved for the finale, when solo baritone and chorus join the orchestra. The preceding three movements, corresponding to sonata first movement, slow movement and scherzo, are fashioned out of individual segments of the folk-tune. There is an obvious conceptual affinity with the *Choral*

Symphony, but with this crucial difference, that whereas Beethoven discards the stuff of his earlier movements as having no relevance to his *dénouement* (*nicht diese Töne*), the import of the first three movements of the *Trees* is made explicit only in the finale. As the composer described it, 'three independent brooks which flow into one stream at the beginning of the last movement.' In fact there is a closer affinity with *Appalachia*, since here too the emotional significance of the material earlier submitted to variation is revealed only in the finale when at the climactic point, solo baritone and chorus take the stand (Hadley directs that his soloist should stand 'behind the orchestra but apart from the chorus yet [as in *Appalachia*] without any air of formality or apparent consciousness of his own importance' – a tall order indeed for the average soloist).

The earlier linked movements all grow in some way out of the ambience of the impending tragedy; they may reflect now the onlooker's reactions to it, now the changing seasons, always the imagined landscape in which the tragedy is set (the 'trees so high'). In the first movement the landscape gradually blossoms into life, a gradual unfolding and expanding of texture,

Ex.36(a)

(b)

sonority and movement – the birthpangs of spring sowing in their wake
(thematically) the seeds of things to come, summer, autumn and winter.
The first phrase of the tune becomes a recurrent ground-bass, and a rustling
continuum of thirds (strings) catches the sound of the wind among the
leaves (Ex. 36a). The second movement is warm and green with the
fullness of summer (all the movements merge imperceptibly one into
another, like the cycle of the seasons), a lyrical flowering of the same
phrase which generated Ex. 36a. How naturally and artlessly it lends
itself to strict canon at the octave (Ex. 36b)! A strange rhythmic lament
forms a central section, later to become (in the finale) the wedding music
of the 'pretty lad' – a funeral dirge (intimations of impending catastrophe
are rife throughout the three orchestral movements). The Scherzo is
autumnal, a bustle of wind and rain, and the finale begins quietly but
menacingly: soft cymbal roll, strings voicing *sul ponticello* an icy
chromatic plaint, a savagely dissonant, agonizingly passionate eruption of
elemental forces. The baritone soloist finally enters with the first stanza
of the ballad and (the character variation technique is not unlike that of
Brigg Fair) the music responds with appropriate imagery to every nuance
of the text; the trees, their rustling leaves, the wind on the thatch, the
'huffle of the gale', the ever-changing sameness of the snowfall (strings
passing through the same two notes kept tense yet motionless through a
skilful dovetailing of parts). Incidentally, for all their anonymity, a number
of the stanzas in *The Trees so High* are evidently the work of a true poet:

> I married was, alas
> A lady high to be,
> In court and stall and stately hall,
> and bower of tapestry.

As the music goes forward to its climax the melody is now treated with
the maximum harmonic and textural freedom, dramatically intensified at
the actual point of climax:

> At the age of eighteen, my love,
> His grave it was a-growing green
> And daisies were outspread,
> And buttercups of gold,
> O'er my pretty lad so young,
> Now ceased growing.

An affecting relaxation and alternation of harmony and texture marks the
second line, a sweet semi-chorus with poignantly expressive oboe and

violin solos sing of the flowers growing upon the grave and the tale is done. The leaves rustle in the trees once more, the baritone returns with the valedictory final stanza, the chorus's scattered, sigh-like interpolations pick up the odd word or phrase from the narrative, eventually losing themselves on the soughing and moaning of the wind among the leaves. A last 'farewell' breathed by the basses; timpani, pizzicato, *finis operis*.

The climate of *The Trees* is predominantly Sibelian, bleak and intransigent, the golden string music of the second movement the only relief from the inhumanity of nature. It is what Percy Grainger would have described as 'North Sea' music. In *The Hills*, however – a hymn to the Derbyshire hills whose glories Hadley had already sung in a modest symphonic poem *Kinder Scout* – there is no such hostility: in the thirteen years or so which had elapsed since *The Trees* the idiom has mellowed slightly (the harmonic language is milder) and these hills serve as a sympathetic and benevolent onlooker and participant in the ageless human cycle of life, love and death. There is nothing here of Hardy's granitically impassive conception of nature; instead the score is prefaced by the psalmist's 'I will lift up mine eyes unto the hills'. The hills are an omnipresent force; their general shape and outline is reflected in the character of the music with the same degree of all-pervasiveness as that of the trees in *The Trees so High*. The impetus to composition came not, however, from a folksong in this case, but from the death of the composer's mother in 1940.

The libretto is Hadley's own and has autobiographical connotations. A 'prodigal son' returns home to find his father no more and his mother near to death. Tramping along the Old Buxton–Manchester Coach Road (now just a track) he reaches the place where a magical panorama opens across Chapel Valley with Kinder Scout towering up beyond in the far distance (one needs a clear day for this). He rests surrounded by the great hills which witnessed his parents' first meeting, early courtship and marriage. He bids them tell the tale anew, and falls asleep in their shadow. Here the music conjures up the mountain panorama in the gathering gloom with the lone and distant cries of curlews, and the chorus, personifying the hills, singing in an eerily atmospheric passage to 'oo' (rounded lips). This is Delian nature-mysticism of the purest water.

And now the hills start to tell the story as though it were actually happening once more. They spring into life in a first movement, 'The Hills in Spring' which is magnificent music. First a scherzo to set the scene, a nerve-tingling, bounding 6/8 fairly bursting with energy: 'Spring in the air, breezy and crisp, galloping clouds and fitful sunlight, smell of the peat, squelch of the moss, rollicking waterfalls spraying the fellside, whistling crags, billowing heather, croaking of grouse, screaming curlew:

the hills, spring on the hills. We heave, we surge, we shout and bellow for joy!' This sense of a tumbling, untameable, tumultuous ecstasy is superbly conveyed. Then the hills identify themselves – Chinley Chewn, Rushup Ridge, Crowdon Head, Kinder Low, Cluther Rocks, Edle Moor, Crooston Knoll, Fairbrook Naze and the rest, all names to be found on the map of the Derbyshire 'Peak' district (a misnomer, there is no peak) roughly between Kinder Scout and Featherbed Moss: here the composer takes up a motif presented in the Prologue and associated with the stern rugged beauty of the hills. The real climax is yet to come, however, for the hills now call down to the two young lovers to come up and enjoy the miracle of spring on the heights. A new motif swings and lunges in thirds (Ex. 37) and forces the music ever upward in thrillingly cumulative ecstasy – 'higher now we climb, higher still again, ever striding forth'.

Ex.37

Finally the climax is reached, the couple stand on the roof of the world, and the music erupts in a blazing paean of praise to the hills in all their majesty and splendour with the two soloists (the lovers) riding the crest of the full orchestra and chorus with glorious, wide-flung phrases. 'Hy-ah, ta-ho, hy-ah, ta-ho, come praise the hills for ever.' It is in such music that Hadley both fulfils and transcends his debt to Delius. It voices an ecstasy which we find in miniature format in the spring anthem *My Beloved Spake* (to words from *The Song of Songs*) and in the wartime cantata *Travellers*: the middle section moves to the quiet waters of the River Cam, but at the words 'Your own voice [will] speak of the wonders to be' there is a sudden sunburst of sound with cymbal roll and harp glissandi shooting in both directions.

There follows an interlude 'In Taxal Woods' in which the pair vow eternal love to the sounds of nature – a rapt *Abendstimmung* with serene and restful writing for the two soloists, a trickling harp discreetly impersonating the 'purling gill' (babbling brook), flute arabesques doing duty for the nightingale: the music has a sparely atmospheric quality (particularly in the harp figurations) which foreshadow the character of Britten's nocturnes. The chorus in the third movement, 'Wedding', often sing to nonsense words to point the rhythms and assist resonance: an anticipation here of the 'mouth music' in *Connemara* (vocal articulation of a tune to random syllables). A huge climax is built up crowned by an exultant, forceful return of the motif in thirds from the first movement, which stands both for the bride's last farewell to her beloved hills and for the prodigal son's awakening. The transition from dream back to reality is beautifully effected with wraith-like reminiscences of earlier motifs (principally Ex. 37) encircling the son's nostalgia – 'my soul is thrilled and haunted by that happy tale of long ago'. After a poignant quotation from *In a Summer Garden* on solo violin he hears his mother's last words: 'The hills bring back sweet memories' – and bids them end their song; and the chorus's unaccompanied epilogue, 'The Hills by Moonlight' – one which well reveals the felicities of Hadley's choral writing – comes in the nature of a consolatory requiem and winds *The Hills* to eternal stillness.

Epilogue

The role of England in Delius's life – both personal and professional –
remains, therefore, ambivalent. It is the only country in which his work
has survived as a living tradition, although in more recent years America
has been showing a greater interest than before; yet it was also the country
for which he reserved some of his bitterest and most scurrilous invective.
Herbert Howells has recalled that this bitterness was only too greatly in
evidence even at the time of the 1929 Festival. Delius of course was a
confirmed egocentric, and selfishness and ingratitude were not lacking in
him; but in all fairness we should remember that this ambivalence was not
restricted to England; he seemed to resent being under an obligation to
whatever country. He made his 'home' – or, more properly speaking, his
base – in France for some forty years; yet he knew little of French culture
or of its great spokesmen, disliked the language, was indifferent to most
of its music and remained attached to Grez only inasmuch as it provided
him with the ideal circumstances for his work – idyllicly beautiful countryside and the fleshpots of the big city whenever he felt in need of relaxation or diversion. Reciprocally his work has been and still is ignored by
the French. Nadia Boulanger, in conversation with the present writer,
was surprised to hear that Delius had written a large-scale tone-poem in
praise of the great city where she was born and had worked for most of
her life, and expressed the view that there was in his music 'something
which the French could never recognise as their own'. Germany, fickle as
the *Pöbel* which Delius and the idol Nietzsche detested so vociferously,
fêted him with much ballyhoo and rhodomontade in the early days,
sloughed him off like an unwanted skin later on; nor was *it* spared the
whiplash of his tongue when the occasion arose. To the Norwegian mountain-country he was more attached than to anywhere else, but Scandinavia
as a whole was too cut off from the mainstreams of European culture to
appeal to him with any permanence. He was essentially a 'good European'. For America he felt nostalgia and a lively affection, for it had

been the enchanted wonderland of his youth; it had rescued him from the counting-houses of Bradford and from insufferable parental oppression, and revealed life to him for the first time in all its power and glory. He loved it for its virgin wildness and beauty, its great size and space and peace urged him to express himself in the grand manner, a manner endemic, not feigned. Yet it is inconceivable that Delius could ever have settled there or become a part of American culture, any more than he seemed capable of becoming a part of French, German, or Norwegian culture (and scant interest Norway has ever shown in this spiritual son of hers who set so many of her glories to superlative music).

Delius's feeling towards England in particular definitely fall into the 'love-hate' category. He sensed the debt he owed to England, just as we all owe some kind of debt, for better or for worse, to the circumstances which enfold us for the first twenty years or so of our lives; and he must also have sensed that his music touched a nerve in England, and that England would remain loyal to him long after everywhere else had cast him aside. He sensed this dependence and he resented it, just as he resented being dependent on his wife and his nurses after losing the use of his eyes and limbs. Delius was a proud man, and he was hard.

How then do we rationalise this English loyalty to Delius, so little encouraged by the composer himself? The answer is surely that we cannot rationalise it at all and must simply accept it as an instance of that rare and precious empathy between composer and audience whose secret can never be divulged by analysis. For Delius is certainly not 'English' like Vaughan Williams, whose music can be truly appreciated only in terms of the English scene. The English take the *Serenade to Music* to their hearts because they sense that the English woods, fields and streams which went into its making also went into the making of part of themselves. Delius is not so easily to be tidied away into topographical pigeon-holes. As for France, we cannot identify Delius as positively with any French painter as we can identify Milhaud with Cézanne; Milhaud's Provençal landscapes and Cézanne's are almost one and the same thing. Grieg's Norwegian cameos retain their national characteristics, however far afield they may travel; Delius's vast mountain murals would be understood as well by Emily Brontë as by Caspar David Friedrich. *Appalachia* is not nearly so circumscribed geographically as the 'endless prairie' music of Copland, and we have only to compare *A Mass of Life* with, say, Pfitzner's *Von Deutscher Seele* to realise that, for all their similarities in expressive tone and temper, in no way is Delius extolling Germany or the Germans; there is nothing of the fanatical chauvinistic demagogue about him. Consider also the unmistakable nationalist elements in Mahler's Bohemian and Austrian landscapes; nothing so specific ever obtains consistently in

Delius. The paradox is that he can assume any of these guises if the mood takes him – he can sound English in the English tone-poems, French in the French songs, and so on. But he transcends them all. Try to pin him down to any one port of call, attempt to impose on him any fixity of allegiance, and he eludes the grasp at once.

For Delius is a true cosmopolitan inasmuch as he celebrates the marvel of the earth *in toto,* he glorifies the sacraments of nature as she embraces all things and all peoples. It is worth while remembering that almost every facet of nature is to be found in Delius's poetry, an extraordinarily wide range, in fact – the magistral everlasting song of the hills and the rivers, the breath of the woods at dawn, the wonder of an early summer morning, the green world of the leaves, the mystic hush of noontide, scents of the summer night, the red ceremony of sunset, a white winter world, the yearly miracle of spring – all the endless melody, harmony and rhythm of the earth. He was one of those who angrily turned aside from the stench and filth in which most of us have to stand steeped the livelong day, prisoners of our own baser natures or our own cowardice, generally both. Instead he joined that great caravan of visionaries, which includes the Dark Fiddler as well as Sali and Vrenchen, the bargemen, Hassan and the unknown singer 'going down the river in the morning' – that multitude that no man can number which goes ever onwards and upwards, singing its litanies in the High Hills, ever in quest of the City that hath foundations.

Delius in truth was a man of vision. As Arthur Hutchings has pointed out, no man without could have penned the ecstatic valediction of:

'Joy, shipmate, joy! Pleas'd to my soul at death I cry'

and

'Depart upon thy endless cruise old sailor'.

Consider also the mighty hymn of praise to the omnipotence of the Will and to Destiny in *A Mass of Life,* that 'great worthy final destiny' for which he who so grandly envisaged it in musical terms requested – nay, insisted – that he be saved: destiny of a romantic and visionary.

Delius's vision was not, however, the first paradise that lies behind the memory of the world as in Ravel's marvellous sunrise-scenes. The 'Lever du jour' in *Daphnis et Chloë* may be the nearest man has ever attained to a music of Paradise, or of a rose-garden at dawn; but Delius's Hy Brasil was something very different. In the finale of *Ma Mère l'Oye* the dawn breaks over a garden of primordial innocence which knows nothing of any Tree

191

or any Fruit. Delius on the other hand accepts both the Tree and the Fruit and glories in the accepting. His garden, his world, has to be lived in and loved; he sings of Whitman's 'Life immense in passion, pulse and power', above all in passion: for it was love which first revealed the earth to him in all its fairness and fullness, love which raises all things to a higher power, much as Machen's Lucian Taylor creates his mystic Garden of Avallaunius out of his love for Annie, the girl from the wild parts of his land. For Delius all the wonder of the world was transmuted into a symbol of the Beloved, and he worshipped the world in honour and remembrance of her. Hardly a bar but does not testify to the shattering ecstasy of their fire.

It has often been claimed that Delius's reputation suffered a fatal blow in the death of Sir Thomas Beecham in 1962. Certain it is that Beecham was an ideal interpreter, and Sargent's arrogant claim that 'his actual presence and personality was so demoniacally essential to the hearer that his best recordings lose much when heard on the gramophone or radio' is glib nonsense. Certain is it too that the present cultural age is temperamentally as alien to Delian romanticism as it could possibly be. The spiritual grandchildren of those who did their best to hound and starve Debussy during his lifetime now have the impertinence to hail him, not as the man who raised the musical language to a new dimension of poetry and magic, but as herald's blazon of the new Dark Age in music which is presently come upon us. Delius, fortunately, has been spared this kind of obscene cruelty. He of course during his lifetime came under the sort of heavy critical fire that all artists of his temperament and outlook seem to provoke, and had his share of finger-wagging (if basically well-disposed) advisers who predicted that he might possibly turn out all right in the end, although he still had much to learn. Fortunately his natural shrewdness, faith in himself and his sharp tongue rendered him proof against the majority of these attacks, and his music is far too transparently 'reactionary' for any extravagant claims to be voiced on his behalf as an innovator.

These practical considerations aside, however, it is improbable that Delius's art is any better or any worse appreciated in our day than in his. Such artists in whatever medium of creativity they are active can never be popular, *ex opere operato*. The highly specialised nature of their work renders it inaccessible to all but a select band of initiates. There is of course no question here of the composer deliberately and cold-bloodedly lowering the communicative potential of his music to a minimum, as frequently happens today. Delius's is an altogether different kind of specialisation, to explain which involves delving deep into the complex relationship between the artist and the public to whose needs he is traditionally required to minister. This public, unfortunately, by no means only consists of those who sit back in chairs and listen. Now men like Delius are not in the vanguard of anything; they do not spend their time obsequiously cultivating non-entities who 'matter' for their money or their influence; they disapprove of, and are disapproved of by, academics and the musical Establishment; their craving for independence frequently robs them of security, not only in the financial sense but in the matter of the kind of ready public acceptance which many artists of less integrity are automatically guaranteed. No, Delius and his ilk have to be content with, in his own words, 'the few there are who love and understand. The rest are not worth bothering about'. Eric Fenby adds that Delius's music has never been loved by the many, but it has always been loved, and dearly loved, by the few. This is not the fault of the many, still less of Delius. It is of the very nature of things. For Delius, as we have noted on many occasions, was a poet and a visionary. You and I, the men in the street, may follow the visionary some of the way into his vision; to some it is given to follow more deeply than others. But with the best will in the world there is a certain barrier beyond which none of us are able to penetrate, for if we were we would be poets and visionaries ourselves. Every response is therefore in some degree a compromise, even for the best and finest natures; that being the case, what hope is there for those who are constitutionally incapable even of setting out upon the journey? It is in this way that the man of the hyper-imaginative or visionary cast of mind, like Delius, pays heavily for his great gifts; and it will always be a question whether the value received be out of all proportion to the price exacted.

Delius was of the decided opinion that it was not. He drank deeply of the loveliness inherent in all the many parts of the world with which he became familiar, and in that he wrote a truly cosmopolitan music, transcending national bounds with a sureness, and yet an elusiveness, which have somehow eluded all other composers, he repaid them in kind and in full measure. The value of his legacy lies not merely in its great glory as art *per se,* but in its ability to stir its recipients to some hazy awareness of their own latent imaginative powers and to an eventual realisation that, the longer and the better they live in Delius and all other fine music, the more their awareness of the wonder of the world will be increased, the more grateful will they be for the privilege of being alive. Frederick Delius, the last of the great pagan poets in music, belongs to the company of those true artists for whose life and work the world is a better place to live in, and of whom surely is composed, in a literal sense,

> . . . the choir invisible
> Whose music is the gladness of the world.

Select Bibliography

An exhaustive Delius bibliography, compiled by Lionel Carley, is to be found in Alan Jefferson's *Delius* (Dent's 'Master Musicians'). The present list is merely an acknowledgment to those sources the author has found especially helpful while working on this study.

CHAPTER 1 : AMERICA

GRAY, Cecil : *Musical Chairs*, London 1948
JAMES, Burnett : Essays on Jazz, London 1961
LAMBERT, Constant : *Music Ho!* New Edition, London 1965
MELLERS, Wilfrid : *Music in a New Found Land*, London 1964
RANDEL, William : 'Koanga and its libretto' *Music & Letters*, April 1971, 141–156

CHAPTER 2 : SCANDINAVIA

LOWE-DUGMORE, Rachel : 'Frederick Delius and Norway' in *Studies in Music*, University of Western Australia Press, No. 6, 1972, 27–41
GLYN-JONES, W : 'Delius and Jacobsen : a novel and its opera' in *Denmark*, Winter 1968, 13–14

CHAPTER 3 : GERMANY

BOULTON SMITH, John : 'Delius and Munch – Portrait of a Friendship' in *Apollo*, 1966, 38–47
CARLEY, Lionel : 'Hans Haym : Delius's Prophet and Pioneer', *Music & Letters*, Jan. 1973, 1–24
CLAPP, Philip Greely : 'All in the Family' in *Chord and Discord*, 1951, 33–41
HUTCHINGS, Arthur : 'Nietzche, Wagner and Delius' *Music & Letters*, July 1941

CHAPTER 4: FRANCE

CARLEY, Lionel:	'Jelka Rosen Delius, Artist, admirer and Friend of Rodin. The correspondence, 1900–14', in *Nottingham French Studies*, vol. IX, No. 1 (1970) 16–30; No. 2, 81–102
LOCKSPEISER, Edward:	*Music and Painting,* London 1973

CHAPTER 5: ENGLAND

COPLEY, I. A:	'Warlock and Delius: a catalogue' in *Music & Letters,* July 1958, 213–218
GRAY, Cecil:	*Peter Warlock,* London 1934
SCOTT-SUTHERLAND, Colin:	*Arnold Bax,* London 1973
SHEAD, Richard:	*Constant Lambert,* London 1973

Index